ESSAYS TODAY 7

ESSAYS TODAY

7

William T. Moynihan, Editor
University of Connecticut

HARCOURT BRACE JOVANOVICH, INC.
New York   Chicago   San Francisco   Atlanta

ISBN: O-15-522946-X

Library of Congress Catalog Card Number: 55-2286

Printed in the United States of America

Contents

Preface

      The modern reader is in a hurry. Time is short, and the information explosion threatens to bury him in details. Books take too long to read, fiction is too indirect, poetry is short on facts. But periodical journalism has an immediacy and directness that books seldom achieve, and in these periodicals the dominant literary form is the essay.

      Michel de Montaigne (1533–1592) first applied the term *essai* (a try, an attempt) to his rambling, whimsical, autobiographical speculations on a wide variety of topics. The form was soon adopted by other writers, who used it for the same informal purposes, but it was also adopted by scientists and others who needed a form for direct, clear discussion of facts and ideas. Their adaptations created another kind of essay, tightly organized and impersonal, and led to the development of still other categories —narrative, descriptive, expository, and argumentative, for instance. This multiplicity of styles and purposes makes it difficult to say precisely what an essay is, but such adaptability also explains why contemporary essays contain some of the best and most significant writing of our time.

      This edition of *Essays Today* has the same purpose as its six predesessors—to present a sampling of the most interesting and effective essays published during the last year or so in the leading journals of the United States and Great Britain. While they represent a wide variety of styles and purposes, there is, nevertheless, a common note in many of them—that the world of the 70's is a world in crisis. The essays are organized in the direction of increasing complexity; the descriptive and informal pieces come early, the argumentative, analytic, even philosophic, pieces come later.

      "The Cheetah" by the D'Aulaires is not only a description of a marvelous animal; it is another tale of a threatened species. Sheila Burnford's account of her stay in an Indian village in the far north is also an account of survival where food is scarce and compassion is nonexistent. By humorous contrast Robert Campbell's story of his affair with an automobile reveals a crisis of $1,500 garage bills.

      The next three essays, "Encounter with the Archdruid" about David Brower, founder of the Sierra Club, "A Man Called Perry Horse" about an Indian living in Washington, D.C., and "On Being a Scientist," are biographical. They describe the lives of men trying to make or find a more habitable world. What exactly is happening to that world, and specifically to its ecology, is the subject of the three essays by Ritchie-Calder, Westing, and Jacoby: "Mortgaging the Old Homestead," "Ecocide in Indochina," and "The Environmental Crisis."

Social, educational, and ethical concerns are the subject of the next half-dozen essays. Catherine Drinker Bowen describes the challenge of being a woman writer; Charles Reich questions the morality of some police actions. Ivan Illich and Philip D. Ortego deal with the failures and possibilities of education in the "third world" and among Mexican Americans. A self-styled burgher, Joseph Whitehill, describes what effect his visits to a prison had on his middle-class attitudes. And Michael Novak, a philosopher from a white minority background, reveals the frustration and bitterness that exist among white ethnic groups.

Alfred Kazin's critical-biographical essay on Joyce Carol Oates is the first of five pieces on the arts and literature. Recent movies receive a critical appraisal from Harold Clurman, who finds that the old god Mammon remains the chief director—even in most films made in the last few years. Irvin Stock and Nick Aaron Ford present differing estimates of the role of Black literature in the college curriculum. Yevtushenko's autobiographical account of the attention and criticism accorded to a famous writer gives an insight into the hazards of creativity and fame.

The final three essays present a wider view of some of the major dilemmas of the present age. Jack Newfield calls for a new political coalition; Robert Jay Lifton warns of moral insensitivity to mass slaughter; and John Passmore, a philosopher, examines the long-range implications inherent in the attitudes and beliefs of the "Now" generation.

The casual, detached style of Montaigne's essays is hardly to be found among the essays collected here. Almost all of these essayists are concerned, involved, and excited about issues of immediate interest to readers in a time when even the arts share a sense of urgency. The nature of the essay fits it to express and evoke this sense, as readers of this book will soon discover.

W. T. M.

ESSAYS TODAY 7

EMILY and OLA D'AULAIRE

The Cheetah

The enormous, blood-red sun was setting behind Kenya's rolling Ngong Hills as the big cat crouched low in the tall, dry grass. Every muscle aquiver, he watched a Thomson's gazelle in the distance. Then, with movements as smooth and deliberate as pouring honey, he began slinking forward.

Slowly, cautiously, the big cat approached unnoticed until he was just 100 yards away. Suddenly, like a golden missile set loose on the darkening plain, he launched into open attack, streaking toward the startled Tommy, who at once began a desperate pattern of run, weave and dodge. But the gazelle had sensed its danger too late. Even with its 45-mile-per-hour speed—plenty to escape from a lion or leopard attacking from any distance—the gazelle was no match for the cheetah. The drama ended quickly, in an explosive cloud of red dust.

The cheetah is the fastest wild animal on earth. From a crouching start, he can reach 45 mph in two seconds. A second or two more and he's careening along at over a mile a minute, his long, thick tail acting as a counterbalance so he can corner like a jackrabbit. Zoologists estimate the cheetah's top speed to be a scorching 75 mph!

One hundred thirty pounds of rangy muscle (relatively lightweight compared to other big cats), the cheetah is clearly built for speed. Long-limbed and lean, he stretches more than seven feet from nose to tail tip and stands two and one-half feet high at the shoulder. His head is small and streamlined, with markings like tear-shaped ebony stains that run from the corners of his eyes to his mouth. His body is gracefully tapered from chest to waist, his coarse yellow fur punctuated with black dots.

Ironically, the cheetah may be rushing headlong into the mists of legend. He has already been wiped out in India, the land that gave him his name (*chita* means "spotted" in Hindi). There, where until the end of the last century cheetahs roamed by the uncounted thousands, not one has been sighted since 1952. East Africa is his final stronghold—and no one knows just how long he can survive there.

There are many who confuse cheetahs with leopards—even Africans, who used to call both animals by the same Swahili name: *ngari*. Indeed, at first glance they look enough alike to be twins—both are tawny-furred, spotted cats. But beyond this superficial similarity, they are as different as a *sumo* wrestler and a ballerina.

THE CHEETAH: NATURE'S SPEED KING Reprinted with permission from *International Wildlife* (January–February 1971). Copyright 1970 by The Reader's Digest Assn., Inc.

The thick-set leopard, heavier by 30 pounds, operates in the shadows of the night, relying on heavy cover, stealth and close-up ambush tactics. The trim cheetah is a creature of the day who likes open spaces and long vistas. His eyesight, like that of all cats, is keen, enabling him to pick out even well-camouflaged prey at great distances.

The cheetah is distinguished even further from the leopard—and other felines—by some distinctly un-catlike features. His legs are long and thin-boned, like a dog's. His head looks too small for his body, and his jaws and teeth are undersized. Even such feline basics as tree-climbing do not always come easy to him. In the Nairobi National Park we watched one playful cheetah try to scramble up an acacia trunk. He made it about half-way to the lowest branches. There his claws lost their grip and, still clutching the tree, he slid indecorously to the ground. The trouble was that a cheetah's claws are not fully retractable and therefore grow worn and blunted—again like a dog's.

For all his tremendous speed, the cheetah has one serious shortcoming: lack of endurance. He is a sprinter, not a long-distance runner. If an all-out chase lasts for more than about 300 yards, he runs out of steam. We once watched a cheetah stalk a young impala. Too soon the impatient cat broke into full pursuit, long tail streaming as he twisted and turned after his prey. Just before he got within striking distance, his gait faltered. He slowed to a walk, then sank to the ground, his sides heaving from exhaustion as he watched the impala trot to safety.

The cheetah seems almost painfully aware that he lacks the power, presence and savagery of the other king-sized tooth-and-clawers. Except on rare occasions, he goes only after the smaller antelopes, killing quickly and cleanly. It is in keeping with his character that when he tries to roar, the sound that comes out is more like a "meow." In moments of contentment he may even chirp like a bird.

The cheetah's family life is generally uneventful. When a female is in season, several males may court her at the same time with little or no rivalry between them. After mating, she is left to herself. Gestation lasts about 90 days, and the female must hunt for her own food right through the last stages of pregnancy. The average litter size is four or five, with the newborn cubs looking as if their spots had gotten wet and the colors had run, turning their soft fur a neutral gray. (It is weeks before the cheetah gets well-defined spots.) After about ten days, the cubs' large eyes open, and after two or three weeks they are walking steadily on enormous feet. In a month or two, the young are ready to accompany their mother on hunts, learning as they go.

One evening in Kenya we watched a mother with four 10-month-old cubs. For a while she trotted along aimlessly as the cubs explored behind her, sniffing each rock and termite mound, and giving playful chase to the silver-backed jackals who were following the family in hopes of scrounging leftovers.

Soon the mother spotted a herd of Grant's gazelles, and froze. In an instant the cubs were at her side, sitting as erect as garden statues, ears perked up, watching the grazing antelope. As the mother went in for the kill, they followed slowly behind, not breaking into full speed themselves until the prey was down. Before their mother had released the gazelle's throat, the hungry cubs had begun to feed.

Once in Tanzania, a game warden watched a cheetah run down a small Thomson's gazelle, then bring it still alive to her young and release it, giving them first-hand practice in the chase. The lesson over, the mother stepped in for the kill and the whole family feasted.

During the learning process, cheetahs, who are normally solitary animals, travel together in family groups (fathers not included) until the young make their first kill—at about 12 months. Then the mother begins to leave them alone for longer periods each day until, after about 18 months, she abruptly departs for good. Only then does she mate again.

The cheetah's chief domain is some 400,000 square miles of African countryside, ranging from dry, almost desertlike scrubland (where water is a problem, cheetahs can subsist on the body fluids of their prey) to open, rolling grasslands dotted with thorn bush and stately umbrella acacias. One afternoon we spotted a cheetah resting on a hillock in just such a landscape. As we watched, a game warden drove up in his Land Rover and the cheetah strolled over to the jeep, put its forepaws on the door and stretched. The warden rolled down his window and scratched the cheetah behind the ears. "I've known that fellow since he was a tiny cub," the warden later explained. "But you'd never catch me doing that to a leopard, no matter how familiar he was to me."

The cheetah's mild nature makes it one of the easiest of all wild animals to domesticate. There is no record of an unprovoked attack on man. In fact, once tamed, they seem to take an almost doglike pleasure in pleasing. They are eager to learn, can be taught to retrieve sticks and balls, and are totally attached to their masters. They seem quite content with several cans of dog food, a fresh chicken and perhaps some frozen horsemeat in place of their daily ration of gazelle.

About the only prerequisite for owning one is affluence; they cost about $2,200 apiece at exotic pet stores. History contains plenty of precedent for keeping one as a pet. Genghis Khan owned one of the beasts and Charlemagne ruled most of medieval Europe with one dozing at his feet. (Even today, Haile Selassie, the Emperor of Ethiopia, is highly partial to his spotted speedster.) In India, mogul emperors, princes and maharajas kept cheetahs by the thousands and even trained them for the hunt.

Today the cheetah is the hunted. Its cured pelt is worth $1,200, and, until recently, fashionable women gladly paid $10,000 for a chic cheetah-skin coat. For each coat purchased, six cheetahs have found themselves in the sights of a poacher's gun. Skins also go into such souvenir items as fur-covered hatbands, lamp bases, pen holders, keychains, watchbands and even snap-on bow ties. But times are changing, and public sentiment is rising against such use of cheetah skins. Many leading furriers refuse to sell them.

Obviously big money outweighs risks, and though East African governments have proclaimed the cheetah a protected species and established stiff penalties, poaching remains prevalent. There are many loopholes in the law and often the offender gets away with only a token fine. In Ethiopia and Somalia, enforcement is practically nonexistent.

Other dangers, too, face the cheetah. Its domain is threatened as the open-bush and low-hill country of Africa increasingly comes under cultivation. The problem is worsened by the cheetah's notoriously slow breeding habits—each female produces only one litter about every two years. And infant mortality is high: of the average litter, only two or three survive to maturity.

Adults, too, are vulnerable. Although they can live to be 12 years old, not many do. Their fragile legs are easily broken, rendering them helpless to feed or flee. Lions and hyenas are their greatest natural enemies and will stalk and kill them if they can. But it is man's poaching which could push the animal over the brink of extinction.

Pessimistic conservationists give the cheetah about ten years before total eclipse. [Former] U.S. Secretary of the Interior Walter Hickel has added the Asiatic cheetah to his list of wildlife seemingly doomed to extinction, and has recommended that the United States prohibit the importation of skins or other parts, except for research.

Others are more optimistic. In addition to the growing conservation-mindedness of people the world over, they point to East Africa's many increasingly well-managed game reserves. Hopefully, it is not too late to turn the tide. In any case, it is a sad commentary on a speed-oriented age that the survival of nature's most magnificent entry into that field should now be in question.

SHEILA BURNFORD

Ohenemoos: The Indian Dog

Ohnemoos is the Ojibwa Indian word for dog; if there is more than one dog, it becomes Ohnemoosuk. And there always *is* more than one Indian dog: there is, in fact, a great unwanted surplus of Ohnemoosuk, and nowhere is one more conscious of this than at Big Trout Lake. I have been in many Indian villages in the extreme Northwest of Ontario, that territory ending on the desolate shores of Hudson Bay, and, while always conscious of dogs as a background as natural as woodsmoke, muskeg, and forest, mostly I retain the more vivid impressions of the inhabitants.

The settlement of Big Trout is on a small island; the time was spring, when the ice was newly gone out, and to the ranks of the already undernourished canine population were added the dogs that had followed families back across the ice from the winter's traplines, and were now marooned there on a few hundred acres of barren land. One could no more escape their presence than they could escape themselves. It would be the rare dog who would depart again before freeze-up; who would be valued enough to take up space in a family canoe, and reach the canine paradise of the summer fishing camps, there to gorge on fish guts and suckers.

Poor dog, poor Ohnemoos, is just another mouth to fill in a harsh country, and as such to be disregarded by the Indian, who has a hard enough job filling his children's mouths. The dog is back almost where he started in his relationship with nomadic man, one of a ring of hopeful jackals or wolves circling the seasonal camps, already convincing himself that some benefit must stem from an association with man. He must fight for his existence, starve or survive; this is the inexorable rule of nature which has governed man's own evolvement and which prevails still in the attitude of the Indian to Ohnemoos today: nature is of necessity pitiless.

The canine word has gone around that the white man is notoriously wasteful with his potato peelings and eggshells, his bits of gristle, burned toast, or apple cores. Besides, often he feeds at least one extra waif along with his own dog: today might be the very day he will take on two. Round and round the island the scavengers go, ever hopeful that the next round will produce some minor miracle—perhaps a beaver pelt, scraped clean and stretched to dry on a frame, will blow down from a roof's safekeeping; perhaps a snowshoe, with a tasty moose-hide thong, or a moccasin stitched with nourishing deer sinew, from a platform cache; perhaps, with any luck, there will be a chocolate-smeared child's face to lick, a fish bone here, a fledgling there. Whatever it might be, the lean snarling bitches with litters will almost certainly pounce first. And I, exploring the island on my own rounds, come to recognize each one of the pack: thin, often mangy or lame, fiercely cringing, warily aggressive, sneaky-eyed, for the most part unlovely pariahs.

Or so I thought at first, shocked and unhappy, fresh from a society that must pay for the privilege of owning a dog, and is liable to prosecution for neglecting it. But when I came to know them better, Ohnemoosuk of Big Trout Lake taught me an affecting lesson: ragged and gaunt they might be, an SPCA nightmare, but they had an unquenchable spirit and ebullience. One day, I watched a mangy half-grown pup drag up an old fishing net from the sand and tear off along the beach with the whole sorry pack in high delight after him in a glorious tumbling game of tag, and I realized that we do dog an anthropomorphistic injustice when we link him with terms of pathos and maudlin sentiment: dog is an incurable optimist, whatever his circumstances.

Pepra was a good example of a super-scrounger, and the one I came to know the best. Thin as a greyhound, blond and leggy, with artful wolf eyes that could take on a professionally abashed expression calculated to melt the stoniest heart, she looked as though she had not had a square meal since the day she was weaned. Theoretically she was not ownerless, belonging to one Susannah, a somewhat flighty character who had other things on her mind—such as an assortment of children and no husband. Pepra must have had me marked down from the moment I stepped out of the Cessna onto the dock, for she came begging around the door of my shack almost before I had unrolled a sleeping bag, and soon established herself as the top dog cleaner-upper after meals.

I encouraged her, for her very obvious attempts to charm amused me; then one cold evening I made the fatal mistake of allowing her to push her way in for a warm by the stove, after which she became extremely possessive. No sooner had she established her status than she dealt briskly and forcibly with any other beggars at the door. She is bound up inextricably with memory of Big Trout, for Pepra was not going to lose sight of her meal ticket for one minute if she could help it. Every inch that I explored of the island was in her company; and as she seemed to have innumerable friends and relations among the other hunger-restless dogs, they usually tagged along too. After a while I became resigned to the fact that if I wanted to search for fossils or flowers or artifacts, every stone that I turned over, every plant, was going to be examined by my interested following as well.

They were a raggle-taggle train for the most part, often snarling and fighting among themselves over some morsel picked up on the way. At first if their quarrels took place too close for my comfort (I am unreasonably terrified of the noise of dogfights), all I had to do was pick up a stick or stone, brandish it threateningly, and all would cringe off with flattened ears and lowered tails—a parody of servility, for their eyes remained bright and watchful. They were either very intelligent or very anxious to please, for in a remarkably short time quarreling was confined to a tolerable distance; they seemed to be only token demonstrations, teeth and noise and little else. After a while all I had to do was say "*psssss*," a noise I found no dog could stand, and order was instantly restored.

Having no option, I spent many hours observing the individual and pack reactions. Pepra had developed a fascinating technique that some of the smaller dogs were just beginning to adapt for themselves: she would collapse on her back at the first warning snarl over some tidbit, the traditional surrendering, but taking care to collapse her hips on the morsel. Meek and apologetic, she would lie there, tail tip quivering placatingly, while tradition now demanded that the victor step back stiffly to acknowledge her acknowledgment of defeat; then, quick as lightning, she would stretch her head backward along the ground, swiveling her hips while at the same time the middle of her body was righting itself; and before the other dog had time to grasp the meaning of this U-bend wriggle, she would be off with the morsel, fast as the ludicrous shaggy greyhound she resembled.

There were two pups in the pack that interested me particularly as a study in contrasts. They were very alike in coloring and height and the shape of their heads, and may well have been litter brothers, but while one was plump and jolly, the other was very thin and nervous. The plump and jolly one I knew was regularly fed at the nursing station, and only came along for the fun: he was the good-natured butt of the rest of the party, being forever jumped on, rolled over, or buffeted. The other was a sickly, irritable thing, with little energy, forever sitting down to scratch. One day he sat down near me to have a prolonged session with his fleas, and I noticed that he had a rope collar on. It was already straining cruelly around his growing neck, so I cut it off. Where the woolly fur had been chafed away on his throat there was a raw crescent of skin. He was such a poor little runt that I could not overcome the eternal (white man's) urge to be a do-gooder: I had a tube of calamine-based ointment in my pocket that I always carried around to stop me from scratching mosquito bites, and I applied some of this to the raw throat. I should have known better. Within seconds he had disappeared entirely from view under a scrimmage of excited dogs. Whether it was the calamine or the base, it was obviously a canine delicacy. When the pup eventually emerged he had been licked clean and his throat was twice as raw from the rasping tongues. And before I had time to put my glove back on I thought my

ointment-smeared fingers were going to be sucked into the avid mouth of
Walleye Junior, an unprepossessing character with one blind eye, who
looked like a small moth-eaten wolf. I never interfered again.

Walleye Junior and Walleye Senior were an interesting couple who
used to join us from the other end of the island. Senior was one of the
oldest, a most indomitable dog, with half of his left ear missing, two toes
on his left front paw, and almost all the hair from his left flank. I used
to try to imagine what possible combination of circumstances had brought
about these losses. He was a surly dog, which was hardly surprising.
He and Junior made an eerie picture together: about the same height,
they always ran with the opaque white eyes between them, so that one
got the strangest impression of a kind of dual three-eared head with a
pair of tinted glasses on the inner eyes, and an outer pair of sharp up-
ward-slanted eyes enclosing them. Of course I tried to convince myself
that they stayed together as an arrangement of mutual benefit, but common sense tells me now that the blind eyes likely were congenital, and
that the pair were probably siblings and had always naturally run together.
At the time I was watching them I was so engrossed in an atmosphere
of the fiercest determination of survival that I would have believed anything.
Sometimes I returned to the shack after one of these afternoon
expeditions along the trail that passed close to the fenced-in compound
of the weather station. There, in safe and solitary glory, sat the only
pedigreed dog on the island, a springer spaniel: from his smooth-domed
head with the long marcelled ears to his frilly leggings and gleaming
Fauntleroy shirtfront, he was immaculate—and as exotic there as the
Little Lord himself in the Northern bush. My scaramouch friends gazed
through the fence in silent awe; there were never any rude scufflings or
derisive barks; Ohnemoos knew his place apparently (although I must
admit I wondered if he would have kept it, and what he would have
done to those ears, if the fence had not been there). Lord Springer in
return gazed through and beyond the hungry peasants at his gate. I
thought he looked infinitely bored and rather stupid. At the end of two
weeks I had added "effete" into the bargain and felt positively sorry for
him.
I was fascinated and also strangely moved by my following's reaction
to me over the time I spent with them. Apart from Pepra, there was no
association with food, for after the ointment episode I never carried so
much as a piece of chocolate with me: I had seen how easily one might
become a rather battered bone of contention. And apart from that, they
were too many; anything left over to share after Pepra had been around
would have been a useless drop in the bottomless maw of their hunger.
They got nothing from me except my remote and somewhat school-
marmish presence. They came only because of their strange, age-old
craving for man's company. I began to understand why the Ojibwa had

placed them uniquely somewhere between man and spirit animal in the mythology evolved countless centuries ago.

Ohnemoosuk of Big Trout lead a most wretched bare existence by any standards, yet the overall impression was that they were not turned mean by it. The skeptic might say that they were too weak from general malnutrition to be savage, and to that I can only point out that any excess energy I saw was spent in chasing one another in play. Yet less than a hundred miles away in another Ojibwa settlement, Ohnemoos of Fort Severn gave a very different impression.

One day, lured by the prospect of fossils to be found on the riverbed, and tales of monster speckled trout just beyond the outgoing ice on the Pippiwatin River, I went up to Fort Severn with one of the nurses bound on her monthly visit. We flew there in a Cessna, and I watched below me the spruce and poplar of Big Trout change to barren land—at one point so desolate in its conformation of wavelike ridges, the long-drawn-out gleam of lakes lying in the hollows, that it looked as though the whole empty arc of world had been left when some global tide went out forever at the beginning of time. The horizon seems so round, the earth so flat there, that Hudson Bay was not visible where it merged with the tundra until we were almost on it—an endless stretch of bleak ice, with a thin line of clear blue water lying offshore.

The tiny windswept community is huddled on the high clay banks of the majestic Severn River just before it sweeps into the bay. It was free of ice now, and the Cessna landed in midstream, then taxied in until the floats rested against the landing at the bottom of a forty-foot clay bank. As I climbed out onto the slippery, treacherous clay, two small balls of fur detached themselves from the carcass of a gull and went for my boots; getting a firm grip on the lace holes they started worrying them like the gull so that I lost my balance and nearly fell in. They clung like furry limpets until the Indian who was holding the wing kicked them, whereupon they fell upon one another. One was snow white, with long guard hairs, like a polar bear cub, and the other was its chocolate-colored brother, both with the most savage demoniacal little faces I have ever seen on puppies, without a trace of the milk-blue innocence one usually finds in the eyes of anything so young. I met them again later, and they were fighting for possession of what I thought was a bone, but on closer examination turned out to be a dog's foreleg. Probably Mum's, I thought; it would be in keeping with their characters if they had polished her off when she weaned them.

They were my introduction to the dogs of Fort Severn: better-looking than their brothers of Big Trout in that they were bigger, with more Husky in them than Indian dog, but the fiercest dogs that I have ever come across. There was not one answering spark of canine good feeling in their cold eyes when they lit on anyone who was not their owner. The largest, the sled dogs, which were still plentiful here, were—thank heaven—staked out, their eyes wicked, their teeth bared as one passed by. Those wandering along the river path were thin and small, of the type that slinks off with raised lip when threatened, then creeps up stealthily behind with teeth at the ready for unwary heels. Plainly the smell of a white person was anathema to the lot of them. For the first time in my life I felt uneasy—to put it mildly—among dogs. Walleye Senior was a veritable Nana compared with this lot: I would not have trusted one further than I could kick it—and then with armor-plated boots.

Fortunately my faith in canine nature at Fort Severn was restored by one half-grown pup. He was a most engaging character, an indeterminate fawn and brown, the thick woolly coat making him seem quite substantial—until one patted him and felt the ribs sharp beneath—with one amber and one greenish blue eye in a pointed intelligent little face. I met him at Father Saigan's, the Oblate missionary, which explained his unusual friendliness, for the kindly little father had been feeding him scraps occasionally from what must have been his own very meager larder: it had been eight months since the supply boat, and another two would pass before it could return through the ice of Hudson Bay.

I was on my way to look for fossils, and stopped by at the tiny shack that was his rectory to see what he had found. He showed me some beautiful specimens; so I borrowed his rubber boots, the pup crawled out from his refuge behind a pile of logs, and we set off along the path that gradually sloped down from the riverbank—a dirty walk in ankle-deep clay.

It was an enchanting day, with a soft spring wind blowing, and at last a mile or so of beach in tide-washed smoothness, marred only by my Father Saigan footprints and those of the running, leaping, spring-mad puppy. The brown tundra landscape was desolate, Daliesque, with house-sized slabs of graying ice piled haphazardly on top of one another at the edge of the tidal limits, as though giant children had been playing there with building blocks; and all the time a background of noise, rumblings and growlings, grindings and sighings, as huge chunks crumbled and fell. My heart was in my mouth several times when the pup climbed up the rotten ice, jumping from block to block after gulls; but he must have been an old hand at the game, for always he leaped to safety just before a segment roared apart.

We walked on, and soon the settlement was far behind, and there was just the pup and myself in the whole world, walking, it seemed, nearly at its rim, two infinitesimal figures in the vast primeval emptiness. Because these terrestrial proportions so diminished us, because the pup was reduced to the whole proportionate measure of my circumscribed world, it was as though I saw every detail of him intensely magnified and clear: the fleeting lights in his tawny and blue-green eyes, every responsive quiver to the wind in the curved side slits of nostrils, each individual whisker antenna above his eyebrows, beneath his chin, standing out singly, even the separate action of his claws in the sand. I can see them yet in a clear timeless photograph taken by the heightened perception that was my mind's eye that day.

He chased sandpipers that rose in a wheeling group only to settle again further on, he rushed barking to the water's edge whenever an Arctic tern broke off from its watchful circling and plummeted down to the water, he dug for digging's sake as I turned over occasional smooth glacial boulders in my fossil quest. His enthusiasm so infected me at one point that I ran too; and my enthusiasm infected him in turn so that he leaped at me and grabbed the canvas shoulder bag and made off along the edge of the water, my precious specimens scattering as he went. But nothing mattered on a magic day like this. The fossils had been there for a million years and more: they could wait another million before I returned to pick them up.

Sometimes we looked up to the quick winging of paired ducks, and once to the slower majestic beat of Canada geese, flying so low that I could see the workings of the pinion feathers and the two neat contrasting lines that were the feet, tucked demurely into the snowy rump. They seemed to awe the pup as much as they did me; as he gazed up in wonder, the strap of the satchel dropped from his mouth, and I was able to retrieve it at last.

We turned when the tide came flooding back, for I had no wish to be caught leaping not so lightly on the piled-up ice blocks. I returned to Big Trout that evening with no fossils, no specimens of anything, but with the most vivid and exhilarating memory of an afternoon spent with a strange vagrant dog, part Husky, part wolf, part Indian dog, who had thrown in his lot with a stranger human for a day. He followed me down the steep, slithery ramp to the Cessna, when the land was washed by the mellow glow of the late Northern sunlight that turned his eyes to mismatched topaz, and bathed him in the short golden glory by which I shall always remember him.

And I wondered for the hundredth time as we flew back, what quirk of evolution thousands upon thousands of years ago impelled dog, alone of all the animals in the world, to throw in his lot with man, even as this pup had done this afternoon. He had no evolutionary need of man either: as his cousins wolf and jackal can testify, he could get along perfectly well without him. He chose deliberately, uniquely, his lot. The enigma fascinates me.

Pepra was waiting for me at Big Trout; protesting her undying love and admiration, she indicated that she had spent a hungry day. I taught her that evening to bark "please" and offer a paw for the reward of food. She learned both within about ten minutes. By the time I left Big Trout she was greeting me with her new repertoire on every possible occasion, and I felt that her future subsistence was assured at the hands of all visitors to the island: only a heart of solid stone will resist the frantic message of that disarming paw.

| ROBERT CAMPBELL

With Thee . . . I Plight My Troth

The two young cyclists came to a skidding halt and turned to stare as I eased the throbbing, supercharged Bugatti into the elevator of a New York garage.

"What's *dat?*" asked the girl incredulously.

"San ahmah'd cah," replied her boy companion.

"Ha'jah know san ahmah'd cah?" persisted the girl, somewhat dubiously.

"I know an ahmah'd cah when I sees one," snapped the boy, shutting off any further questions.

Such are the incidents that keep the true Bugatti owner going. It doesn't much matter whether the observations are accurate. The important thing is that they should occur with a high rate of frequency, for they provide a direct transfusion to what otherwise would be a seriously damaged ego. Without these little interludes few mortals could withstand the doubts, frustrations and anguish that assail a Bugatti owner as he sets out on the open road, the loneliest driver there because he knows full well that in so doing he is putting himsef several hundred, or perhaps a thousand, miles away from the nearest human being who has the faintest idea of what makes this particular machine tick.

By now it is almost common knowledge that the Bugatti is the greatest automobile ever made. There is an aura and mystique about these cars that applies to no other known vehicle. Throughout the 1920s and 1930s they swept the racing circuits of Europe, amassing an overall victory total that has yet to be surpassed. Top speed in some of the last models reached 180 mph, quite a clip even for today. To own a Bugatti was to possess what Sir Malcolm Campbell described as "a car in a class by itself." *"Pur sang"* was the term the aficionados used—thoroughbred. There is a story, possibly apocryphal but completely credible, about a Frenchwoman who poisoned her husband to collect his insurance—so she could buy her lover a Bugatti.

World War II put an end to the Bugatti era when the factory at Molsheim in eastern France was overrun by the German army. Ettore Bugatti, the Italian automotive genius who moved to France as a young man and designed the cars that bore his name, died shortly afterward. Hugh

WITH THEE . . . I PLIGHT MY TROTH By Robert Campbell. Reprinted by permission from *Sports Illustrated,* November 9, 1970. © 1970 Time, Inc.

Conway, a Briton and world authority on the cars, estimates that around 6,000 were produced during the 30-odd years of the era and that roughly 1,200 have survived. A few models even appeared in the postwar years. But the spark was gone. Yet, though more than a quarter century has passed, the Bugatti mystique remains as alive as ever. Two magazines in circulation today are devoted purely to Bugatti matters, a fact unique in automotive history. It is as though the era never ended. And in a way it hasn't, for some people anyway, as I discovered on seeing my first Bugatti.

The encounter took place in the summer of 1952. The car, a sleek gray convertible, had been brought to New York from Europe by an engineer friend who was also a sometime racing driver. I had practically lost all interest in automobiles at that point, though I retained vivid child-hood memories of the classic American cars of the '30s—my first hair-raising ride in a boat-tailed Auburn Speedster, then hours of curbside watching with the gang in our small town, hoping for a glimpse of one of the great Packards or Cadillacs or Lincolns and later the Cords. But something happened to cars after World War II.

One day in New York I met my friend's Bug (a frequently used diminutive, not a mechanical term). My first reaction was: "What a queer-looking automobile!" And indeed it was, completely unlike any other machine I had ever seen or even imagined. I circled the car warily, looked under it and sat in it as my friend chatted about finned racing brakes, the unique front axle, precise steering, instruments and so on. I still didn't get the idea though. Then he took me for a ride.

We headed uptown through Central Park. The engine made quite a racket. The springs were unyielding. We stopped for a red light just short of the S turns at the north end of the park. Two hopped-up motor-cyclists on gooked-up motorcycles pulled alongside, gave us the eye and emitted a challenging "vroom, vroom." The light changed and the Bugatti took off, accelerating with breathtaking speed. It took the sharp curves effortlessly, with but a slight movement of the steering wheel, as though the whole car were hung on rails. The motorcyclists fell behind and dropped from view. We returned to my friend's apartment and I took a second look at the car. This time I got the point.

The car looked exactly like what it had just done. Its design gave the impression of something light and poised, impatient and self-confident, capable, ready to spring alive at the slightest touch and take you whistling down the road at top speed, negotiating the tightest curve with ease, on and on to the end of the world if need be—and you'd better hop in right now or it might just up and depart without you. This pure expression of function and purpose had resulted in a uniquely beautiful automobile. There wasn't a single false note to the design. Every feature served and was subservient to the basics: acceleration, speed, road holding and endurance. Moreover, the design represented what would be called in mathematicians' terms the elegant solution to a problem, as opposed to solving it by brute force. Ettore Bugatti achieved his racing objectives with elegance and finesse, and that is just the way his cars look.

This, I think, is what lies at the core of the Bugatti mystique. There is a look about a Bugatti that says, "I am the Eternal Machine." Closer scrutiny will reveal the barest trace of a smile that says, "I am the Infernal Machine, too." But a novice like myself would not notice that. I was simply hooked. I had to have one of those cars. I had been bitten by the Bug bug but had no way of realizing the virulence of this disease. It has no known cure. It runs a long course, periodically racking the host in feverish convulsions until, hopefully, some immunity sets in. Even then the patient is never quite the same again.

The Bugatti hangup is a transcendental experience in the true sense, with the pilgrim progressing through levels of understanding as though through a series of veils, moving ever onward toward the True Reality, the Ultimate, the One—in this case a true perception of the Eternal Machine. Only a few make it through the full course of this disease. In this respect the Bug hangup is different from more popular indulgences such as glue sniffing and LSD popping, which produce hallucinations. But however gaudy and exciting these hallucinations may be, they have no objective reality. This is merely a form of self-induced schizophrenia. Bugatti owners, on the other hand, are not the least bit schizzed. A Bug is, after all, a real thing—just as real as Ahab's whale.

At the time I got hooked I realized I lacked several important qualifications for owning a Bugatti. It seemed to me that to maintain such a machine it was necessary to be either rich or a good mechanic, and preferably both. Since the latter course was the only one reasonably open to me, I set out to acquire some knowledge about automobile engines. I read a book. Then, for $150, I bought a disheveled 1927 Rolls-Royce touring car and hauled it out to a small garage in New Jersey. I took it apart—and over a year of weekend work went by before I got the Rolls back together. Surprisingly enough it actually ran. I drove the car around the block and back to the garage. Then I returned proudly to the city. The next day it turned cold and the Rolls' block cracked.

The week after that I sold it to a fellow from Wilkes-Barre for $75. It was a beautiful, sunny day and as the Rolls disappeared I sat down on the curb and almost cried. Had I known at the time the true meaning of all the weekends I had invested I might very well have shot myself. For one could spend a whole lifetime working on Rolls-Royces and hardly learn anything relating to Bugattis, as I found out later on.

Now thinking myself prepared, I set out in search of a Bugatti. And five years after being bitten by the Bug bug I had a shot at one—a sleek, white, supercharged, four-door bomb, a late 1939 tourer and one of the last Bugattis made. I phoned a crotchety old Alsatian mechanic I had become acquainted with; I was at least smart enough to know I would need a consultant.

"Charlie, I'd like you to take a look at a Bugatti I want to buy."

"Dun't buy it."

"But I want to buy it."

"Dun't buy it."

"But I *want* it!"

"Are you rich?"

"No."

"Dun't buy it."

"But I'm in love with the car, Charlie."

"So marry it. But dun't buy it."

I brought the car to Charlie's shop. He contemplated it dubiously. He stuck a finger up the tail pipe and looked at the black smudge that resulted. Dubiously. He lifted the hood, picked up a yard-long stick of wood, pressed one end to the engine and the other to his ear, and listened, dubiously. The stethoscope effect, I thought to myself cheerily, admiring Charlie. "What do you think of her, Charlie?" He arched his eyebrows, hunched his shoulders and curled down the corners of his mouth, all dubiously. "It runs," he said. Then he walked away.

For a modest investment of $2,000 I became what is known in some quarters as a *Bugattiste*. I experienced instantly what might be described, in transcendental terms, as the "novitiate's bends." I finally had my hands on the Ultimate Automobile. And I felt I now stood in the presence of some Final Revelation.

The Bugatti did everything in its power to encourage this deception—by continuing to run, for example. In buying it I had also become a member of what must be the world's most exclusive key club. The ignition keys of most of the later-model cars are identical. A distinct touch! *Un vrai beau geste!* What owner of a Bugatti would conceivably make off with another's machine?

Our first outings together were a success, both socially and sonically. Driving along to the supercharged whine of the engine was pure joy. It was also marvelous for the ego. Pedestrians stared. Crowds gathered. Notes with messages and phone numbers were stuck under the windshield wipers: "Call me immediately! Desperate!" "Take $6,000 cash?" A Britisher with a highly pinstriped suit, a spanking-new Rolls-Royce and a complete Arthur Treacher accent pulled alongside one evening:

"Oh, I say! Booghhatti, isn't it?"

"Yes it is."

"Late model, what?"

"Fifty-seven C—late '39."

"Thought so. Mahhhvelus to see one. Simply mahhhhvelus. Luck, old chap!"

There are, one should admit, sexual overtones to such an ego-expanding machine. "Good God!" exclaimed a friend's wife at her first sight of the car. "That's the biggest phallic symbol I've ever seen!" A stop at a favorite French restaurant one evening produced similar results. Guy the bartender, the *patron* and his wife and half the clientele poured out to the sidewalk to admire this particular piece of French pastry. Guy drew me aside and whispered with an air of Gallic savoir faire, "She eez gude for getteeng zee girls, *non?*"

I began to venture out on longer trips, explaining to my wife all the instruments, levers and buttons on the dash, the trick of revving up the engine, double-clutching and shifting down just at the right sound (which, if missed, produces a nerve-shattering grind from the gearbox) and other features of the car. I even let her drive it (she's a good driver). She accepted the hangup with a kind of serene confidence that I wasn't totally balmy or worse and even came to enjoy the car to some extent, I think. That's important. For, short of bringing some young thing home to live with you, I can't imagine anything that could break up a marriage quicker than a Bugatti. It is totally impossible to explain the hours over at the shop doing little things like polishing the brake drums or repacking the water pump or searching through store after store for some obscure kind of grease that hasn't been made in 30 years. In all that time who knows what you've been up to?

A notice appeared once in the sports section of the Sunday *Times* advertising two Bugattis for sale. It concluded with: "Wife says must go." I couldn't help feeling that if that was the way it was with them the fellow would have been better off keeping the cars instead.

On the open road I developed a facile habit of turning small defects into large virtues that, at the least, must have been mildly infuriating. One Christmas we started out for Maryland in a light snowstorm to spend a few days with my mother. We were hardly under way when the windshield-wiper motor quit. "Ha!" I said to my wife. "Now you'll see that Mr. Bugatti thought of everything." I reached for a walnut knob on the walnut dash. This knob connected directly with the wipers and by turning it left right, left right the wipers did the same. For 250 miles I worked the wipers by hand. A pessimist might have said that the car needed that knob because the wiper motor was none too reliable. But I didn't look at it that way. I couldn't afford to, emotionally.

We arrived at my mother's house and were greeted with the news that my old friend Bill was having a cocktail party and we were definitely expected. We went, and my old friend Bill held out a drink for me. I accepted it in the wiper hand, curling my stiff fingers around the glass. Immediately and automatically the hand rotated gently to the left and dumped the drink down my old friend Bill's shirt.

In the course of such trips I became superstitious about the car, convinced that it was inhabited by some druidlike spirit. Once I took it out while a bit tipsy. The motor gradually died and the Bug refused to budge. I attributed this to a kind of self-preservation instinct on the part of the car. The next day it ran perfectly. On one of those hypnotic hauls up the New Jersey Turnpike the sound of the motor seemed to rise and fall rhythmically. It alarmed me. I couldn't understand it. I popped my ears.

The rhythm persisted. I finally concluded that the car had undertaken to keep the driver awake.

Approaching New York at dawn I glanced in the rearview mirror. An enormous cloud of white smoke was billowing out behind the Bugatti. "My God!" I thought. "The Red Baron has shot us down!" I pulled off the road and lifted the hood. Nothing. I started up again. Nothing. No smoke, no nothing. We finished the trip, wide awake but quite without incident.

This mixture of awe and superstition, fantasy, fright and rationalization presents a reasonably accurate sketch of the classic fool's paradise. Somewhere in the back of my mind was developing a terrible, unformulated thought, "I really don't know a blinking thing about this automobile." My ego bubble was about to burst. One "pop" and all that élan would vanish. It was time for me to be graduated from the Lower Level to the Second Stage. I was quite unaware of this, thinking somewhat foolishly that I had already arrived.

Graduation exercises took place on a trip to Richmond with a film producer friend named Larry Madison. I picked up Larry at his house, handed him a stick of gum and asked if he would mind chewing some. "We have an oil leak," I explained as we headed south. (Charlie had told me that gum was a good leak sealer in a pinch.) We made Richmond with only a few stops for gum and water for the radiator and headed back the next afternoon. In the middle of nowhere, the bad news came in the form of a loud rapping sound in the engine. "Sounds like a connecting rod," said Larry. We limped into a little one-horse town and up to a garage. A mechanic came out.

"My friend is sick," I said.

"Mebbe I can hep ya."

"No, sir, I don't think you can."

The mechanic seemed insulted. He lifted the hood, took one look at the supercharged Bugatti engine and slammed the hood down again.

"No, suh, I don't think I can eitheh."

"Well, tell us how to get the bus to Fredericksburg and mail me the car."

The next morning, back in New York, I called Charlie:

"Our mutual friend is sick."

"*Qu'est-ce qu'il y a?*"

"*Il y a un* burned-out bearing, I think."

Charlie just whistled.

Several days later the Bugatti arrived at Charlie's shop on a truck. It was pushed against the side wall along with a Lagonda, a Delahaye, a Hispano-Suiza, a Packard tourer and several Rolls-Royces that awaited the Master's attention. I asked him what he thought a job like mine would run. "Don't count on getting out of here for less than $750" was as far as he would go. I volunteered to help out on weekends, doing uncritical chores like taking off nuts and bolts and cleaning up parts and so on, with some vague idea that I would thereby learn something and possibly also cut costs. Charlie agreed.

My racing friend took a dim view of this plan, pointing out that there were a lot of things about Bugatti engines that you really have to know in order to rebuild one properly, that tolerances, nut tightnesses and things like that are critical in a racing engine, even a detuned touring version of the engine. He urged me to send the engine back to the factory in France. I refused, feeling that if I did I would end up knowing no more about the car than I did to start with, whereas if I helped out around Charlie's shop I would discover what made the thing tick. Secretly, of course, I was actually blowing up a new ego balloon to replace the one that had just popped. This balloon, appropriate to the Second Stage, would be labeled with the following doubtful proposition:

List all possible false starts. What then remains is the right way. The proposition is suspect because with a Bugatti there are an infinite number of possible false starts.

Work began in Charlie's shop, which on a Bugatti is not easy, because the engine must be removed completely from the car before anything significant can be accomplished. To get it out, the hood, side panels, front fenders and radiator have to come off. Only then comes the really unique challenge of the celebrated Bugatti power plant. It is put together with dozens and dozens of little nuts and bolts, like an airplane engine, instead of a lesser number of larger ones. "Must have had someone working full time just making nuts and bolts," muttered Charlie. The nuts and bolts also come in a fantastic variety of sizes, requiring not only a full complement of European metric wrenches but some British and American wrenches and a few pure Bugatti wrenches. Some nuts are almost impossible to get at without hiring a part-time midget or bending a perfectly good wrench into some corkscrew shape. Watching Charlie struggle with one particularly inaccessible nut behind the water pump, I remarked with some pride: "I guess Mr. Bugatti built his cars to stay together, not come apart." Charlie exploded: "Damn guinea ought to have been a Swiss watchmaker!"

After several weeks of this the famous Bugatti crankshaft came out. Unlike most crankshafts, which are cast, this remarkable object was machined out of a solid billet of steel—journals, counterweights and all. "It's beautiful," I said. "A work of art," commented Charlie grudgingly. "Didn't nobody make *that* in a day. Well, no use just standing here looking at it." Somehow that's what happened, though, for almost two years.

In an effort to keep things going I fiddled around with trivial matters like scraping 25 years of gook off the chassis with a putty knife, getting small parts rebuilt and taking the eight-day stop clock to the watchmaker. From time to time Charlie would look at the parts scattered about his old, dingy shop and remark: "Yes, sir. We gotta be sober when we put *that* back together."

Finally Charlie got around to me. I found him with my pistons lined up on a workbench. "Watcha doin'?" I asked with as much casualness as I could muster. "Knurling up your pistons. Makes 'em a little larger." This, Charlie had reasoned, would compensate for the fact that pistons and cylinder walls had undoubtedly become somewhat worn through use. I pointed out to Charlie that I had backtracked on the history of the car and discovered it already had oversized pistons in it. A previous owner had demanded that it run quieter. "When you leave here you're gonna have a nice tight engine, son" was Charlie's only response.

The engine gradually resumed its original shape. And then came the problem of getting it back into the car. Charlie devoted a whole day to squeezing the engine back in—pulling, pushing, turning, wiggling and kicking at it in the process. Every now and then his pressure valve let go: "A lot of other people made automobiles that stood up, didn't they? Him and his crazy ideas." Later, in a muffled singsong from beneath the car: *"La Misère. La Misère de Bugatti"* (imparting to the name the full flavor of its proper pronunciation—Boo-gha-tee). Finally he succeeded, crawled out from under the car and kicked it viciously. "Any man ever made a crazy automobile, this is it! Mr. Bugatti, I hate you!"

Charlie started the car. It ran, in a somewhat ragged fashion. Charlie fiddled around, and the engine sounded smoother. His assistant suggested that maybe now the fenders and hood could go back on. "No sir," snapped Charlie, "not until the engine is running perfectly."

The car was run in the shop periodically for several days, and then the old man took it out and drove it around the block. Hood and fenders went back on. After that the Bugatti refused to run at all. Charlie stared at the car in disbelief. "Heartbreaking automobile," he said. He fiddled some more. "It's some damn little thing about this big," he said, holding up two fingers about two inches apart.

I called a Bugatti expert in Connecticut to ask if he would take a look. He couldn't but said he would send someone. The next day a little man arrived with a little Bugatti emblem in the lapel of his coat, which somehow infuriated me. The little man removed a sparkplug and took a compression check. There was a slight whistling sound but no compression. The same was true in other cylinders. "The valves are all bent," the little man said. Then he went home.

Charlie couldn't believe it. Summer came and went and he still couldn't believe it. Apparently there are things about a Bugatti that elude a good Rolls-Royce man. But in the fall he went at it again, took the engine out, dismantled it, straightened the valves and reassembled the car once more. In the latter operation he followed a suggestion made by the Connecticut consultant to make assembly easier. He glued the piston rings to the cylinders to make inserting them easier. Then he poured solvent through the sparkplug holes to dissolve the cement and release the rings, draining the resulting gunk out of the bottom of the engine. Then came the day for the Great Road Test.

I had a business date at a research lab in New Jersey, and Charlie agreed that a run out there would be a good first trip. Early the next morning I arrived at the shop. The car was poised and ready to go, all warmed up and with a blanket over the classic, horseshoe-shaped radiator. Charlie was ready to go, too. No coveralls for a classy test like this. Instead a tweed suit and golf cap. We made the 35-mile trip without incident, and I waved goodby to Charlie as he headed back to the city. By mid-afternoon, unable to bear the suspense any longer, I called the shop.

"How are things?"

"Not so good."

"What happened?"

"You know that long, slow grade up to the George Washington Bridge?"

"Yes."

"Burned out a bearing."

This time it was my turn to whistle. I returned to the city, got to the shop as soon as I could and looked at the fine-mesh wire screen that forms the car's oil filter. It was completely covered with a kind of gooey slop. The recommended solvent had dissolved the glue, all right. But Charlie had not gotten it all out of the engine. The residue had clogged off all oil circulation, which is as good a way as any to burn out a bearing. Charlie took the hood and fenders off again.

I made the next road test myself, down the West Side Highway, around the Battery and up the FDR Drive, where I knew I could keep moving and the car would not overheat. But at the Battery it began to overheat. And by the time I reached the 96th Street exit it was boiling. I pulled off and stopped. The car spat out several quarts of boiling water. I sat there waiting for it to cool down. "Charlie made me a nice, tight engine all right," I thought, "and it'll take about 10,000 miles to break it in."

I speculated briefly on what people would think of an ad in the *Times* that read: *"Owner* says must go!" I rejected the idea as being unfair to the Bugatti—humiliating, even. After all, it was not *its* fault that it had become involved in some affair of the halt leading the blind into one cul-de-sac after another. It was not *its* fault if it became overheated. To hell with élan and all that. To hell with *my* ego. What about *its* ego? The car deserved better than this.

At this point, unaware as ever, I was beginning to move from the Second Level to the Third Level, where the split occurs between Bugatti fanciers and Bugatti lovers. I very well might have decided that the car was just too much trouble, persuaded Charlie to get it running somehow and unloaded it on the next unsuspecting fancier. I imagine quite a few Bugattis change hands at this stage. But I couldn't do it. I cared about the car and wanted to see it functioning properly. And, despite the hangups, I had learned enough to become convinced of something that is the definition of the Third Level: No matter what anyone says, there *is* a Right Way.

"Bugattis run hot," Charlie had said. I was quite certain by this point that only sick Bugattis ran hot. After all, the engine was designed to run wide open for 24 hours straight in a race like Le Mans, for example. So why should it boil over tooling around Manhattan at 35 or 40 mph? Charlie had obviously made the pistons too tight. And there were probably several dozen other things wrong with the engine that I didn't know about. But I was quite sure by now that there was a Right to it and that in some ultimate way a Bugatti engine did make sense. Further, I was hooked on the thought of one day knowing what *that* engine would be like.

I tried to start the car but the engine had seized and would not turn over at all. A tow truck hauled us back to Charlie's shop. Charlie broke the engine loose by applying a crowbar to the flywheel and presented his bill—$1,500. My jaw sagged. Charlie was a sport about it, though. He knew I wanted to keep the car in his shop. There were still a million little things to attend to. And he let me pay him in the course of the next month or so.

Good times returned. I ran the car carefully and managed to keep it below boiling. Gradually it loosened up and cooled down, and the joys of the open road returned. We had the car on Nantucket one whole summer, and it enjoyed the cool climate. The Bugatti went to the store and performed other minor errands, just like any family car. But time finally ran out on another trip back from Maryland. The oil pressure dropped, and again came the telltale hammering. This time the engine went back to the factory. Quite a few letters were exchanged. A query as to what had gone wrong evoked the stark reply: *"Le passage d'huile des manetons du vilebrequin était complètement bouché."* Which is to say that the oil channels of the crankshaft were plugged up. More of that glue-and-solvent gunk, no doubt.

In due time the engine returned from the factory completely rebuilt to original Bugatti specifications. It sounded great—very strong. It ran at a cool 65° centigrade, just like my old manual said it should. I broke it in carefully and began to take it up slowly to the higher rpms. It, in turn, began to run hot. The radiator was flushed out. Still it ran hot. Once on the open road it boiled over quite unaccountably. After that a slight rapping sound could be heard when the engine was cold. The sound disappeared once it was warmed up, which meant that when I took the car to a mechanic to ask about it, it wouldn't make its noise.

Disaster came on a long trip to upstate New York with a friend named Dunbar. We were climbing a long grade near the little town of Herkimer when suddenly smoke began to pour up from beneath the floorboards, accompanied by a death rattle from the engine. Dunbar remarked: "Bubbie, I do believe we're afire." I pulled off the road. The engine stopped with a clunk that had all the finality of a prison gate being slammed shut. I lifted the hood. The No. 1 spark was covered with a whitish paste that I could only imagine was vaporized aluminum from a piston. We were only a few miles short of our destination and soon managed to get a push to the motel. I put in a call to Bob Schultze, the best mechanic I know, who has a shop in New Jersey near where I now live. "We've come a cropper," I said.

Bob closed his shop at noon the next day and came to fetch us.

Quite unbelievably it turned out that The Works, as the Bugatti factory is sometimes called, had blundered. Someone had installed the No. 1 piston and connecting rod backward, which put a lot of pressure on the weak side of the piston. This, in turn, had made for excessive friction and explained the overheating. Under the strain the piston had finally exploded into two fragments. This discovery restored my confidence in the rightness of the engine. Once more a defect in execution, not in design.

A month later I set out on a business trip to the West Coast. I wrapped up one of the good pistons and rods in a paper bag and put it in my suitcase. "If anything happens to the airplane," I told my wife, "and the FAA finds this piston while they're poking around in the rubble, it'll take them three months and cost the Government $10,000 to figure out where it came from." I had a side destination on the Coast, the shop of O. A. Phillips near Pasadena. Bunny, as he's called, is the honorary chairman of the American Bugatti Club. He had the original Bugatti agency in Hollywood in the 1930s, raced the cars then and has worked on practically nothing but Bugattis since. If anyone in the world knows the Right of it, I figured, it's got to be Bunny.

We talked for three hours about little details and touches I'd never heard of or even imagined, and when I returned home I shipped Bunny my engine.

Later, Bob and I contemplated the body. It, too, clearly needed attention to prevent it from deteriorating. We put it on a truck and carted it off to the obvious mecca for bodies, Earl Lewis' Restoration Shop near Princeton. Ultimately the chassis, too, will be towed to still a third mecca for rewiring and a few other things, a place known as Vintage Auto Restorations, Inc. run by an East Coast Bug expert named Donald Lefferts.

That's about as far as you can scatter an automobile. But I know now that it's the Right Way. Old Charlie was right about one thing at least, asking, "Are you rich?" But I cannot let that nagging question interfere now. For somewhere along the line I took another piece of his advice and married the car, for better or worse (and in sickness and in health). I now stand on the threshold of the Fourth Level where, like Ahab's whale, the Eternal Machine beckons. I know now that there is indeed such a thing as a real Bugatti, a car that will run to the end of the world if need be, with that feeling of joy and response I have had but the faintest glimpse of so far. And I have my hands on one—almost. All that remains is for it to come together. Somewhere in my future there is the Ultimate Automobile. Name: Bugatti. I hope we make it.

JOHN McPHEE

From Encounters with the Archdruid

David Brower, who talks to groups all over the country about conservation, refers to what he says as The Sermon. He travels so light he never seems far from home—one tie, one suit. He calls it his preacher suit. He has given the sermon at universities, in clubs, in meeting halls, and once in a cathedral (he has otherwise not been in a church for thirty years), and while he talks he leans up to the lectern with his feet together and his knees slightly bent, like a skier. He seems to feel comfortable in the stance, perhaps because he was once a ski mountaineer.

Sooner or later in every talk, Brower describes the creation of the world. He invites his listeners to consider the six days of Genesis as a figure of speech for what has in fact been four billion years. On this scale, a day equals something like six hundred and sixty-six million years, and thus "all day Monday and until Tuesday noon, creation was busy getting the earth going." Life began Tuesday noon, and "the beautiful, organic wholeness of it" developed over the next four days. "At 4 P.M. Saturday, the big reptiles came on. Five hours later, when the redwoods appeared, there were no more big reptiles. At three minutes before midnight, man appeared. At one-fourth of a second before midnight, Christ arrived. At one-fortieth of a second before midnight, the Industrial Revolution began. We are surrounded with people who think that what we have been doing for that one-fortieth of a second can go on indefinitely. They are considered normal, but they are stark, raving mad."

Brower holds up a photograph of the world—blue, green, and swirling white. "This is the sudden insight from Apollo," he says. "There it is. That's all there is. We see through the eyes of the astronauts how fragile our life is, how thin is the epithelium of the atmosphere."

Brower has computed that we are driving through the earth's resources at a rate comparable to a man's driving an automobile a hundred and twenty-eight miles per hour—and he says that we are accelerating. He reminds his audiences that buffalo were shot for their tongues alone, and he says that we still have a buffalo-tongue economy. "We're hooked on growth. We're addicted to it. In my lifetime, man has used more resources than in all previous history. Technology has just begun to happen. They are *mining* water under Arizona. Cotton is subsidized by all that water. Why grow cotton in Arizona? There is no point to this. People in Texas want to divert the Yukon and have it flow to Texas. We are going to fill San Francisco Bay so we can have another Los Angeles in a state that deserves only one. Why grow to the point of repugnance? Aren't we repugnant enough already? In the new subdivisions, everybody can have a redwood of his own. Consolidated Edison has to quadruple by 1990. Then what else have you got besides kilowatts? The United States has six per cent of the world's population and uses sixty per cent of the world's resources, and one per cent of Americans use sixty per cent of that. When one country gets more than its share, it builds tensions. War is waged over resources. Expansion will destroy us. We need an economics of peaceful stability. Instead, we are fishing off Peru, where the grounds are so rich there's enough protein to feed the undernourished of the world, and we bring the fish up here to fatten our cattle and chickens. We want to build a sea-level canal through Central America. The Pacific, which is colder than the Atlantic, is also higher. The Pacific would flow into the Atlantic and could change the climate of the Caribbean. A dam may be built in the Amazon basin that will flood an area the size of Italy. Aswan Dam, by blocking the flow of certain nutrients, has killed off the sardine fisheries of the eastern Mediterranean. There is a human population problem, but if we succeed in interrupting the cycle of photosynthesis we won't have to worry about it. Good breeding can be overdone. How dense can people be?"

More than one of Brower's colleagues—in the Sierra Club, of which he was for seventeen years executive director, and, more recently, in his two new organizations, Friends of the Earth and the John Muir Institute for Environmental Studies—has compared him to John Brown. Brower approaches sixty, but under his shock of white hair his grin is youthful and engaging. His tone of voice, soft and mournful, somehow concentrates the intensity of his words. He speaks calmly, almost ironically, of "the last scramble for the last breath of air," as if that were something we had all been planning for. "There is DDT in the tissues of penguins in the Antarctic," he says. "Who put the DDT in Antarctica? We did. We put it on fields, and it went into streams, and into fish, and into more fish, and into the penguins. There is pollution we know about and pollution we don't know about. It took fifty-seven years for us to find out that radiation is harmful, twenty-five years to find out that DDT is harmful, twenty years for cyclamates. We're getting somewhere. We have recently found out that polychlorinated biphenyls, a plastic by-product, have spread throughout the global ecosystem. At Hanford, Washington, radioactive atomic waste is stored in steel tanks that will have to be replaced every fifteen years for a thousand years. We haven't done *anything* well for a thousand years, except multiply. An oil leak in Bristol Bay, Alaska, will put the red salmon out of action. Oil exploration off the Grand Banks of Newfoundland will lead to leaks that will someday wreck the fisheries there. We're hooked. We're addicted. We're committing grand larceny against our children. Ours is a chain-letter economy, in which we pick up early handsome dividends and our children find their mailboxes empty. We must shoot down the SST. Sonic booms are unsound. Why build the fourth New York jetport? What about the fifth, the sixth, the seventh jetport? We've got to kick this addiction. It won't work on a finite planet. When rampant growth happens in an individual, we call it cancer."

To put it mildly, there is something evangelical about Brower. His approach is in some ways analogous to the Reverend Dr. Billy Graham's exhortations to sinners to come forward and be saved now because if you go away without making a decision for Christ coronary thrombosis may level you before you reach the exit. Brower's crusade, like Graham's, began many years ago, and Brower's may have been more effective. The clamorous concern now being expressed about conservation issues and environmental problems is an amplification—a delayed echo—of what Brower and others have been saying for decades. Brower is a visionary. He wants—literally—to save the world. He has been an emotionalist in an age of dangerous reason. He thinks that conservation should be "an ethic and conscience in everything we do, whatever our field of endeavor" —in a word, a religion. If religions arise to meet the most severe of human crises, now and then religions may come too late, and that may be the case with this one. In Brower's fight to save air and canyons, to defend wilderness and control the growth of population, he is obviously desperate, an extreme and driven man. His field, being the relationship of everything to everything else and how it is not working, is so comprehensive that no one can comprehend it. Hence the need for a religion and for a visionary to lead it. Brower once said to me, "We are in a kind of religion, an ethic with regard to terrain, and this religion is closest to the Buddhist, I suppose." I have often heard him speak of "drawing people into the religion," and of being able to sense at once when people already have the religion; I also remember a time, on a trail in the Sierra Nevada, when he said, "We can take some cues from other religions. There is something else to do than bang your way forward."

Throughout the sermon, Brower quotes the gospel—the gospel according to John Muir ("When we try to pick out anything by itself, we find it hitched to everything else in the universe"), the gospel according to Henry David Thoreau ("What is the good of a house if you don't have a tolerable planet to put it on?"), the gospel according to Buckminster Fuller ("Technology must do more with less"), and the gospel according to Pogo ("We have met the enemy and he is us"). A great deal of the sermon is, in fact, a chain of one-liners from the thinking sector: "The only true dignity of man is his ability to fight against insurmountable odds" (Ignazio Silone), "Civilization is a thin veneer over what made us what we are" (Sigurd Olson), "Despair is a sin" (C. P. Snow), "Every cause is a lost cause unless we defuse the population bomb" (Paul Ehrlich), "The wilderness holds answers to questions man has not yet learned how to ask" (Nancy Newhall).

Brower has ample ideas of his own about what might be done. He says, "Roughly ninety per cent of the earth has felt man's hand already, sometimes brutally, sometimes gently. Now let's say, 'That's the limit.' We should go back over the ninety and not touch the remaining ten per cent. We should go back, and do better, with ingenuity. Recycle things. Loop the system." When he sees an enormous hole in the ground in the middle of New York City, he says, "That's all right. That's part of the ninety." In non-wilderness areas, he is nowhere happier than in places where the ninety has been imaginatively gone over—for example, Ghirardelli Square in San Francisco, a complex of shops and restaurants in a kind of brick Xanadu that was once a chocolate factory. When someone asks him what one person can do, Brower begins by mentioning Rachel Carson. Then he tells about David Pesonen, a young man in California who stopped a nuclear-power station singlehanded. Then he sprays questions. "Are you willing to pay more for steak, if cattle graze on level ground and not on erodable hills? Are you willing to pay more for electricity, if the power plant doesn't pollute air or water?" He taunts the assembled sinners. "You are villains not to share your apples with worms. Bite the worms. They won't hurt nearly as much as the insecticide does. You are villains if you keep buying automobiles. Leave these monsters in the showroom." Invariably, he includes what must be his favorite slogan: "Fight blight, burn a billboard tonight!"

The cause is, in a sense, hopeless. "Conservationists have to win again and again and again," he says. "The enemy only has to win once. We are not out for ourselves. We can't win. We can only get a stay of execution. That is the best we can hope for. If the dam is not built, the damsite is still there. Blocking something is easiest. Getting a wilderness bill, a Redwoods Park bill, a Cascades Park bill, is toughest of all."

Brower is somewhat inconvenienced by the fact that he is a human being, fated, like everyone else, to use the resources of the earth, to help pollute its air, to jam its population. The sermon becomes confessional when he reveals, as he almost always does, that he has four children and lives in a redwood house. "We all make mistakes," he explains. His own mistakes don't really trouble him, though, for he has his eye on what he knows to be right. After he gave a lecture at Yale once, I asked him where he got the interesting skein of statistics that six per cent of the world's population uses sixty per cent of the world's resources and one per cent of the six per cent uses sixty per cent of the sixty per cent. What resources? Kleenex? The Mesabi Range?

Brower said the figures had been worked out in the head of a friend of his from data assembled "to the best of his recollection."

"To the best of his *recollection?*"

"Yes," Brower said, and assured me that figures in themselves are merely indices. What matters is that they feel right. Brower feels things. He is suspicious of education and frankly distrustful of experts. He has no regard for training per se. His intuition seeks the nature of the man inside the knowledge. His sentiments are incredibly lofty. I once heard him say, "It's pretty easy to revere life if you think of all the things it's done while it was onstage." He is not sombre, though. Reading a newspaper, he will come upon a piece by a conservation writer and say, "I like that. He's neutral the right way."

Brower is a conservationist, but he is not a conservative. I have heard him ask someone, "Do you like the world so much that you want to keep it the way it is?"—an odd question to be coming from David Brower, but he was talking about the world of men. The world of nature is something else. Brower is against the George Washington Bridge. He is against the Golden Gate Bridge. He remembers San Francisco when the bridge was not there, and he says the entrance to the bay was a much more beautiful scene without it. He would like to cut back the population of the United States to a hundred million. He has said that from the point of view of land use the country has not looked right since 1830. There are conservationists (a few, anyway) who are even more vociferous than Brower, but none with his immense reputation, none with his record of battles fought and won—defeater of dams, defender of wilderness. He must be the most unrelenting fighter for conservation in the world. Russell Train, chairman of the President's Council on Environmental Quality, once said, "Thank God for Dave Brower. He makes it so easy for the rest of us to be reasonable. Somebody has to be a little extreme. Dave is a little hairy at times, but you do need somebody riding out there in front."

| JOHN CORRY

A Man Called Perry Horse

"We used to say, 'Were you scared?' and he'd say, 'Gee, man, of course,' and then he'd tell us how they had old men riding along with them, and how the job of the old men would be to keep talking to the young guys, telling them to keep their courage up, and not to get scared." The man saying this is a young man, and he is talking about conversations with his great-grandfather, who died in 1953 at the great age of 106, and was called Man Who's Hunting for a Horse. The young man himself is called Perry Horse, and he thinks that when he has children he may call them something like Hunting Horse, which is closer to his great-grandfather's name than just plain Horse, and more distinctive, too. Great Grandfather once rode like hell through Texas and Mexico, shooting citizens and stealing horses, and when he died so many years later, being practically a monument at the time, and getting buried in moccasins and an old soldier's uniform, it took six buses just to carry his friends and relatives to the funeral, not to mention the Congressmen and other prominent people who showed up. Perry Horse, the great-grandson, remembers him well, and he remembers him talking about his own father, who, of course, would be the great-great-grandfather of Perry Horse. When Great Great Grandfather was just a shaver, he was captured by a mean Pawnee with one eye, and years later, when the Pawnees and the Kiowas met in solemn council to conclude a treaty of peace, Great Great Grandfather fell upon the mean Pawnee with one eye, busting his head open with a mighty blow, and nearly ending the peace council then and there. Great Great Grandfather, you see, was a Kiowa, and even now Perry Horse, who has a flag decal stuck on the window of his car, and lives in a big brick apartment building in Alexandria, Virginia, and has his own parking place outside a government office in Washington, even now, with all that, Perry Horse says, "I think of myself as a Kiowa first, an American citizen second." Perry Horse is not romantic about this, and he is not uppity, either, and he does not much give a damn what your feelings are about it at all. "When I was in the fourth grade," he says, "I had this white friend, who was my best buddy, you know, and then one day he said that he'd invite me to his house, but that his folks wouldn't understand. *That* was when I knew I was an Indian." To hell with it, he said to himself subsequently, and now in the evenings he sits in his apartment building, which is called the Sherwood, and is full of airline stewardesses and government people and military men, and when he gets to feeling lonely he thumps on an Indian drum and sings old Kiowa songs without words that he learned when he was a boy in Oklahoma. Perry's mother died when he was four, and he was pretty much raised by his grandmother, Mabel Hummingbird, who never had much to say to him at all in the way of English except, "Talk Kiowa."

"If I really wanted to tease her," Perry says, "I'd say that someday I'd marry a white girl, and then she'd start to ranting and raving. My grandmother, you know, always lived the Indian way."

Now, in fact, Perry Horse did not marry a white girl, and neither did any of his brothers, two getting wed to other Kiowas, and one, like Perry, getting into a mixed marriage of sorts when he wooed a Choctaw. Perry himself married Ella Mae Webber, a Cherokee, and he was first attracted to her, he says, because she really looked like an Indian. The Cherokees were lobbying in Washington, and sending people into polite society, and marrying whites when the Republic was still very young, and Perry says that when he sees a guy who looks white, but says he is an Indian, he figures he is a Cherokee. Perry would have none of this, wanting a wife who was not only *de jure,* as it were, but also *de facto* Indian. The history of the Indian in this country is a history of misery and other people's duplicity, which you know from having seen the movie, of course, but what you probably do not know is that the Winnebagos had big heads, and that the Utes were short and squat, and that the Crows were long and lank. Physically, the tribes did not share much other than black hair, dark eyes, and some tint of copper color; and at the time Columbus got here they had about three hundred languages, no two of which were greatly related to one another. Perry says that when two Indians meet, and cannot tell right off what the other's tribe is, they say something like, "Where you from, man?" and figure it out from there. Perry says that whites are forever taking him for Spanish, Mexican, or Filipino, but that a bright Indian who has spent a lot of time around other Indians can usually come up with Kiowa pretty quickly, and that this has something to do not just with his appearance, but with the way he talks and the ways he sits and the way he stands. "I know who I am," Perry says, "and I don't have to prove it to anybody. I like being an Indian."

Now, there is a fair amount of nonsense put about on the Indian, and it distresses Perry no end. Mostly, he says, it is the romanticizing of it all that gets to him, although he is not very happy with the stuff about the poor drunken Indian, either. He says that when he and the other Indian boys went to the movies in Oklahoma, they would all cheer when it came time for the cavalry to come in and gun down the bad Indians, and that they cheered because there were human values involved, and the Indians in the movie really were bad guys, and to hell with all that stuff about racial self-hatred. Not long ago, some swells who bleed a lot in public had a big cocktail party for Americans for Indian Opportunity, which is run by Mrs. Fred Harris, who is herself part Comanche, and is the wife of the Senator from Oklahoma. The party was held at a great big summer mansion in Southampton, Long Island, and Perry and his wife were there, along with a bunch of other Indians, few of whom had ever been in such a nifty place, or seen such nifty people before. "I've loved Indians all my life," a very rich lady said to Perry, and for all he and his friends knew maybe she really did have a thing about them, but when she started to talk about "My Indians" and "Our Indians," then it did seem proprietary to them, and Perry felt his innards freeze up. "The people who had the party were real nice, and they made us feel right at home, but some of the other people," Perry says, "oh, man. None of us Indian guys had ever been in a mansion like that before, and it was real funny. We went walking on through, and there on the lawn we saw a helicopter. We just naturally thought it belonged to the people who were having the party, until we found out it was the cops' and that they'd just parked it there. I sure learned a lot about people that day. All the Indian guys were wearing jackets and ties, and the people at the party were wearing feathers and beads and things that I guess they thought were Indian. There was one lady with a long skirt with fringes all around the bottom, and one of our guys said, 'Man, that's either high fashion, or the dogs got to her on the way over.' Someone asked Ella Mae why she wasn't in Indian garb, and she said she didn't have to wear it because she already knew she was an Indian. Oh, I really did learn a lot that day. All those rich people on the lawn just kept on circling one another, like they were, you know, *detached* from one another. Now it wasn't like a bunch of Kiowas getting together. With Kiowas you'd know right off whether they liked each other or not, but with those people you couldn't tell a thing."

Perry attended Haskell Institute, an Indian college in Kansas, and after that he "bummed around," as he says, in California, worked for a while as a clerk in the Bureau of Indian Affairs in Washington, and then spent three years in the Army, being trained as a court reporter, and getting stationed in a number of places, including Korea. He says that he did not feel any particular warmth for Orientals and, indeed, that when he saw so many poor people at one time they congealed and became indistinguishable, which is the way poor people generally look to all the rest of us, too. After his discharge, he went back to Washington, married Ella Mae, and began to toil once more in the Bureau of Indian Affairs, rising to the rank of GS–9 in the Civil Service, and electing to spend his time on the problems of Indian education. A government agency is a kind of whispering gallery, wherein the employees, being greatly dependent on the election returns and the caprice of the White House, fill their idle hours by talking about proposed reorganizations and new programs. The Bureau, being like any other government agency, has a fair amount of this, and what is more it is ethnic, too. About half the people who work there are Indians, dealing with other Indians, and some of them are full of zeal. Nonetheless, the Bureau of Indian Affairs, or BIA, is a dirty word among the young Indian red hots, the militants, and they have approximately the same feeling for it that the Black Panthers have for the Urban League, or the NAACP. This makes them think of Perry as an Uncle Tom, and he, in turn, thinks that a lot of them aren't real Indians. "They try so hard to be Indian," he says, "and, you know, I feel kind of sorry for some of them. They wear their hair long, and they have headbands, but they don't even know a real Indian hair style." You might think that an Indian kid wearing a headband is roughly the same as a black kid wearing a dashiki, and in a way you are right because neither a headband nor a dashiki has anything to do with anything other than itself. The Indian battle, though, is different from the black battle because there are far fewer Indians than blacks, and most Indians live in the back of beyond, which is not a good place to start a revolution. The Indian, in fact, needs an advocate in the seat of government, and young Indians like Perry sometimes join the Bureau because for them it is the only real game in town.

So, here is Perry, pulling into his parking space just before 8:30 in the morning, having arisen at 7:30, skipped breakfast, and perhaps picked a few chords on his guitar, which he does sometimes in the morning and sometimes in the evening for the simple joy of picking. He wears $40 boots with pointy toes, a Madras jacket, pants with a great wide belt, and an Indian necklace in place of a tie. When he walks he throws those $40 boots out in front of him, coming down heel first, and sometimes hooking his thumbs in the side pockets of his pants, the general picture being a little like Captain Ahab keeping his balance on the deck of the Pequod, or Lyndon Johnson pacing off his back 40, or maybe a GS-9 Kiowa from southeastern Oklahoma, getting ready to answer his mail in the bowels of a government building. Perry Horse works in the Office of the Director of Education of the BIA, and he begins his day by reading letters, some of which are from people who want to teach in Indian schools, and some of which are from college students just asking about the possibility of teaching in Indian schools, and a few of which are from hippies and other folks mad to start a commune on a reservation. Perry Horse answers all the letters, including those from the commune folk, whom he tells that the U.S. government cannot do much about communes, but maybe some local tribal councils can. Once Perry was sent out to visit colleges and universities to recruit kindergarten teachers for Indian schools at $7,000 and up, and he found that the students he had to be most wary of, aside from the young men who just wanted to beat the draft, were the ones he came to think of as missionary types, lusting after the satisfaction that comes only from the uplifting of someone else. Indian schools are not like Andover Academy, and an Indian boy who lives in rural poverty, and wants to drop out as quickly as he can, is not Dink Stover. The isolation gets to some people who teach school on Indian reservations, the disciplinary problems get to others, and sometimes it is just the burden of living in someone else's culture. Perry himself went to public schools in Carnegie, Oklahoma, where Indians made up only about a fourth of the students, and he says it was fine, except that he never got anything about Indian history. "You'd be an Indian kid, and you'd be sitting there," he says, "and you'd be told that Columbus discovered America. Hell, they should qualify it and say he discovered it for the Europeans. I'm surprised now at how we all sat there and took it. I remember taking an oral history exam once, and the teacher asked me who discovered the Pacific, and I kind of laughed, and said, 'Some Indian guy.' But, shoot, besides that I never did a thing."

It is changing, however, and many people want to do *something* about it, and now the thinking in the Bureau and in other high places is that Indians ought to minister to other Indians, without anyone being made over into whites, which sensible Indians, of course, don't want anyway. "An Indian kid hears all these stories about what I guess you'd call witchcraft, and he believes them," Perry says. "Most tribes have stories like that, you know, but then the Indian child goes to school, and he starts to learn about science, and he's told that the stories are all wrong. He gets mixed up. He doesn't know what to believe." Perry says that Indians do not talk to whites about all the things they know and hear, and that some tribes cannot stand the sight of an anthropologist, while other, more elfin, tribes see in an anthropologist a figure of great hilarity, although not necessarily someone they ought to be talking to, either. Some Indian things stay intact because Indian people do not talk about them to outsiders, which only would dissipate them, and Perry says he knows of things that would be comprehensible only to another Kiowa.

When Perry was a boy, his aunt, suffering from blood clots, was treated by an Indian man who followed the old ways of medicine. Perry says that when the man called upon his aunt, the man gave him a beer bottle, and told him to go into the yard and break it into shards. Then, after boiling the shards in water, Perry says, the man used them to make tiny incisions on his aunt's body. Then he took a hollowed out buffalo horn, placed it over the incisions, and began to suck hard at the small end of the horn. All the while, Perry says, the man chewed a big wad of gum, and whenever he stopped sucking on the buffalo horn he stuck the wad at the small end, making the horn into a vacuum. Perry says that the man got the blood clots out this way, and that he saw him do it, and that his aunt was fine afterwards. This, of course, would be perfectly understandable to a student of Chinese acupuncture, but a graduate of Harvard Medical School might never believe it. Just so, there is the story of Satank, a famous Kiowa warrior who chose death before dishonor. Satank, captured by the Army in the years after the Civil War, was being led somewhere in chains and manacles when he whirled on the soldiers, and tried to slice them up with a butcher knife. He was shot to death, and the question was, Where did he get the knife? The Army said Satank had been twice searched, but that he probably had hidden the knife in his hair. This never made much sense, except to maybe the Army Inspector General, and the Kiowas always have said that Satank conjured up the knife, which is really a more satisfying thing to think. The Kiowas do not expect white people to agree with them on this, and some of them hope the white people, in turn, will not press them too hard on things like the Trinity and the Virgin Birth.

Perry is not much concerned himself with the Christian mysteries, even though on his father's side he descends from a couple of Methodist preachers. His grandfather, in fact, was probably the first Kiowa Methodist minister, and the other thing he was known for was that he weighed about 300 pounds, and could fill up two seats in a buggy. Perry's father is also a Methodist preacher, and when Perry was a boy he spent a fair amount of time at church services and prayer meetings, although he says now that if he ever got back to an Indian community he might look into the Native American Church, the peyote religion. The peyote services that he knew of at home were held in a tepee, which would always be set up facing the west, and which would have inside to the east a dirt altar shaped like a crescent. The service would be precisely orchestrated, and would last from sundown to sunup, with men sitting in a circle in the tepee, each holding a gourd, a staff, and a fan, and each having four ritual songs to sing. Some songs in the service have no words, being sung no less carefully for that, and Perry's uncle, who lives among the Crow people in Montana, is known as a famous singer of the peyote songs.

Since his marriage, Perry has been exposed to an even more authentic Indian religion than the Native American Church—which has bits and pieces of Christianity strewn about it—and that is the Cherokee worship. Perry's brother-in-law is the keeper of the sacred Cherokee fire, which is supposed to have been kindled in North Carolina, and then carried by the Cherokees on their long march to Oklahoma. In their rituals, seven arbors are set up around the flame, and sermons in Cherokee are preached at each one. Perry has walked from arbor to arbor, while his brother-in-law translated the sermons for him, and he says that the Indian preachers were exhorting their listeners to do good, to hurt no man, and to live industriously. He says that he had heard much the same kind of morality in the traditional Kiowa stories, and that they were so much a part of his childhood that he no longer remembers where it was, or from whom, that he first heard them.

Perry was born in a tent outside Carnegie, Oklahoma, in 1940, and shortly after that his family moved to a home in the Wichita Mountains, which Perry says is now two hours away from Carnegie by car, but was then two days away by horse and wagon, with a stop overnight at some relative's house. The wagon had rails on the sides, and sometimes a canvas was stretched across the top, under which Perry and his brothers would sleep. Perry remembers his early childhood as more or less idyllic, despite, or maybe because of, the kerosene lamps, wood stoves, and well water, and he says that he and his brothers could pack a few biscuits and bacon sandwiches, and disappear into the hills for a day at a time. Once Perry and his brothers were poking around with a sawed-off .22 rifle, and they shot a fox, which made Perry feel bad, and he says that since then he has had small use for either guns or hunting. Eventually, his family left the Wichita Mountains, which were really just rolling hills, and drifted back to a home outside Carnegie, which was not a bad place for an Indian community, there being other towns in Oklahoma that were really lousy. Perry remembers seeing signs outside places in Clinton that said, "No Indians Allowed," while in other towns, like Ponca City, it was better if an Indian didn't show up at all. ("You know when a place is going to be tough, like Ponca City," Perry says. "I don't know all the ways it's tough, but a lot of Ponca and Pawnee guys could tell you.") Carnegie was better, although in Perry's high school white gangs and Indian gangs periodically would punch one another around. Perry and his friends wore their hair very long, and slouched around without belts in their levis, and after one fight they were punished by being ordered to cut their hair, and to put back their belts.

You may think there is a great unity among the Indians of Oklahoma and elsewhere, what with all the small white slights, and great white oppressions, but in fact Indians have always fought more among themselves. The Kiowas now bicker with the Comanches and the Kiowa-Apaches, and when Perry was a boy he was told to watch out for the Utes and the Navahos. For that matter, Kiowa grandmothers would frighten children with tales of menacing Negroes, and when he first saw a couple of Negroes on a street corner in an Oklahoma town, Perry was stricken with dread.

"Indians are different than other people," Perry says. "There is the feeling for the land. Kiowas call the sun our father, but the earth is our mother. Indian people who live in cities, you never see them go to Europe on a vacation. They always go home, where they grew up. So many black people want to be like whites, I think. Not Indians, they want to be only what they are." Perry, living in Alexandria and working in Washington, has no white friends, which is something he neither regrets, nor even thinks about much. Last New Year's Eve he and Ella Mae were at a party, where there were no whites until late in the evening, when a few of the host's neighbors dropped in. The change in atmosphere, Perry says, was palpable. He and the other Indians began to feel uncomfortable, and they did not stop feeling that way until the whites had left. It was the same, Perry says, when he and Ella Mae were at a party where most of the guests were black. Indians, he says, simply prefer being alone with their own. Perry owns a $500 Trini Lopez electric guitar, and for a while he played with a rock group, three guitarists, a drummer, and a vocalist, and they were all Indians, too. He has studied art at the Corcoran Gallery in Washington, getting an A in painting, and finding that mostly he prefers to paint Indian things. Perry's brothers, who are younger, hardly speak Kiowa at all, and if Perry and Ella Mae have children, the children probably will never know a word of an Indian language, or of a great many other things that are important to their parents. Perry says the day may come when he will move back to an Indian community, and that one reason he would do this would be so any child of his could know who *he* is, just as Perry Horse does himself.

MITCHELL WILSON

On Being a Scientist

To the outside world, the word *scientist* refers to a jumble of strange bedfellows—physicists, chemists, biologists, and at least thirty other clans—who spend their lives among the riddles and realities of nature. Each man is convinced that his particular science is more important than the others—and totally different in the intellectual and temperamental qualities it requires. Physicists speak of organic chemistry as being as boring as bookkeeping. Biologists retort that the intellectual austerity of physics is as airless and soul-numbing as the inside of an ether cone. Lord Todd, white-haired Nobel laureate in organic chemistry, once while telling how he had taken over a problem from biochemistry, assured me that the two chemistries were totally different disciplines, even though to a nonscientist they seem to be concerned with almost identical material.

With preferences so passionately defended, and distinctions so finely drawn, one would assume that a man ought to be able to tell you why he made his particular choice. I. I. Rabi at Columbia said flatly: "Because physics is the only basic science there is. Everything else is to the right of it and depends on it. Nothing is to the left of it."

Max Perutz in Cambridge said just as flatly: "Molecular biology is the basic science of life; it is now the only way one knows what one is talking about."

Allan Sandage at Mount Palomar says: "Astronomy and cosmogony—that's where the great questions still have to be answered."

Jacques Monod of the Pasteur Institute says: "Why biology? Well, because I felt that was where the most work was to be done."

ON BEING A SCIENTIST By Mitchell Wilson. From *The Atlantic Monthly,* September 1970. Reprinted by permission of International Famous Agency. Copyright © 1970 by Mitchell Wilson.

Picasso, when asked why he chose to be an artist, lost his temper and retorted that when a man finds himself asking why he is doing what he is doing, it is time for him to give it up. The men of science whom I questioned kept their tempers; still, what they gave me were not reasons at all but only statements of preference. These highly analytical men were no more able to describe precisely what had captured their minds than is any young lover to explain why he is deeply in love with a particular girl and not her sister. They knew there would never be wealth as the world measures it, nor even success in the popular sense. Why, then, do they do what they do? They don't know.

I had assumed, too, that the scientist's objectivity would enable him to discern not only new ideas but the men who generate new ideas. Among physicists, the saying goes that "there are really only two categories of men who become theoreticians; the geniuses, and the men who are merely brilliant. Those less than brilliant needn't bother to come around." Scientists themselves, of course, know their ranks include a great many who are far from brilliant, and some who are incompetent. They know, too, that among them are science snobs and climbers who want to be—and be seen—in the presence of famous and accomplished scientists. There are also the science politicians and influence brokers. But no matter how contemptible, foolish, fatuous, or venal a man may be, the work he does and has done weighs more with his fellow scientists than the ugliness which is all the outside world may see.

In the end, among themselves, scientists respect only one quality—excellence. No scientist cares that Newton could be meanly vindictive, that Michelson compulsively chased girls, that Pauli's wit could be malevolent and destructive. The scientist reveres talent when it exists, but the men whose careers are dedicated to increasing man's perception of the universe are not always able to perceive among themselves those who will emerge and tower over everyone else.

Albert Einstein was thought to have so little promise at graduation that no school or university bothered to offer him a job. Five years later, in 1905, at the age of twenty-six, the still supposedly untalented man working as an obscure patent clerk in Bern published three original papers in a single year, each of which was destined to become a classic of scientific thought. The response from the world of science to this unprecedented performance was total indifference. That silence persisted for another five years.

When Niels Bohr in 1913—also in his twenties—worked out the bizarre conditions under which an atom could have the planetary structure which experiment seemed to call for, it was only one of dozens of alternative atomic theories that had been appearing in the journals month after month for decades. No one paid very much attention even though, a few months after publication, Einstein confided to a friend that Bohr's ideas, however radical, were of the greatest importance. "I once had similar ideas but I didn't dare publish them!" was his amazing confession. Albert

Szent-Gyorgyi, who has ranged over half a dozen fields in the life sciences with brilliance and Hungarian wit, admits that he once so despaired of any recognition in his early years in biochemistry that he actually determined on suicide.

There are instances of overlooked talent far worse than these—cases where true ability went unacknowledged until ten, twenty, thirty years after the man's death. The monk Mendel, for example, founded the science of genetics in a monastery garden; the physician Semmelweis was hounded out of Vienna for pioneering prophylaxis; and even Sadi Carnot's membership in one of France's more eminent families did not keep his work on thermodynamics from being totally ignored during his lifetime and for twenty years after his death.

Currently an attempt is being made to soften the latent but growing hostility to technology and science by insisting that the scientist *is* really quite human. Just like everyone else, he likes tennis, sports cars, cookouts, his family. The DuPont Corporation assures you that their scientists are just as active in local and community affairs as their neighbors—if not more so. A recent book stated that its "main aim is to present to the reader the American scientist just as he is—a person who happens to enjoy science as much as a lawyer enjoys law, or a doctor enjoys the practice of medicine, or a businessman enjoys the daily hassle of business."

Well, "enjoy" is a pretty pale word for what goes on. The scientist is like everyone else *only* if "everyone else" is restricted to that infinitely small number of fortunate men who manage to find in life precisely that one pursuit that engages their best abilities, their minds and passions, with more felicity than most wives ever do.

There is pleasure—profound pleasure, both of touch and mind—to the experimentalist in the manipulation of apparatus. If he has designed it himself, there is the added pleasure of seeing it perform its delicate intricacies exactly as he conceived it, under his direct control. The theorist, in addition, has the overwhelming satisfaction of feeling that he has been intuitively attuned to the subtlest nuances of nature when one of his hypotheses turns out to be true.

Richard Feynman at fifty wears his Nobel Prize like an open-collared shirt. Twenty-five years ago at Los Alamos, he was an *enfant terrible,* bubbling with quick brilliance on the theoretical problems of bomb-building that came his way. "It was a succession of successes—but easy successes. After the war, I moved over to the kind of problems [like the self-energy of the electron] that men spend years thinking about. On that level there are no easy successes; and the satisfaction you get when you're proved right is so great that even if it occurs only twice in a lifetime, everything else is worth it!"

Recently, Jack Peter Green, who does pharmacology in terms of quantum chemistry, was polishing a research paper during a country weekend. He had spent more than a year working over the molecular structure of a number of chemically diverse hallucinogens—LSD, mescaline, and others—and was finally able to prove that one specific atomic configuration can be discerned somewhere in the molecular structure of each. I was amazed to hear sounds of private satisfaction come from his room; but later when he was discussing his results, it was clear that his delight had nothing to do with pride in his own performance or with the prestige that would be coming to him for his discovery. It was purely aesthetic pleasure in the exquisite way nature ordered things. "How elegant it is!" he kept saying. "And so simple!"

A young Italian scientist's English was slow and meticulous. "I feel guilty about coming back to the lab after hours to get a little more done, and still I always come back," he said to me. "I know very well that whether I come in or not on Sunday, there will be no great change in science. I neglect my wife and my little daughter for those few extra hours—yet I keep coming. Why? Is it really only curiosity? Because if that's all that's driving me, then it's wrong for me to come for that additional time." "Then why *do* you come in?" I persisted. "Because it is my happiness," he said simply. "This is where I want most in the world to be—this is what I want most in the world to be doing."

Only young artists, actors, musicians, and writers know the same immersion, because what is involved is the deep engagement of a talent; and only a talent at work allows the hours, days, and years of a life to roll by without being counted. That is why, in such lives, there is a far more dangerous risk than failure—there is the terrifying possibility that some day the love affair may stop. Then, tragically, all that is left is the pain of disillusion and the stunned sense of all those wasted years. A scientist, like the artist, is not only different from other men; he had better go on being different!

Whatever is different about the scientist must begin with the particular kind of intelligence such a man possesses. It is said that the scientist must have an inquiring mind—which is true; and that he must also be one of those people who take deep pleasure in learning—which is also true, and also superficial; because both these qualities are demanded also by any number of other disciplines. The particular kind of sensibilities required by a scientist are more complicated.

Begin with his intense awareness of words and their meanings. While the poet's affinity for words makes him sensitive to their sound, emotion, and rhythm, the scientist uses them as instruments of precision. He must be capable of inventing new words to express new physical concepts. He must be able to reason verbally by analogy—to explain "how this thing is like that thing," and to be able to fit the many resemblances into one single generalization that covers them all.

The scientist must also think graphically, in terms of dynamical models, three-dimensional arrangements in space. The dynamical model of a bacterial cell, for example, is a hollow rigid capsule that may be either spherical or tubular, containing an otherwise shapeless living cell enclosed within a soft sac, the plasma membrane. Niels Bohr's dynamical model of an atom is a miniature solar system with relatively enormous electrons orbiting about an almost inconceivably small sun—the atomic nucleus—a tremendous distance away. Scientists keep these three-dimensional pictures in mind as vividly as if they were actually seeing them. Formulas and equations printed on a two-dimensional page have three-dimensional meanings, and the scientist must be able to read in three dimensions to "see the picture" at once. There is nothing "abstract" about a scientist's thinking.

This visualization is so vivid that a scientist examining a theoretical problem is really like a jeweler peering through his loupe at a gem which he holds close to his eye, turning it over and over in his fingers. To Einstein, there was nothing abstract about his theory of relativity. Even the slightest apparent deviation from the hard world of physical reality made him intellectually uncomfortable. For more than a decade, meeting at international science conferences, he and Bohr, by then both in middle age, had monumental arguments over the meaning of the uncertainty principle, with Einstein the one who stuck stolidly to the basic mechanistic principle of cause and effect. "I cannot believe that God throws dice," he said.

The split between the so-called "Two Cultures" is much more than a matter of humanists learning more about science, and the scientists spending more time on aesthetics. Unless a man has some kind of spatial imagination along with his verbal sensibility he will always be—as far as understanding science goes—in the role of the tone-deaf struggling with a course in music appreciation. On the other hand, the possessor of both verbal and spatial sensibility will rather quickly be bored if asked to limit his imagination to only the verbal domain, in the case of the humanities; or to only the spatial domain, in the case of the graphic arts.

A man accustomed to working at the peak of his powers has no patience with anything that calls on him to work at only half-load. With this dual sensibility then, the true scientist would find it difficult "to be like everyone else" even if he wanted to.

Not only is there a split between scientists and other people, there is also a sharp split among scientists themselves. Within specializations, a division runs across every field—a sort of trans-science geological fault, which results from the fact that there are two kinds of scientific knowledge. Claude Bernard, the founder of experimental medicine, pointed out that there is the knowledge we already possess, and there is the knowledge we still have to discover. One type of scientist—the man with encyclopedic knowledge of past and current thought in science—can make an inspiring teacher or a brilliant research administrator, but he is not necessarily the man who is most creative. The other type of scientist—a beachcomber on the edge of the sea of the unknown—may be so haphazardly versed in the literature of his own field that he sometimes invents and discovers things that have been invented and discovered before.

Szent-Gyorgyi says he feels embarrassed, isolated, and ignorant at meetings in the presence of these highly articulate scientists who seem to have all knowledge at their fingertips, even though he is the one with the Nobel Prize and they are not. The Polaroid inventor, Edwin Land, feels that discoveries are made by those scientists who have freed themselves "from a way of thinking that is held by friends and associates who may be more intelligent, better educated, better discipined, but who have not mastered the art of the fresh clean look at the old, old knowledge."

In the main it is these intellectual ragamuffins who are responsible for the great advances; just as the great novels and poems are not written by men of the widest erudition and critical ability. History is a cruel book-keeper and carries on its ledgers only the names of those who create what is enduring; it drops forever the men who appear to scintillate in their own times with the knowledge only of their own time. J. Robert Oppenheimer was a brilliant administrator of other men's work; he was a brilliant interpreter of other men's work, and a judge who could make piercing evaluations of other men's work. But when it came time—figuratively speaking—to write his own poetry in science, his work was sparse, angular, and limited, particularly when judged by the standards he himself set for everyone else. He knew the major problems of his time; he attacked them with style; but he apparently lacked that intuition—that faculty beyond logic which logic needs—in order to make great advances. If one were speaking not of science but of religion, one could say that Oppenheimer's religiosity was the kind that could make him a bishop but never a saint.

This particular quality which is so essential to the scientist is almost indefinable. Years ago, as a graduate student, I was present at a three-way argument between Rabi, Szilard, and Fermi. Szilard took a position and mathematically stated it on the blackboard. Rabi disagreed and rearranged the equations to the form he would accept. All the while Fermi was shaking his head. "You're both wrong," he said. They demanded proof. Smiling a little, he shrugged his shoulders as if proof weren't needed. "My intuition tells me so," he said.

I had never heard a scientist refer to his intuition, and I expected Rabi and Szilard to laugh. They didn't. The man of science, I soon found, works with the procedures of logic so much more than anyone else that he, more than anyone else, is aware of logic's limitations. Beyond logic there is intuition, and the creative scientist often is out there, rather than within the exquisitely arranged landscapes of rigorous logic.

For eighteen years before Newton wrote down the general law of gravitational attraction, he had an intuitive perception that the earth's gravitational force extended at least as far as the moon and was responsible for the moon's motion. Even then, another year passed before it became clear that an assumption basic to the whole idea had still not been proven—and the matter was brought to Newton's attention. He went to work on it at once. The next day he handed over a few sheets of paper containing the mathematical proof that a spherical mass, no matter how large—earth, moon, or sun—behaves gravitationally as if all its mass were concentrated into a single point at its center. Newton had assumed intuitively for years that something like this might be the case, and for all those years had never for a moment thought that everyone else did not share his perception.

A composer looked at me with surprise when I happened to mention that the scientist experienced creativity in exactly the same way as the artist. "But what does he create?" he asked. "I thought he dealt only with logical processes—deductions from experiment."

Creativity for the scientist does have certain characteristics that are unique. To begin with, the scientist picks his problem because he knows enough about it to know that no one knows very much about it—except that there are unanswered questions there. Out of insight or inspiration, he suggests a possible answer to one of the questions: for example, What *is* a possible structure for the atom? What *does* bind the atoms together to form molecules? By *what* means does the living cell store the chemical energy released within its walls? The creative moment occurs when the suggested answer is being formed. Naturally, the scientist would like to be proved right, and so the performance of the deciding experiment can never be the dispassionate exercise it is popularly thought to be. Experiment carries all the emotion of a contest. Objectivity lies in the scientist's willingness to accept, however reluctantly, evidence that his brilliant conception is wrong. Once Nature gives its decision, there is no appeal. In fairly short order then, the scientist is ruthlessly informed whether his creation is valid or not. The artist, on the other hand, has no such objective standard. He can always find, or invent, an aesthetic system to justify his creation.

There are several other important differences between creativity for the artist and for the scientist. If Shakespeare had never written *Hamlet,* if Beethoven had not lived to create *Eroica,* no one else would have brought these works into existence. Other artists would have created other works. In science, though, if Einstein had never lived to work out relativity, if Maarten Schmidt hadn't recognized the nature of the quasars in the sky, or if Crick and Watson had not solved the structure of DNA, other scientists would have done so. The world of art is infinite in creative possibilities, the world of science is restricted: there is only one Nature to be discovered.

Again, no work of art has ever had—ever can have—the revolutionary impact on man and his society the way the introduction of a new technology can. With the artist, a moment of history comes to an end when he finishes his particular work and the act of creation is completed. With the scientist, it is that precise moment that a new phase of history begins, even though he himself cannot possibly foresee what future generations will add to his contribution or choose to do with it. This is where he is the prisoner of his own time.

Faraday couldn't conceivably guess that dropping a small bar magnet down the center of a coil of wire would mean that a hundred years later millions of miles of electric power lines would flash billions of kilowatt-hours back and forth across the earth. Nor could Semmelweis know that his campaign to save women from death by puerperal fever was one of the several steps that would help lead—five generations later—to the threat of such world overpopulation that mass starvation looms as one of man's possible fates.

Not long ago, I asked Otto Robert Frisch, who, with his aunt, Lise Meitner, had actually been the first to realize that uranium atoms were indeed undergoing nuclear fission with enormous emissions of energy, whether at that point (1939) he had any sense of what his work was to lead to. He had been a young man then, a refugee from Hitler's Austria.

"My aunt and I spent the weekend together in the Swedish country-side," he said. "She told me what she had just heard from Hahn in Berlin. We discussed it over and over as we walked through the woods; and the more we talked, the more we became convinced that the uranium nuclei were indeed breaking up—*fission* was *her* word for it. We wrote up a short joint paper on this completely unsuspected nuclear process before we separated. She went back to Stockholm, and I went back to Copenhagen to the Bohr Institute. I had a vague sense that we were onto something that might be important, but I couldn't say how. I remember writing to my parents that we might have a tiger by the tail, but believe it or not I couldn't think of an experiment to do until Plazcek—do you remember him; the most skeptical man in the world?—Plazcek said he didn't believe any part of it, and that made me so angry that I said I'd prove it to him, and I did. But you see, that was all still months before Joliot in Paris detected the emission neutrons ejected during each fission, which meant that a chain reaction was possible. I had no way of guessing that this would be so."

The inventors of radically new machines always judge the value of what they create, but their judgment is embedded in the standards and needs of their own times. Dr. Richard Gatling, a Union Army surgeon, appalled by the bloody cost of the American Civil War, reasoned that he could reduce the number of losses by reducing the size of armies. He developed a gun with a tenfold firing power so that one man could do the work of ten. The Gatling gun—the first modern machine gun—turned out to have a very different effect.

The Wright brothers seriously weighed the possible future effects of their invention. They saw their airplane as a sort of air scout able to fly over enemy lines and detect every movement. Military surprise would be impossible, and from then on wars would be useless.

When Einstein's work on relativity led him to the historic discovery of the convertibility of mass and energy, he did not foresee how his principle would act as a guide to the release of nuclear energy. Is he to be held responsible for the deaths at Hiroshima? Does history hold Newton guilty for every artillery barrage laid down by all the armies of the world in every war of the past three hundred years because one of the outcomes of Newton's laws of dynamics was the artillerist's science of ballistics?

Yet because of the scientist's inability to look over the walls of history and foresee what subsequent generations will do with the fruits of his discovery, society today blames the scientist for what it wrenched from his hand and turned into engines of evil, poisoning the earth's atmosphere, crust, and waters. The scientist is bewildered to find himself considered the villain. It is as if Prometheus were chained to the rock—not by the gods from whom he stole the fire, but by the men he tried to help, because, as they claim, he had now made it possible for them to burn one another to death. Nevertheless, the very scientists who are being considered the bogeymen are the ones who must still be called upon to use their ingenuity to help undo the damage which society has done to itself. They are more than anxious to meet the challenge.

LORD RITCHIE-CALDER

Mortgaging the Old Homestead

Past civilizations are buried in the graveyards of their own mistakes, but as each died of its greed, its carelessness or its effeteness another took its place. That was because such civilizations took their character from a locality or region. Today ours is a global civilization; it is not bounded by the Tigris and the Euphrates nor even the Hellespont and the Indus; it is the whole world. Its planet has shrunk to a neighborhood round which a man-made satellite can patrol sixteen times a day, riding the gravitational fences of Man's family estate. It is a community so interdependent that our mistakes are exaggerated on a world scale.

For the first time in history, Man has the power of veto over the evolution of his own species through a nuclear holocaust. The overkill is enough to wipe out every man, woman and child on earth, together with

MORTGAGING THE OLD HOMESTEAD By Lord Ritchie-Calder. Reprinted by permission from *Foreign Affairs,* January 1970. Copyright © 1970 by the Council on Foreign Relations, Inc., New York.

our fellow lodgers, the animals, the birds and the insects, and to reduce our planet to a radioactive wilderness. Or the Doomsday Machine could be replaced by the Doomsday Bug. By gene-manipulation and man-made mutations, it is possible to produce, or generate, a disease against which there would be no natural immunity; by "generate" is meant that even if perpetrators inoculated themselves protectively, the disease in spreading round the world could assume a virulence of its own and involve them too. When a British bacteriologist died of the bug he had invented, a distinguished scientist said, "Thank God he didn't sneeze; he could have started a pandemic against which there would have been no immunity."

Modern Man can outboast the Ancients, who in the arrogance of their material achievements built pyramids as the gravestones of their civilizations. We can blast our pyramids into space to orbit through all eternity round a planet which perished by our neglect.

A hundred years ago Claude Bernard, the famous French physiologist, enjoined his colleagues, "True science teaches us to doubt and in ignorance to refrain." What he meant was that the scientist must proceed from one tested foothold to the next (like going into a mine-field with a mine-detector). Today we are using the biosphere, the living space, as an experimental laboratory. When the mad scientist of fiction blows himself and his laboratory skyhigh, that is all right, but when scientists and decision-makers act out of ignorance and pretend that it is knowledge, they are putting the whole world in hazard. Anyway, science at best is not wisdom; it is knowledge, while wisdom is knowledge tempered with judgment. Because of overspecialization, most scientists are disabled from exercising judgments beyond their own sphere.

A classic example was the atomic bomb. It was the Physicists' Bomb. When the device exploded at Alamogordo on July 16, 1945, and made a notchmark in history from which Man's future would be dated, the safe-breakers had cracked the lock of the nucleus before the locksmiths knew how it worked. (The evidence of this is the billions of dollars which have been spent since 1945 on gargantuan machines to study the fundamental particles, the components of the nucleus; and they still do not know how they interrelate.)

Prime Minister Clement Attlee, who concurred with President Truman's decision to drop the bomb on Hiroshima, later said:

> We knew nothing whatever at that time about the genetic effects of an atomic explosion. I knew nothing about fall-out and all the rest of what emerged after Hiroshima. As far as I know, President Truman and Winston Churchill knew nothing of those things either, nor did Sir John Anderson who coordinated research on our side. Whether the scientists directly concerned knew or guessed, I do not know. But if they did, then so far as I am aware, they said nothing of it to those who had to make the decision.[1]

[1] "Twilight of Empire," by Clement Attlee with Francis Williams. New York: Barnes, 1961, p. 74.

That sounds absurd, since as long before as 1927, Hermann J. Muller had been studying the genetic effects of radiation, work for which he was awarded the Nobel Prize in 1946. But it is true that in the whole documentation of the British effort, before it merged in the Manhattan Project, there is only one reference to genetic effects—a Medical Research Council minute which was not connected with the bomb they were intending to make; it concerned the possibility that the Germans might, short of the bomb, produce radioactive isotopes as a form of biological warfare. In the Franck Report, the most statesmanlike document ever produced by scientists, with its percipience of the military and political consequences of unilateral use of the bomb (presented to Secretary of War Henry L. Stimson even before the test bomb exploded), no reference is made to the biological effects, although one would have supposed that to have been a very powerful argument. The explanation, of course, was that it was the Physicists' Bomb and military security restricted information and discussion to the bomb-makers, which excluded the biologists.

The same kind of breakdown in interdisciplinary consultation was manifest in the subsequent testing of fission and fusion bombs. Categorical assurances were given that the fallout would be confined to the testing area, but the Japanese fishing-boat *Lucky Dragon* was "dusted" well outside the predicted range. Then we got the story of radiostrontium. Radiostrontium is an analogue of calcium. Therefore in bone-formation an atom of natural strontium can take the place of calcium and the radioactive version can do likewise. Radiostrontium did not exist in the world before 1945; it is a man-made element. Today every young person, anywhere in the world, whose bones were forming during the massive bomb-testing in the atmosphere, carries this brandmark of the Atomic Age. The radiostrontium in their bones is medically insignificant, but if the test ban (belated recognition) had not prevented the escalation of atmospheric testing, it might not have been.

Every young person everywhere was affected, and why? Because those responsible for H-bomb testing miscalculated. They assumed that the upthrust of the H-bomb would punch a hole in the stratosphere and that the gaseous radioactivity would dissipate itself. One of those gases was radioactive krypton, which quickly decays into radiostrontium, which is a particulate. The technicians had been wrongly briefed about the nature of the troposphere, the climatic ceiling which would, they maintained, prevent the fall-back. But between the equatorial troposphere and the polar troposphere, there is a gap, and the radiostrontium came back through this fanlight into the climatic jet-streams. It was swept all around the world to come to earth as radioactive rain, to be deposited on food-crops and pastures, to be ingested by animals and to get into milk and into babies and children and adolescents whose growing bones were hungry for calcium or its equivalent strontium, in this case radioactive. Incidentally, radiostrontium was known to the biologists before it "hit the headlines." They had found it in the skin burns of animals exposed on the Nevada testing ranges and they knew its sinister nature as a "bone-seeker." But the authorities clapped security on their work, classified it as "Operation Sunshine" and cynically called the units of radiostrontium "Sunshine Units"—an instance not of ignorance but of deliberate non-communication.

One beneficial effect of the alarm caused by all this has been that the atoms industry is, bar none, the safest in the world for those working in it. Precautions, now universal, were built into the code of practice from the beginning. Indeed it can be admitted that the safety margins in health and in working conditions are perhaps excessive in the light of experience, but no one would dare to modify them. There can, however, be accidents in which the public assumes the risk. At Windscale, the British atomic center in Cumberland, a reactor burned out. Radioactive fumes escaped from the stacks in spite of the filters. They drifted over the country. Milk was dumped into the sea because radioactive iodine had covered the dairy pastures.

There is the problem of atomic waste disposal, which persists in the peaceful uses as well as in the making of nuclear explosives. Low energy wastes, carefully monitored, can be safely disposed of. Trash, irradiated metals and laboratory waste can be embedded in concrete and dumped in the ocean deeps—although this practice raises some misgivings. But high-level wastes, some with elements the radioactivity of which can persist for *hundreds of thousands* of years, present prodigious difficulties. There must be "burial grounds" (or euphemistically "farms"), the biggest of which is at Hanford, Washington. It encloses a stretch of the Columbia River in a tract covering 575 square miles, where no one is allowed to live or to trespass.

There, in the twentieth century Giza, it has cost more, much more, to bury live atoms than it cost to entomb the sun-god Kings of Egypt. The capital outlay runs into hundreds of millions of dollars and the maintenance of the U.S. sepulchres is over $6 million a year. (Add to that the buried waste of the U.S.S.R., Britain, Canada, France and China, and one can see what it costs to bury live atoms.) And they are very much alive. At Hanford they are kept in million-gallon carbon-steel tanks. Their radioactive vitality keeps the accompanying acids boiling like a witches' cauldron. A cooling system has to be maintained continuously. The vapors from the self-boiling tanks have to be condensed and "scrubbed" (radio-active atoms removed); otherwise a radioactive miasma would escape from the vents. The tanks will not endure as long as the pyramids and certainly not for the hundreds of thousands of years of the long-lived atoms. The acids and the atomic ferments erode the toughest metal, so the tanks have to be periodically decanted. Another method is to entomb them in disused salt mines. Another is to embed them in ceramics, lock them up in glass beads. Another is what is known as "hydraulic fraction": a hole is drilled into a shale formation (below the subsoil water); liquid is piped down under pressure and causes the shale to split laterally. Hence the atoms in liquid cement can be injected under enormous pressure and spread into the fissures to set like a radioactive sandwich.

This accumulating waste from fission plants will persist until the promise, still far from fulfilled, of peaceful thermonuclear power comes about. With the multiplication of power reactors, the wastes will increase. It is calculated that by the year 2000, the number of six-ton nuclear "hearses" in transit to "burial grounds" at any given time on the highways of the United States will be well over 3,000 and the amount of radioactive products will be about a billion curies, which is a mighty lot of curies to be roaming around a populated country.

The alarming possibilities were well illustrated by the incident at Palomares, on the coast of Spain, when there occurred a collision of a refueling aircraft with a U.S. nuclear bomber on "live" mission. The bombs were scattered. There was no explosion, but radioactive materials broke loose and the contaminated beaches and farm soil had to be scooped up and taken to the United States for burial.

Imagine what would have happened if the *Torrey Canyon*, the giant tanker which was wrecked off the Scilly Isles, had been nuclear-powered. Some experts make comforting noises and say that the reactors would have "closed down," but the *Torrey Canyon* was a wreck and the Palomares incident showed what happens when radioactive materials break loose. All those oil-polluted beaches of southwest England and the coasts of Brittany would have had to be scooped up for nuclear burial.

II

The *Torrey Canyon* is a nightmarish example of progress for its own sake. The bigger the tanker the cheaper the freightage, which is supposed to be progress. This ship was built at Newport News, Virginia, in 1959 for the Union Oil Company; it was a giant for the time—810 feet long and 104 feet beam—but, five years later, that was not big enough. She was taken to Japan to be "stretched." The ship was cut in half amidship and a mid-body section inserted. With a new bow, this made her 974 feet long, and her beam was extended 21 feet. She could carry 850,000 barrels of oil, twice her original capacity.

Built for Union Oil, she was "owned" by the Barracuda Tanker Corporation, the head office of which is a filing cabinet in Hamilton, Bermuda. She was registered under the Liberian flag of convenience and her captain and crew were Italians, recruited in Genoa. Just to complicate the international triangle, she was under charter to the British Petroleum Tanker Company to bring 118,000 tons of crude oil from Kuwait to Milford Haven in Wales, via the Cape of Good Hope. Approaching Lands End, the Italian captain was informed that if he did not reach Milford Haven by 11 P.M. Saturday night, he would miss highwater and would not be able to enter the harbor for another five days, which would have annoyed his employers. He took a shortcut, setting course between

Seven Stones rocks and the Scilly Isles, and he finished up on Pollard Rock, in an area where no ship of that size should ever have been.

Her ruptured tanks began to vomit oil and great slicks spread over the sea in the direction of the Cornish holiday beaches. A Dutch tug made a dash for the stranded ship, gambling on the salvage money. (Where the salvaged ship could have been taken one cannot imagine, since no place would offer harborage to a leaking tanker.) After delays and a death in the futile salvage effort, the British Government moved in with the navy, the air force and, on the beaches, the army. They tried to set fire to the floating oil which, of course, would not volatilize. They covered the slicks with detergents (supplied at a price by the oil companies), and then the bombers moved in to try to cut open the deck and, with incendiaries, to set fire to the remaining oil in the tanks. Finally the ship foundered and divers confirmed that the oil had been effectively consumed.

Nevertheless the result was havoc. All measures had had to be improvised. Twelve thousand tons of detergent went into the sea. Later marine biologists found that the cure had been worse than the complaint. The oil was disastrous for seabirds, but marine organic life was destroyed by the detergents. By arduous physical efforts, with bulldozers and flame-throwers and, again, more detergents, the beaches were cleaned up for the holiday-makers. Northerly winds swept the oil slicks down Channel to the French coast with even more serious consequences, particularly to the valuable shellfish industry. With even bigger tankers being launched, this affair is a portentous warning.

Two years after *Torrey Canyon* an offshore oil rig erupted in the Santa Barbara Channel. The disaster to wildlife in this area, which has island nature reserves and is on the migratory route of whales, seals and sea-birds, was a repetition of the *Torrey Canyon* oil-spill. And the operator of the lethal oil rig was Union Oil.

III

Another piece of stupidity shows how much we are at the mercy of ignorant men pretending to be knowledgeable. During the International Geophysical Year, 1957–58, the Van Allen Belt was discovered. This is an area of magnetic phenomena. Immediately it was decided to explode a nuclear bomb in the Belt to see whether an artificial aurora could be produced. The colorful draperies and luminous skirts of the aurora borealis are caused by the drawing in of cosmic particles through the rare bases of the upper atmosphere—ionization it is called; it is like passing electrons through the vacuum tubes of our familiar fluorescent lighting. The name Rainbow Bomb was given it in anticipation of the display it was expected to produce. Every eminent scientist in the field of cosmology, radio-astronomy or physics of the atmosphere protested at this irresponsible tampering with a system which we did not understand. And typical of the casual attitude toward this kind of thing, the Prime Minister of the day, answering protests in the House of Commons that called on him to intervene with the Americans, asked what all the fuss was about. After all, they hadn't known that the Van Allen Belt even existed a year before. This was the cosmic equivalent of Chamberlain's remark about Czechoslovakia, at the time of Munich, about that distant country of which we knew so little. They exploded the bomb. They got their pyrotechnics and we still do not know the cost we may have to pay for this artificial magnetic disturbance.

In the same way we can look with misgivings on those tracks—the white tails of the jets, which are introducing into our climatic system new factors, the effects of which are immeasurable. Formation of rain clouds depends upon water vapor having a nucleus on which to form. That is how artificial precipitation is introduced—the so-called rain-making. So the jets, crisscrossing the weather system, playing noughts and crosses with it, can produce a man-made change.

In the longer term we can foresee even more drastic effects from Man's unthinking operations. At the United Nations' Science and Technology Conference in Geneva in 1963 we took stock of the effects of industrialization on our total environment thus far. The atmosphere is not only the air which humans, animals and plants breathe; it is also the envelope which protects living things from harmful radiation from the sun and outer space. It is also the medium of climate, the winds and the rain. Those are inseparable from the hydrosphere—the oceans, covering seven-tenths of the globe, with their currents and extraordinary rates of evaporation; the biosphere, with its trees and their transpiration; and, in terms of human activities, the minerals mined from the lithosphere, the rock crust. Millions of years ago the sun encouraged the growth of the primeval forests, which became our coal, and the plant growth of the seas, which became our oil. Those fossil fuels, locked away for aeons of time, are extracted by man and put back into the atmosphere from the chimney stacks and the exhaust pipes of modern engineering. About 6 billion tons of carbon are mixed with the atmosphere annually. During the past century, in the process of industrialization, with its release of carbon by the burning of fossil fuels, more than 400 billion tons of carbon have been artificially introduced into the atmosphere. The concentration in the air we breathe has been increased by approximately 10 percent, and if all the known reserves of coal and oil were burnt at once, the concentration would be ten times greater.

This is something more than a public health problem, more than a question of what goes into the lungs of an individual, more than a question of smog. The carbon cycle in nature is a self-adjusting mechanism. Carbon dioxide is, of course, indispensable for plants and is, therefore, a source of life, but there is a balance which is maintained by excess carbon being absorbed by the seas. The excess is now taxing this absorption because of what is known as the "greenhouse effect." A greenhouse lets in the sun's rays but retains the heat. Carbon dioxide, as a transparent diffusion, does likewise. It keeps the heat at the surface of the earth and in excess modifies the climate.

It has been estimated that, at the present rate of increase, the mean annual temperature all over the world might increase by 3.6 degrees centigrade in the next forty to fifty years. The experts may argue about the time factor and even about the effects, but certain things are apparent, not only in the industrialized Northern Hemisphere but in the Southern Hemisphere also. The North-polar icecap is thinning and shrinking. The seas, with their blanket of carbon dioxide, are changing their temperature, with the result that marine plant life is increasing and is transpiring more carbon dioxide. As a result of the combination, fish are migrating, changing even their latitudes. On land the snow line is retreating and glaciers are melting. In Scandinavia, land which was perennially under snow and ice is thawing, and arrowheads of over 1,000 years ago, when the black soils were last exposed, have been found. The melting of sea ice will not affect the sea level, because the volume of floating ice is the same as the water it displaces, but the melting of icecaps or glaciers, in which the water is locked up, will introduce additional water to the sea and raise the level. Rivers originating in glaciers and permanent snow fields will increase their flow; and if ice dams, such as those in the Himalayas, break, the results in flooding may be catastrophic. In this process the patterns of rainfall will change, with increased precipitation in some areas and the possibility of aridity in now fertile regions. One would be well advised not to take ninety-nine year leases on properties at present sea level.

IV

At that same conference, there was a sobering reminder of mistakes which can be writ large, from the very best intentions. In the Indus Valley in West Pakistan, the population is increasing at the rate of ten more mouths to be fed every five minutes. In that same five minutes in that same place, an acre of land is being lost through water-logging and salinity. This is the largest irrigated region in the world. Twenty-three million acres are artificially watered by canals. The Indus and its tributaries, the Jhelum, the Chenab, the Ravi, the Beas and the Sutlej, created the alluvial plains of the Punjab and the Sind. In the nineteenth century, the British began a big program of farm development in lands which were fertile but had low rainfall. Barrages and distribution canals were constructed. One thing which, for economy's sake, was not done was to line the canals. In the early days, this genuinely did not matter. The water was being spread from the Indus into a thirsty plain and if it soaked in so much the better. The system also depended on what is called "inland delta drainage," that is to say, the water spreads out like a delta and then drains itself back into the river. After independence, Pakistan, with external aid, started vigorously to extend the Indus irrigation. The experts all said the soil was good and would produce abundantly once it

got the distributed water. There were plenty of experts, but they all overlooked one thing—the hydrological imperatives. The incline from Lahore
to the Rann of Kutch—700 miles—is a foot a mile, a quite inadequate
drainage gradient. So as more and more barrages and more and more
lateral canals were built, the water was not draining back into the Indus.
Some 40 percent of the water in the unlined canals seeped underground,
and in a network of 40,000 miles of canals that is a lot of water. The
result was that the watertable rose. Low-lying areas became waterlogged,
drowning the roots of the crops. In other areas the water crept upwards,
leaching salts which accumulated in the surface layers, poisoning the
crops. At the same time the irrigation régime, which used just 1½ inches
of water a year in the fields, did not sluice out those salts but added,
through evaporation, its own salts. The result was tragically spectacular.
In flying over large tracts of this area one would imagine that it was an
Arctic landscape because the white crust of salt glistens like snow.

The situation was deteriorating so rapidly that President Ayub
appealed in person to President Kennedy, who sent out a high-powered
mission which encompassed twenty disciplines. This was backed by the
computers at Harvard. The answers were pretty grim. It would take
twenty years and $2 billion to repair the damage—more than it cost to
create the installations that did the damage. It would mean using vertical
drainage to bring up the water and use it for irrigation, and also to sluice
out the salt in the surface soil. If those twenty scientific disciplines had
been brought together in the first instance it would not have happened.

One more instance of the far-flung consequences of men's localized
mistakes: No insecticides or pesticides have ever been allowed into the
continent of Antarctica. Yet they have been found in the fauna along the
northern coasts. They have come almost certainly from the Northern
Hemisphere, carried from the rivers of the farm-states into the currents
sweeping south. In November 1969, the U.S. Government decided to
"phase out" the use of DDT.

Pollution is a crime compounded of ignorance and avarice. The great
achievements of *Homo sapiens* become the disaster-ridden blunders of
Unthinking Man—poisoned rivers and dead lakes, polluted with the
effluents of industries which give something called "prosperity" at the
expense of posterity. Rivers are treated like sewers and lakes like cess-
pools. These natural systems—and they are living systems—have strug-
gled hard. The benevolent microorganisms which cope with reasonable
amounts of organic matter have been destroyed by mineral detergents.
Witness our foaming streams. Lake Erie did its best to provide the oxygen
to neutralize the pickling acids of the great steel works. But it could not
contend. It lost its oxygen in the battle. Its once rich commercial fishing
industry died and its revitalizing microorganic life gave place to anaerobic
organisms which do not need oxygen but give off foul smells, the mortu-
ary smells of dead water. As one Erie industrialist retorted, "It's not our
effluent; it's those damned dead fish."

We have had the Freedom from Hunger Campaign; presently we shall need a Freedom from Thirst Campaign. If the International Hydrological Decade does not bring us to our senses we will face a desperate situation. Of course it is bound up with the increasing population but also with the extravagances of the technologies which claim that they are serving that population. There is a competition between the water needs of the land which has to feed the increasing population and the domestic and industrial needs of that population. The theoretical minimum to sustain living standards is about 300 gallons a day per person. This is the approximate amount of water needed to produce grain for 2½ pounds of bread, but a diet of 2 pounds of bread and 1 pound of beef would require about 2,500 gallons. And that is nothing compared with the gluttonous requirements of steel-making, paper-making and the chemical industry.

Water—just H_2O—is as indispensable as food. To die of hunger one needs more than fifteen days. To die of thirst one needs only three. Yet we are squandering, polluting and destroying water. In Los Angeles and neighboring Southern California, a thousand times more water is being consumed than is being precipitated in the locality. They have preempted the water of neighboring states. They are piping it from Northern California and there is a plan to pipe it all the way from Canada's North-West Territories, from the Mackenzie and the Liard which flow northwards to the Arctic Ocean, to turn them back into deserts.

V

Always and everywhere we come back to the problem of population— more people to make more mistakes, more people to be the victims of the mistakes of others, more people to suffer Hell upon Earth. It is appalling to hear people complacently talking about the population explosion as though it belonged to the future, or world hunger as though it were threatening, when hundreds of millions can testify that it is already here —swear it with panting breath.

We know to the exact countdown second when the nuclear explosion took place—5:30 A.M., July 16, 1945, when the first device went off in the desert of Alamogordo, New Mexico. The fuse of the population explosion had been lit ten years earlier—February 1935. On that day a girl called Hildegarde was dying of generalized septicaemia. She had pricked her finger with a sewing needle and the infection had run amok. The doctors could not save her. Her desperate father injected a red dye into her body. Her father was Gerhard Domagk. The red dye was pronto-sil which he, a pharmaceutical chemist, had produced and had successfully used on mice lethally infected with streptococci, but never before on a human. Prontosil was the first of the sulfa drugs—chemotherapeutics, which could attack the germ within the living body. Thus was prepared the way for the rediscovery of penicillin—rediscovery because although Fleming had discovered it in 1928, it had been ignored because neither he nor anybody else had seen its supreme virtue of attacking germs within the living body. That is the operative phrase, for while medical science and the medical profession had used antiseptics for surface wounds and sores, they were always labeled "Poison, not to be taken internally." The sulfa drugs had shown that it was possible to attack specific germs within the living body and had changed this attitude. So when Chain and Florey looked again at Fleming's penicillin in 1938, they were seeing it in the light of the experience of the sulfas.

A new era of disease-fighting had begun—the sulfas, the antibiotics, DDT insecticides. Doctors could now attack a whole range of invisible enemies. They could master the old killer diseases. They proved it during the war, and when the war ended there were not only stockpiles of the drugs, there were tooled up factories to produce them. So to prevent the spread of deadly epidemics which follow wars, the supplies were made available to the war-ravaged countries with their displaced persons, and then to the developing countries. Their indigenous infections and contagions and insect-borne diseases were checked.

Almost symbolically, the first great clinical use of prontosil had been in dealing with puerperal sepsis, childbed fever. It had spectacularly saved mothers' lives in Queen Charlotte's Hospital, London. Now its successors took up the story. Fewer mothers died in childbirth, to live and have more babies. Fewer infants died, fewer toddlers, fewer adolescents. They lived to marry and have children. Older people were not killed off by, for instance, malaria. The average life-span increased.

Professor Kingsley Davis of the University of California at Berkeley, the authority on urban development, has presented a hair-raising picture from his survey of the world's cities. He has shown that 38 percent of the world's population is already living in what are defined as urban places. Over one-fifth of the world's population is living in cities of 100,000 or more. And over one-tenth of the world's population is now living in cities of a million or more inhabitants. In 1968, 375 million people were living in million-and-over cities. The proportions are changing so quickly that on present trends it would take only 16 years for half the world's population to be living in cities and only 55 years for it to reach 100 percent.

Within the lifetime of a child born today, Kingsley Davis foresees, on present trends of population-increase, 15 billion people to be fed and housed—nearly five times as many as now. The whole human species would be living in cities of a million-and-over inhabitants, and—wait for it!—the biggest city would have 1.3 billion inhabitants. That means 186 times as many as there are in Greater London.

For years the Greek architect Doxiadis has been warning us about such prospects. In his Ecumenopolis—World City—one urban area like confluent ulcers would ooze into the next. The East Side of World City would have as its High Street the Eurasian Highway stretching from Glasgow to Bangkok, with the Channel Tunnel as its subway and a built-up area all the way. On the West Side of World City, divided not by the tracks but by the Atlantic, the pattern is already emerging, or rather, merging. Americans already talk about Boswash, the urban development of a built-up area stretching from Boston to Washington; and on the West Coast, apart from Los Angeles, sprawling into the desert, the realtors are already slurring one city into another all along the Pacific Coast from the Mexican Border to San Francisco. We don't need a crystal ball to foresee what Davis and Doxiadis are predicting; we can already see it through smog-covered spectacles; a blind man can smell what is coming.

The danger of prediction is that experts and men of affairs are likely to plan for the predicted trends and confirm these trends. "Prognosis" is something different from "prediction." An intelligent doctor having diagnosed your symptoms and examined your condition does not say (except in novelettes), "You have six months to live." An intelligent doctor says, "Frankly, your condition is serious. Unless you do so-and-so, and I do so-and-so, it is bound to deteriorate." The operative phrase is "do so-and-so." We don't have to plan for trends; if they are socially undesirable our duty is to plan away from them; to treat the symptoms before they become malignant.

We have to do this on the local, the national and the international scale, through intergovernmental action, because there are no frontiers in present-day pollution and destruction of the biosphere. Mankind shares a common habitat. We have mortgaged the old homestead and nature is liable to foreclose.

ARTHUR H. WESTING

Ecocide in Indochina

All wars raise havoc with the land on which they are fought. However, our war in Indochina has been, and continues to be, particularly disruptive of the environment.

The country is largely rural, and the enemy is dispersed in the fields and forests, in the mountains and swamps. This enemy matches his numbers and concealment and persistence against our wealth and technology and persistence. They hide and we seek.

In an attempt to cope with that elusive enemy, dispersed and hidden in the wild stretches of Vietnam, the United States military employs two

ECOCIDE IN INDOCHINA By Arthur Westing. © *Natural History Magazine,* March 1971. Reprinted by permission.

major tactics: bombing on a staggeringly unprecedented scale and laying bare vast stretches of terrain. Both tactics are enormously disruptive of the ecology (and economy) of Vietnam.

When an area is found to contain—or is even suspected of containing —Vietcong, it is subjected to intensive aerial bombardment. Hundreds of bombing sorties are flown each day. Some three million bombs are dropped annually, for a total now of more than ten million tons, and the program is being intensified daily. In flying over the country, as I did last August, one is overwhelmed by the endless craters, each 20 or 30 feet deep and 30 to 40 feet across. These ubiquitous craters are (at least during the rainy season) usually filled with water and provide an ideal breeding habitat for malarial mosquitoes. The long-term ecological effects, possibly for centuries, of this massive intrusion of the environment have attracted little attention.

The other massive ecological disturbance is our program of defoliation: the destruction of vast stretches of vegetation in order to deny cover and sanctuary to the enemy. This is done in two major ways. One rather straightforward approach is to bulldoze the countryside. Using giant tractors equipped with sharpened Rome-plow blades, we have now cleared a 1,000- to 2,000-yard strip along most major transportation routes. Most of these swaths—often scraped down to the infertile subsoil—are barren and subject to erosion. The remainder are largely weed-choked wastelands. They will be difficult to reclaim and rehabilitate after the war.

In addition to roadside clearing, large contiguous areas of countryside are Rome-plowed to deny them to the enemy. At least one-half million acres of forest were cleared through 1969, according to information released by the Army. This program continues unabated. In the words of the commanding officer of this operation, "The B-52 bomber is the battle-ax of this war, and our plow is the scalpel."

The second and much more extensive means we have devised for denying wild land cover and sanctuary to the other side is the aerial application of plant poisons, or herbicides. This aspect of the war drew me to Indochina twice, most recently in August, 1970, as director of the Herbicide Assessment Commission of the American Association for the Advancement of Science (AAAS). There is no precedent for the massive use of herbicides in a tropical environment and thus no way of reliably predicting the full extent and seriousness of the damage being inflicted upon the ecology of Vietnam. The likelihood of serious long-term damage to the environment has been a major concern of many scientists in this country and elsewhere. In December, 1970, the Council of the AAAS resolved to urge the United States to renounce the military use of herbicides.

War against the plants of Vietnam began in late 1961 and, according to a recent Department of Defense news release, was inflicted upon some 5½ million acres through 1969. Since the program continues to this day, the current figure can be estimated to be in excess of 6½ million acres.

(A half million or more acres classified as agricultural have been sprayed.) All told, one acre in six in South Vietnam has now been sprayed.

To illustrate the extent of environmental disruption more graphically: South Vietnam approximates the size of New England; the area sprayed is larger than Vermont; the area bulldozed almost that of Rhode Island. While none of Vietnam's 43 provinces has escaped, some have been attacked herbicidally with particular intensity and frequency. Among these are the Rung Sat region in Gia Dinh Province southeast of Saigon, Tay Ninh Province (War Zone C), which is northwest of Saigon, and Long Khanh Province (War Zone D) northeast of Saigon—the last previously contained major stands of South Vietnam's magnificent virgin tropical forest.

Most forest spraying has been done with a 1:1 mixture of 2,4–D and 2,4,5–T, Agent Orange in military terminology; some with a 4:1 mixture of 2,4–D and picloram, or Agent White; and small amounts with dimethyl arsenic acid, Agent Blue. The use of Agent Orange was discontinued in early 1970, largely in favor of Agent White. Agent Orange was applied at the rate of 25 pounds of active ingredients per acre; Agent White at 8 pounds; and Agent Blue at 9.

When an upland forest is attacked with herbicide, the leaves drop after two or three weeks and the trees remain bare for several months. Sunlight, able to reach the forest floor following defoliation, promotes the growth of a luxuriant understory in which certain herbaceous grasses and shrubby bamboos dominate. A tropical forest has an enormous diversity of species, some more sensitive to the spray than others. When refoliation of the trees occurs, about one out of ten trees fails to survive the treatment, perhaps more. This has occurred on more than 5 million acres in Vietnam. The repeated spraying of an additional million acres or so of upland forest has caused even more serious damage. In such areas the proportion of trees killed rises dramatically, as much as 50 percent to 80 percent or higher, depending upon the number of applications, the type of spray, and the local mix of species. An estimated 6½ billion board feet of merchantable tropical timber have been destroyed, plus an indeterminate amount of fuel wood, charcoal wood, and other forest products.

In flying over these hard-hit areas, I was impressed by the widespread invasion of cogon grass (*Imperata*) or, even worse, a variety of low-growing scrub bamboos. These species are aggressive colonizers and prevent the re-establishment of the former high forests. The resultant grass savannas and bamboo brakes have a reduced biomass and an impoverished fauna. Commercially worthless, they will be extremely difficult to eradicate. These vegetational wastelands will remain one of the legacies of our presence for decades to come.

Additional, less obvious ecological damage is likely to occur in a sprayed upland forest. In a tropical forest ecosystem (unlike those of temperate zones) the major fraction of the total nutrient budget is in its biotic component (largely in the leaves and small twigs). Following defoliation, a significant fraction of the leaf-stored nutrients is probably lost permanently in the water runoff. It takes decades for a tropical ecosystem to restore its former productivity following such nutrient dumping.

Herbivorous insect, bird, and bat populations are bound to decline markedly and with them, their pollinating function, which is so important in a tropical forest where individual plants of the same species are usually widely scattered. In the replacement community, particularly following multiple herbicidal attacks, the original set of animal populations will be replaced by a less diverse set. A large number of species will be eliminated and the replacement community will have higher numbers of fewer species, many of them new to the area. In addition, the miles of borders (or ecotones) between divers vegetational types is being greatly increased. Such a fringe habitat supports its own animal community. For example, the scrub typhus mite appears to be restricted to such a niche.

The chemicals used for defoliation missions (largely 2,4-D, 2,4,5-T, and picloram) are potent herbicides but are supposedly not toxic to animals. These chemicals have their main effect on terrestrial animals (both large and microscopic) indirectly via the dependence of these animals on plants for food and shelter. However, at least one of the herbicides, 2,4,5-T, contains dioxin as an impurity. Dioxin is both highly toxic and enormously teratogenetic (causing birth defects) to mammals. Vietnam's countryside has been drenched over the years with some 47 million pounds of 2,4,5-T, with an estimated dioxin concentration of 25 parts per million. This means that more than one thousand pounds of dioxin have been introduced into Vietnam's environment. Dioxin's environmental stability, mobility, and possible points of concentration in the ecosystem are not yet known.

In a different ecological situation, more than one million acres of Vietnam's southerly coastal regions are subject to daily flooding at each high tide. This tidal zone supports a characteristic biotic community known as mangrove swamp. It is an inhospitable region used mainly as a source of charcoal and as sanctuary for the ubiquitous Vietcong. More subtly, it is a crucial breeding and nursing ground for a great variety of ocean fishes and crustaceans and some river fishes.

To date, more than one-quarter of Vietnam's mangrove association has been sprayed and killed. I say *killed* because, through some quirk of nature, one herbicidal attack of this tidal zone literally kills all the plant life that grows there. Moreover, for unknown reasons, the plants do not regenerate. The utter devastation that results is eerie to behold and also frightening because I could find no indication of how soon, if ever, recovery would occur. Tens of thousands of acres sprayed years ago still have no sign of green on them. The web of life on these vast stretches has been destroyed, with ecological ramifications—and even geologic ones via marine erosion—not yet possible to fathom. Whether or not the recent disappearance of the freshwater tarpon, which breeds among the mangroves, from the Mekong Delta is the result of this destruction remains to be determined.

My focus has been on the strictly ecological impact of the military use of herbicides in a tropical setting. What must be left for another time is the impact of this program on human ecology—on the 17 million semi-destitute Vietnamese peasants and primitive hill tribesmen inexorably enmeshed in the vagaries of the war. This unfortunate aspect of the problem has incredibly serious economic, public health, and social welfare dimensions.

Whatever one's political and moral views may be toward the war in Indochina, one has to assume that the war will end some day and that the surviving population must have a natural resource to support itself. The natural resource is the base upon which an underdeveloped country must build its future.

In December (1970) the White House announced a "phasing out" of the use of herbicides. It is my hope that a second statement is imminent announcing the immediate cessation and abrogation of such use of herbicides. I hasten to add that I have little against the discriminate civil use of many herbicides; I am only against their massive and indiscriminate use by the military. One cannot destroy a nation in order to save it.

NEIL H. JACOBY

The Environmental Crisis

Who would have predicted, even as recently as a year ago, the strong ground swell of public concern about the environment that now preoccupies Americans? The great silent majority as well as activists of the left have discovered that our country is running out of clean air and pure water. Suddenly, we all understand that smog, noise, congestion, highway carnage, oil-stained beaches, junk graveyards, ugliness, and blatant commercial advertising not only offend our senses but threaten our health and our very lives.

Now we are trying to identify the culpable parties and to demand corrective action. What are the basic forces behind environmental deterioration and why has a crisis emerged so swiftly? What are the merits of

THE ENVIRONMENTAL CRISIS By Neil H. Jacoby. Reprinted, with permission, from the November 1970 issue of *The Center Magazine,* a publication of the Center for the Study of Democratic Institutions in Santa Barbara, California.

the diagnoses and prescriptions that have been advanced for the environmental problem? How can the environment be improved, and who should pay the costs? What are the respective roles and responsibilities of business and of government in restoring environmental amenities? Above all, what lessons does the environmental crisis teach about the functioning of our political and market systems, and about reforms needed to forestall other crises in the future?

We focus attention upon the urban physical environment, that is, upon the spatial and sensory qualities of the land, air, water, and physical facilities that surround the three out of four Americans who live in towns and cities. This milieu deteriorates as a result of air and water pollution, noise, industrial and household waste materials, declining quantity or quality of housing per capita, crowding, congestion, loss of privacy and recreational facilities, rising accidents and loss of time in urban transportation, and, not least of all, drabness and ugliness.

The physical environment is, of course, only one dimension of the quality of human life. In focusing upon physical factors, one excludes important social and psychological factors such as order and security, social mobility, and the social participation or alienation of the individual. All of these environmental factors, along with per capita income, wealth, health, and education, need enhancement.

Spatially, the urban environment must be viewed as one subdivision of the entire global ecosystem, which also embraces rural lands, the oceans, the atmosphere surrounding the earth, and outer space. Since all parts of this system interact, ideally it should be analyzed, planned, and managed as a whole.

The urban physical environment nevertheless merits a top priority because it affects the majority of our population and, by general assent, its qualities are below the threshold of tolerability. In addition, physical factors powerfully influence the health, mental attitudes, and life-styles of urban residents, and their enhancement will elevate the social and psychological qualities of American society. One is therefore justified in focusing attention upon the physical characteristics of urban life, notwithstanding that it is a partial analysis of the global ecosystem.

Three basic forces have operated to change the urban physical environment for the worse: population concentration, rising affluence, and technological change. The overwhelming tendency of people to concentrate in cities has worsened the environment in many ways. Traffic congestion, crowding, overloading of transportation, marketing and living facilities, delays and loss of time, along with rising levels of air, water, and noise pollution, have been among the social costs of urbanization. During the half-century between 1910 and 1960 the percentage of Americans living in urban areas of 2,500 or more rose from 45.7 to 70, while the number of urbanites tripled from 42 to 125 million. Beyond doubt, the 1970 census will reveal an accelerated urbanization. Urbanization clearly brings benefits to people—wider job opportunities, richer educational and cultural fare, more individual freedom from social constraints —or else it would not have been so powerful and enduring a movement. Yet, beyond some levels of population size and density, the total costs of urbanization begin to exceed the total benefits. Discovery of the optimum size of cities and optimum density of their populations are vitally important tasks confronting national planners.

A second prime mover in environmental change has been rising affluence—the expansion of annual real income and expenditure per capita. Real income per person (measured in 1958 dollars) more than doubled during the eighteen years, 1950–1968, from $1,501 to $3,409. As real incomes have mounted, each person has bought and consumed more tangible goods, thrown them away more quickly, and generated solid waste. Each person has traveled more miles per year, multiplied his contacts with other people, and rapidly expanded his usage of energy. All of this has increased air, water, and noise pollution, crowding, congestion, and traffic accidents. With the number of urbanites doubling and per capita real incomes quadrupling every forty years, the problem of supplying urban amenities is exploding. One shudders to contemplate the environmental degradation that would occur if 525 million Indians, now crowded 417 per square mile, were each to spend as much as 200 million Americans living only 60 per square mile. India seeks affluence, but could she stand it?

Environmental degradation is not, of course, inherent in rising affluence. Only the particular forms and methods of production and consumption to which our society has become accustomed degrade it. Rising affluence can and should be a source of environmental enhancement.

It is often overlooked that rising per capita income results in an increased demand for environmental amenities. People naturally demand better public goods—more comfort and convenience and beauty in their communities—to match the better private goods and services their rising incomes enable them to buy. One reason for the environmental "crisis" is the frustration felt by the public with a short supply of environmental amenities available to meet a rising demand for them.

The physical environment of large American cities has not degenerated absolutely in an overall sense, but probably has been improving. People easily forget amenities taken for granted today that were lacking half a century ago. Examples are air-conditioned offices, restaurants, and homes; thermostatically controlled electric and gas heat; underground utility wires and poles; paved boulevards and auto freeways. These have widely replaced the crowded slums, the filth of unpaved streets, the drafty cold-water flats and belching chimneys of winter, and the steaming miseries of unrefrigerated summers. Even in the inner city, people today live longer, healthier, and more comfortable lives—if not happier ones—than they did before World War I. What has happened is that the overall supply of urban amenities has fallen far short of the rising effective demand for them, and the supply of certain critical goods, such as pure air and water, has virtually vanished.

The third source of the environmental problem is technological change. Advancing technology has expanded the variety of products available for consumption, made products more complex, raised rates of obsolescence and thereby added to waste disposal. It has also added immensely to the per capita consumption of physical materials and energy, with consequent increments of waste and of pollution. It has expanded the amount of information required by consumers to make rational choices in markets, thereby creating market imperfections that are the source of the contemporary "consumerism" movement. Technological change, however, is, like rising affluence, a two-edged sword; it can be used to improve as well as to degrade the environment. Technology can *reduce* material consumption and recycle harmful wastes. Examples are the replacement of bulky vacuum tubes by microminiaturized circuits in computers, or the conversion of sewage into pure water plus fertilizers. Environmental preservation calls for a redirection of our technological efforts, as well as a restructuring of patterns of consumption.

One conspicuous aspect of environmental deterioration has been the disappearance of "free goods"—amenities such as clean air, pure water, and open space—that are in such ample supply relative to the demand for them that they are not economized. Pure air is no longer free. To obtain it one must buy air-conditioning equipment and acquire a home in which to install it. Pure water must be purchased by the bottle, now that the product of many muncipal water systems is barely potable. Most urban dwellers must spend large sums of money for travel in order to gain the privacy and recreation of a natural environment unavailable at home.

A second aspect of environmental change is the fast-rising importance of spatial relationships in the cities. Such factors as building heights and population densities, street layout, park location, and zoning patterns largely determine the life-styles of urban residents and the supply of amenities available to them. The atrociously bad planning of most American cities and the abject perversion of zoning and building requirements to serve short-term commercial interests are well documented. The flagrantly overdense building on Manhattan Island has been permitted only because of popular ignorance and apathy. Now, the public is belatedly recognizing the heavy social costs that its neglect has created. Popular concern with city planning, zoning, and building development is rising. The heavy stake of the individual in the physical attributes of his community is finally being appreciated.

A third aspect of environmental change is the multiplication of interdependencies among individuals. To an increasing extent the activities of each of us impinge upon others. This is so not only because more people live in cities, but also because the scale and variety of each person's activities rise with the amount of real income he produces and consumes. Thus, no one suffered disamenity a generation ago when his neighbor played a phonograph in a suburban home; but many suffer when a neighbor's son now turns up the sound volume of his hi-fi instrument in a high-rise apartment building.

Increasing interdependency is one way of looking at what economists call the "spillover effects" or external costs of production or consumption. For example, paper mills emit chemical wastes into lakes and streams, copper smelters inject sulphur dioxide into the air, and electric generating stations throw off carbon monoxide, radioactive wastes, or hot water, depending upon their fuels. Motor vehicles cause massive air and noise pollution, traffic accidents, and vast expenditures on medical, legal, policing, and engineering services and facilities—all borne mainly by the public. These industries all generate external costs, thrust upon society in the form of loss of environmental amenities. Although reliable estimates are lacking, total external costs in the U.S. economy are of the order of tens of billions of dollars a year.

The speed with which public interest in the environment has mounted may be explained primarily by the swift decline in certain amenities below thresholds of tolerability. Although certain critical amenities, notably pure air, have been diminishing for many years, the public has suddenly become aware of critical deficiencies. Thus, the quality of air in the Los Angeles Basin deteriorated steadily after 1940. Yet only by the mid-nineteen-sixties, after school children were being advised not to exercise outdoors on smoggy days and when smog alerts were being sounded on many days each year, was decisive action taken to reduce air pollution from motor vehicles. By the sixties, people saw that the "capacity" of the atmosphere over the basin to disperse pollutants had been intolerably overloaded.

After the design capacity of any facility has been reached, amenities diminish exponentially with arithmetic increases in the load. For example, when a twenty-first person enters an elevator designed to hold twenty persons, everyone in the elevator suffers loss of comfort; and when a twenty-second person enters, the percentage loss of amenity is much greater than the 4.8 per cent increase in the number of passengers. Similarly, when the five thousand and first automobile enters a freeway designed to carry five thousand vehicles per hour, it puts pressure of inadequate space upon five thousand and one drivers, and not only upon the new entrant.

Another reason for current public concern with the environment is the gathering appreciation of inequity as some groups in society gain benefits at the cost of other groups. The automobilist whose vehicle spews out air pollution gets the benefits of rapid and convenient travel; but he imposes part of the costs of that travel upon people who are forced to breathe bad air and hear deafening noise and who must bear the costs of painting and maintaining property corroded by pollutants. Because this is manifestly inequitable, upgrading the environment by eliminating this kind of pollution will not only add to aggregate real income, but will also improve its distribution.

Before examining effective measures for enhancing the environment let us dispose of a number of partial or superficial diagnoses of, and prescriptions for, the problem. Several schools of thought have arisen.

First, there is the Doomsday School. It holds in effect that the problem of environmental degradation is insoluble. For example, Paul Ehrlich argues in his book *The Population Bomb* that it is already too late to arrest man's inexorable march to racial extinction through overpopulation, malnutrition, famine, and disease. Other criers of doom are the natural scientists who predict changes in the earth's temperature, as a result of accumulating carbon dioxide in the atmosphere, with consequent melting of the polar ice and other disasters. Although laymen are incompetent to judge such matters, they remain moot issues among natural scientists and therefore call for at least suspended judgment. Accumulating evidence suggests that population growth in the advanced nations has already slowed appreciably, and is starting to do so in many less developed lands. In any event, an apocalyptic view of the future should be rejected if only because it leads to despair and inaction. If one really believes that the future is hopeless, one will cease making an effort to improve society.

At the opposite pole is the Minimalist School. It holds that environmental deterioration is a minor problem in comparison with such contemporary issues as poverty, civil rights, and school integration. Its members argue that political leaders calling for a better environment are "eco-escapists," seeking to divert public attention from their failure to resolve these primary issues. What the Minimalists overlook is that the United States is already making progress in reducing poverty, expanding civil rights, and achieving educational integration, while it is still losing ground in arresting the decline of the urban environment. They also forget that attention to the environment does not mean neglect of poverty. On the contrary, central-city areas generally have the worst physical conditions of life and are populated mainly by low-income families. Because the poor stand to gain most from environmental enhancement, a war on pollution is one battlefront in a war on poverty. A vigorous attack on that front need not inhibit action on other fronts.

There is also a Socialist School. Its members view environmental deterioration as an inescapable consequence of capitalist "exploitation." If only private enterprise, market competition, and profit incentives were replaced by central planning and state ownership and management of enterprises, they contend, the problem would disappear. However, the socialist countries are facing more serious problems of pollution as their per capita G.N.P.'s are rising. Managers of socialist enterprises are judged by the central planners on the efficiency of their operations, and are under as much pressure to minimize internal costs and throw as much external cost as possible on the public as are the managers of private firms in market economies who seek to maximize stockholders' profits. Moreover, because a monolithic socialist society lacks a separate and independent mechanism of political control of economic processes, it is less likely to internalize the full costs of production than a market economy, with its dual systems of market-price and governmental controls. Pollution has arisen primarily from the failure of our political system, acting through government, to establish desired standards of production and consumption. If government performs its unique tasks, the competitive market system will operate within that framework to produce what the public demands without harming the environment.

The largest group of new environmentalists appear to be associated with the Zero Growth School. Its thesis is simple: since environmental degradation is caused by more people consuming more goods, the answer is to stop the growth of population and production. Nature has fixed the dimensions of the natural environment; therefore man should fix his numbers and their economic activities. We must establish a stable relationship between human society and the natural world.

Zero economic and population growth could arrest the process of environmental degradation, but could not, per se, restore a good physical environment. Were real G.N.P. constant through time, current levels of air and water pollution, noise, crowding, ugliness, and other negative elements would continue as long as present patterns of production and consumption are maintained.

Zero growth of population and production is, moreover, impossible to achieve. Because economic growth is a product of expanding population, higher investment, and advancing technology, zero growth would call for stopping changes in all three variables. This cannot be done in the proximate future, if at all. A leading population analyst has shown that even if, beginning in 1975, every family in the United States were limited to two children—an heroic assumption—population dynamics are such that this nation would not stop adding people until about 2050 A.D., when it would contain nearly 300 millions. (See Stephen Enke, "Zero Population Growth—When, How, and Why," TEMPO Publication 70TMP35, Santa Barbara, California, June 2, 1970.) While a decline in net savings and investment to zero is possible, it is extremely unlikely in view of the savings and investment rates Americans have maintained during the present century in the face of enormous increases in their real wealth and incomes. (See *Policies for Economic Growth and Progress in the Seventies,* Report of the President's Task Force on Economic Growth, U.S. Government Printing Office, Washington, D.C., 1970.) A static technology of production is inconceivable. As long as Americans remain thinking animals they will increase the productivity of work.

Finally, zero growth is undesirable. A rising G.N.P. will enable the nation more easily to bear the costs of eliminating pollution. Because zero growth of population is far in the distance, and zero growth of output is both undesirable and unattainable, it follows that the environmental problem must be solved, as President Nixon stated in his January, 1970, State of the Union Message, by redirecting the growth that will inevitably take place.

The Austerity School of environmental thought is related to the Zero Growth School. Its members assert that environmental decline is produced by excessive use of resources. They are outraged by the fact that the United States consumes about forty per cent of the world's energy and materials, although it contains only six per cent of the world's population. Believing that asceticism is the remedy, they call for less consumption in order to conserve resources and to reduce production and pollution. We should convert ourselves from a society of "waste-makers" into one of "string-savers."

The basic error here is that it is not the amount of production and consumption per capita that degrades the environment, but the fact that government has failed to control the processes of production and consumption so as to eliminate the pollution associated with them. Without such political action, consumption could be cut in half and society would still suffer half as much pollution; with appropriate political control consumption could be doubled while pollution is radically reduced. The second error of the Austerity School, which distinguishes it from the Zero Growth School, is a notion that the world confronts a severe shortage of basic natural resources. Exhaustive studies by Resources for the Future have shown the contrary: there are no foreseeable limitations upon supplies of basic natural resources, including energy, at approximately current levels of cost. Technological progress is continually opening up new supplies of materials that are substitutable for conventional materials (e.g., synthetic rubber and fibers) and lowering the costs of alternative sources of energy (e.g., production of petroleum products from oil shales, tar sands, and coal). Austerity theorists do make a valid point, however, when they observe that governmental regulation to internalize external costs can cause business enterprises to develop ways of recycling former waste materials back into useful channels.

Finally, there is the Public Priorities School. Its adherents see the problem as one of too much governmental spending on defense and space exploration, leaving too little for environmental protection. The solution, as they see it, is to reallocate public expenditures. There are two responses to this line of reasoning: public expenditures are already being strongly reordered, and in any event reallocations of private expenditures will weigh far more heavily in a solution of the environmental problem. Thus between the fiscal years 1969 and 1971 federal budget outlays on defense and space are scheduled to shrink by ten per cent, from $85.5 billions to $77 billions, whereas outlays on social security and public assistance will rise by twenty-six per cent, from $46 billions to $60 billions. The President has announced plans for further contractions of defense outlays and expansions of expenditures on the nation's human resources.

Environmental restoration does require large increases in public expenditures upon sewage disposal and water purification, parks, housing, urban development, and public transportation. Even more, however, it calls for a reallocation of private expenditures as a result of governmental actions to internalize external costs in the private sector. For example, the purchase price and operating expenses of an automobile that is pollution-free will undoubtedly be higher than for a vehicle that degrades the environment, because the auto user will be paying the full costs of his private transportation. With internalization of costs, spending on private auto transportation may be expected to decline relatively. At the same time, spending on education and housing, which produce external benefits, will increase relatively. In the aggregate, readjustments in patterns of private expenditure will far outweigh reallocation of public expenditure in a total program of environmental restoration.

Because the environmental problem is critically important and is soluble, and neither socialization of the economy, zero growth, austerity, nor new public spending priorities offer a satisfactory solution, a more basic approach must be made. A good policy for environmental improvement should improve the distribution of income among people as well as the allocation of society's resources. Governmental intervention is necessary to attain both ends.

Environmental degradation occurs, as has been shown, when there are significant external costs involved in producing or consuming commodities. A social optimum cannot be achieved when there is a divergence between private (internal) and social (external plus internal) costs. An optimal allocation of society's resources requires that the full costs of production of each good or service be taken into account. The internalization of external costs must therefore be a pivotal aim of environmental policy. (A trenchant description of the external costs of economic growth is given by E. J. Mishan, *The Costs of Economic Growth,* New York: Praeger, 1967.)

Theoretically, perfectly competitive markets in which there are no transaction costs will lead to an optimum reallocation of resources in cases of pollution via bargaining between the polluter and the person harmed by pollution, no matter which party is legally responsible to compensate the other. (See R. H. Coase, "The Problem of Social Costs," *Journal of Law and Economics,* III, October, 1960.) In practice, however, the transaction costs of education, organization, and litigation are excessively high when pollution affects large numbers of people, as it usually does. For this reason it is more efficient for government to resolve pollution problems by legislation or regulation, rather than to leave them to bilateral market bargaining. For example, government can order air polluters to reduce their emissions by x per cent. Polluters then incur (internalize) costs in order to conform to the public regulation, thereby relieving the public of even greater costs of maintaining health and property damaged by pollution.

Prior governmental action is essential because the competitive market system is incapable, by itself, of internalizing the costs of anti-pollution measures. Suppose, for example, that the automobile could be made pollution-free by installing a device costing x dollars. An automobile owner would not voluntarily install the device, because other people would reap the benefits of the cleaner air made possible by his expenditure. General Motors proved this in 1970 by a well-advertised effort to sell motorists in the Phoenix, Arizona, area a pollution-reducing kit costing only twenty-six dollars. During the first month only a few hundred kits were sold in a market with several hundred thousand potential buyers. Auto makers would not voluntarily install the device because to do so would add to their costs and put them at a disadvantage in competition with other manufacturers who did not install it. And antitrust laws prohibit any agreement among all auto manufacturers simultaneously to install, or not to install, pollution-reducing devices. Where large external costs or benefits are involved, there is a conflict between the decision that serves the self-interest of the individual and that which serves the collective welfare of the community. Community welfare can only be given the precedence it deserves by a prior governmental action regulating private behavior, followed by corporation actions to modify products, prices, and allocations of resources in order to conform to the public regulation.

Society cannot reasonably expect individual enterprises or consumers to shoulder external costs in the name of "social responsibility," because the competitive market system puts each firm and household under strong pressure to minimize its costs in order to survive. What is needed is a prior political decision that leaves all producers or consumers in the same relative position.

There are usually alternative solutions to pollution problems; each alternative should be evaluated in order to identify the least costly of them. Consider again the example of smog in the Los Angeles Basin. Among possible ways of coping with this problem are the following: controlling emissions of pollutants from motor vehicles and stationary sources by public regulation; moving people out of the basin; rezoning to reduce building density; building a rapid mass-transit system; imposing heavy taxes on private automobile operation; or subsidizing motorists to limit their auto mileage. The costs and benefits of each alternative, and combinations thereof, should be evaluated before an anti-pollution policy is adopted. The goal should always be the most efficient use of scarce resources.

All desirable things in limited supply have a cost, and there are trade-offs between desirable things. People may gain more of one thing only by sacrificing something else, and the optimum situation is reached when no additional benefits can be obtained by further substitutions. These principles apply to environmental amenities. For example, noise pollution can be reduced with benefits to health and well-being, but at the cost of larger expenditures for insulation or noise-abatement devices or a reduction in the speed or power of engines. Conceivably, utter silence could be achieved by incurring astronomical costs and by making great sacrifices of mobility, power, and time. The public decides the optimum noise level by balancing the benefits of less noise against the costs of attaining it. Government then fixes a noise standard at that point where the costs of reducing noise further would exceed the additional benefits to health and well-being. Although the calculus is necessarily rough, this is the rationale of determining standards to reduce pollution of all kinds.

Just as governmental intervention is needed to bring about the reallocations of resources needed for environmental improvement, so it is also required to levy the costs of such improvement equitably among individuals and groups in society so as to improve—or at least prevent a worsening of—the distribution of income.

There are opposite approaches to the problem of cost allocation. By one principle, polluters should pay the costs of suppressing their pollution; by another, the public should pay polluters to stop polluting. The second principle is defended on the ground that the public benefits from the reduction of pollution and should pay the costs of this benefit. Those who espouse this view hold that tax credits and public subsidies are the proper instruments of a policy for environmental betterment. Libertarians usually favor this approach because of their preference for the "carrot" versus the "stick," and their belief that public boards often come under the domination of those they are supposed to regulate.

Advocates of the first principle argue, to the contrary, that society initiates an anti-pollution policy from a current status of inequity. The problem is to restore equity as between polluters and those damaged by pollution, not to compensate polluters for a loss of equitable rights. They also observe that persons with large incomes generally generate disproportionately more pollution than those with low incomes, so that a policy of internalizing costs in the polluter will tend to shift income from richer to poorer people, with resulting gains in social well-being. The appropriate instruments for dealing with pollution are, in their view, public regulations to reduce harmful activities, or taxes and fines on polluters.

Equity requires that the costs of suppressing environmental damage be borne by those responsible for it. Public restraint of private actions harmful to the environment thus should be the dominant instrument of environmental policy. Assertion of this principle does not, however, preclude the use of taxes, fines, or lawsuits, nor does it rule out the use of public subsidies to enterprises which, through long-continued tolerance of harmful activities vital to their survival, have acquired a certain equity in them. For example, a city council might prohibit billboard advertising of off-premise goods or services, on the ground that the visual pollution costs borne by the public exceed the benefits. To enable outdoor advertising companies to finance an adjustment into other activities, a city might reasonably offer to pay them subsidies over a period of years on a descending scale.

Since the quality of the urban environment is a function of many variables, public policies to enhance the environment must utilize many instruments.

Direct governmental control of emissions of pollutants—audial, atmospheric, olfactory, visual, or health-affecting—is now exemplified in federal and state laws governing air and water pollution, and in federal standards of noise emissions from aircraft engines. Assuming that reduction of emissions is the least costly solution, the main problems are to determine appropriate standards and enforce them. In fixing standards, the state of pollution-control technology is an important consideration. Where such technology exists and can be applied at reasonable cost, the law should simply ban emissions and enforce compliance. This appears to be true of much air and water pollution from fixed sources, such as the chimneys of manufacturing and power-generating plants. Where pollution technology is in process of development, as in the case of automobile emissions, government should fix standards that are progressively raised as time goes on.

Another way to internalize external costs is to guarantee each property owner legal rights to the amenities pertaining to his property. A California court recently awarded substantial damages to home owners near the Los Angeles International Airport to compensate them for demonstrated loss of property values because of excessive noise from airplanes. A constitutional amendment should be enacted guaranteeing every property owner a right to environmental amenities, because this would induce business enterprises to reduce or eliminate pollution in order to escape legal liabilities. However, judicial processes are so costly, time-consuming, and uneven in their results as to make other solutions to environmental problems preferable.

Governments—federal, state, and local—themselves contribute to air and water pollution, especially by discharging untreated sewage into rivers and lakes. They should internalize these costs by massive public expenditures on sewage-treatment and water-purification plants. Such outlays will, of course, ultimately be paid for by a public that presumably values a clean environment more highly than the money paid in taxes to finance such facilities.

Urban planning, zoning, and building regulations are powerful instruments for enhancing the amenities of space, privacy, recreation, housing, transportation, and beauty in our cities. If American cities are to offer ample amenities for living, much stronger governmental controls of the design, quality, height, and density of buildings, and of the layout of transportation, recreation, and cultural facilities will be necessary. Americans will have to put a much higher priority on urban amenities, if strong enough instruments of social control over property usage are to be forged. Such controls will be opposed by builders, accustomed as they are to permissive public regulation that can be bent to their purposes. Yet firm public control of land usage under a long-range metropolitan plan is one reason why such cities as London hold a strong attraction for their residents as well as for millions of foreign visitors.

Enlargement of the supply of urban amenities also calls for immense public and private expenditures on recreational and cultural facilities, housing, and public transportation systems. The many programs coming under the auspices of the federal Departments of Transportation and of Housing and Urban Development serve this end. A whole battery of incentives for the participation of private enterprise in the gargantuan tasks will need to be fabricated, including tax credits, accelerated depreciation, credit guaranties, cost-plus contracts, and direct governmental subsidies. The naive idea that private corporations can or will undertake urban rehabilitation out of a sense of "social responsibility" denies the ineluctable fact that in a competitive market economy the firm cannot devote a material part of its resources to unprofitable activities and survive. Just as government must first create a market for pollution-reducing devices before the enterprise system will produce them, so it must first create adequate incentives to induce enterprises to produce urban housing and transit systems. That the responses are swift when the incentives are strong is shown by the great strength of the housing boom after World War II, triggered by liberal F.H.A. mortgage insurance and Veterans Administration home-loan guaranties.

Above all, a high-quality urban environment requires the public to assign high values to urban amenities—to appreciate them greatly and to work hard and pay for them. So far, too few American urbanites have held such values with sufficient intensity to bring about the necessary political action. Whether recent public outcries for a better environment will be sufficiently strong, sustained, and widespread to change the historical American posture of indifference remains to be seen.

The sudden emergence of the environmental problem raises profound issues about the functioning of our social institutions. Does it betoken an institutional breakdown—a failure to respond to new demands of the public? Has the social system responded, but been seriously laggard in its responses? Does the fault lie mainly in the political or in the market subsystem of our society, wherein there are two methods by which social choices of the uses of resources are made—voting in elections and buying in markets?

Although these questions cannot be answered finally, the most defensible positions appear to be the following. First, the social system has been sluggish in responding to the higher values placed by the public on environmental amenities, but it has not broken down and the processes of resource reallocation have begun. Second, the environmental crisis was generated primarily by tardy responses of the political system, and only secondarily by faults in the market system.

If American society is to attain optimal well-being, its dual set of political and market controls must operate promptly and in the proper sequence in response to changes in social values. Political action is first needed to create a demand for environment-improving products; market competition can then assure that this demand is satisfied economically. Measures are needed to improve both political and market processes.

Our model of the dynamic relationships between changes in social values, government actions, and corporate behavior is shown in the chart below. The primary sequential flow of influence runs from changes in social values, via the political process, to changes in governmental regulation of the private sector and reallocation of public resources; thence, via the market process, to corporate reallocation of private resources. However, changes in social values are not wholly determined by shifts in levels of income and other autonomous factors. They also respond to political leadership in the legislative and executive branches of government and to the public advertising and selling efforts of corporations. Similarly, governmental actions are not responsible exclusively to shifts in the values of the public. They are also influenced in some degree by the political activities of businessmen and by corporate lobbying. These secondary flows of influence also help to determine the performance of the social system.

The model enables us to identify salient points of improvement in the system. They are to reform the political process so that government actions will more rapidly and accurately reflect significant shifts in social values, to reform the market process so that corporate behavior will more rapidly and accurately reflect changes in governmental regulation, and to reform political and business behavior so that their secondary influences will help rather than hinder. Specifically, what changes are needed in each of these three areas?

The environmental problem emphasizes once again the need for a political system capable of translating changes in social values rapidly and accurately into governmental actions. The political apparatus for sensing, recording, mobilizing, transmitting, and acting upon millions of changes in individual preferences must be improved. Our representative system of government must be made more representative. This raises anew the old dilemmas of participative democracy, the weaknesses of political parties, the unrepresentativeness of legislatures, and the inordinate influence of pressure groups in an age of accelerating technological, demographic, and economic change. The basic requirements for greater efficiency of the political system are better education and sustained participation in political affairs by citizens. While one may easily be pessimistic in the light of the past, there is ground for hope of improvement. Americans generally spend only a small fraction of the time and effort they devote to private goods in making choices of the public goods they purchase with their taxes. Yet purchases of public goods and services are now

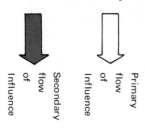

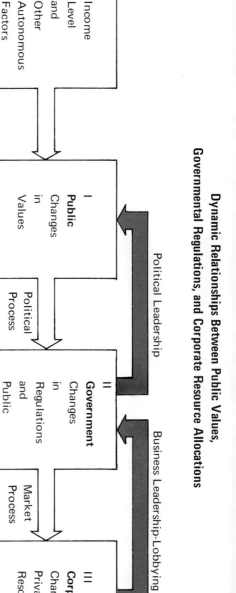

**Dynamic Relationships Between Public Values,
Governmental Regulations, and Corporate Resource Allocations**

nearly one-third as large as purchases of private goods. During 1969 government purchases amounted to $225 billions or twenty-three per cent of a total G.N.P. of $923 billions, whereas private purchases were $698 billions or seventy-seven per cent. Rational behavior in resource allocation requires a massive increase in the time and effort devoted to public decisions. Hopefully, the present egregious under-allocation of time represents a cultural lag which will be rectified in due course.

Changes should be made in the voting process to make it function more like a market. Just as consumers record the relative intensities of their demands for different private goods by the amounts of their expenditures in markets, so voters could be enabled to record the relative intensities of their demands for public goods. Each voter could be given, say, one thousand votes, which he could cast in whatever numbers he chose for alternative aggregate levels of public expenditures and alternative patterns of allocation of each level among different objects. Finally, a maximum usage of direct links between public expenditures and the taxes levied to finance them could help to make the political system more responsive.

The competitive market system must also be made more responsive to shifts in public values and governmental regulations. Despite its undoubted superiority as a device for gauging consumers' wants, the recent rise of the "consumerism" movement reflects, among other things, a disturbing insensitivity of the business corporations to changing public demands and expectations. The foot-dragging behavior of the auto makers in regard to safety and air pollution and of the oil companies in regard to air and ocean-water pollution are symptomatic. Business corporations generally have been reluctant, if not obstructive, reactors to new social values instead of innovative leaders in satisfying them. Either their market researchers have been unable to detect them, or else correct market intelligence has not been utilized by their engineering, manufacturing, and marketing executives.

A reorientation of corporate organization is needed, from the board of directors down through corporate and divisional managers to individual plant and store executives. The board should include one or more "outside" directors chosen especially for their knowledge of corporate relationships to society, including the environment. This need should be met by the normal process of including such nominees in the slate of directors presented by management for stockholder vote, rather than by augmenting the board by special stockholder nominees, as Ralph Nader proposed to General Motors Corporation. The normal procedure is more likely to result in effective board action to improve the environment, because it avoids "bloc" politics within the board. Every single policy and action of the firm should be reviewed for its effect upon the environment. An environmental analyst, assigned to this task as a staff adviser to the chief executive, would help to assure good corporate behavior. Standard corporate policy should require all managers to include in their proposals for new operations of facilities measures for preventing adverse environmental effects. Corporations should also make more penetrating use of consumer surveys and public-opinion polls in order to keep informed of shifts in public tastes and priorities.

Reforms are also needed to insure that the secondary influences upon social values exercised by political and business leaders are facilitative rather than obstructive. These influences are significant. For example, President Eisenhower's sponsorship of the Interstate Highway Act in 1956 and President Kennedy's proposal of a manned round trip to the moon in 1961 mobilized and activated changes in the values of the American people which led to highway and space programs each of the order of five billion dollars a year. President Nixon's leadership in 1970 in a national effort to improve the environment will probably produce even larger reallocations of resources. All three Presidents discerned deep changes in public priorities to which they gave form and implementation. Without such political leadership, readjustments would have been delayed amid mounting public tension and frustration.

American corporate leadership generally has not played a helpful role in implementing changes in social values. Whereas business lobbyists should be informing legislators of new environmental regulations desired by the public, they usually oppose such changes. Most corporate advertising is narrowly focused upon expanding public demand for existing products rather than for new products with superior environmental effects. As Henry Ford recently advised, corporate managers should "stop thinking about changing public expectations as new costs which may have to be accepted but certainly have to be minimized. Instead, we should start thinking about changes in public values as opportunities to profit by serving new needs."

This analysis of deterioration in the urban environment and of means to restore it has unveiled neither a master culprit nor a panacea. It has delineated a complex public problem requiring many instruments of policy for its solution. It has shown that the basic requirement is a citizenry that assigns higher values to urban amenities than it has in the past, and will work harder and pay more to get them. Given new social preferences, new regulations will be imposed and those long-neglected regulations on the statute books will finally be enforced. It is disturbing to reflect that a lawsuit brought by the Attorney General of the United States early in 1970 against several large corporations for polluting the southern end of Lake Michigan was to enforce a federal statute enacted in 1899. Here—as in the administration of urban zoning codes—Americans have not put high enough values upon environmental amenities to insist that private actions conform to existing public laws.

Environmental improvement will call for annual public and private expenditures of tens of billions of dollars indefinitely into the future. Profound changes will be necessary in the structure of relative costs and prices of goods, and in patterns of production and consumption. These readjustments will cause difficulties for individual companies operating on the margin of profitability and unable to pay the full costs of their products. Yet the ability of our profit-oriented enterprise system to adapt to a massive internalization of costs cannot be doubted, when one recalls its successful assimilation of the technological revolution since World War II. Over a period of time the costs and prices of products with large external costs (e.g., automobiles) would rise relatively, while those with large external benefits (e.g., homes) would decline relatively. While consumers would spend relatively less on autos and relatively more on housing, in a growing economy this would mean changes in the growth rates of different industries rather than an absolute decline in the output of any one. Also, new industries would emerge to supply the growing demand for pollution-controlling equipment and services. Profit rates and market signals would continue to guide resources in the directions desired by consumers.

The effects of environmental improvement upon the overall growth of the U.S. economy depend mainly upon how "economic growth" is defined and measured. There is a growing recognition that the true end of public policy is a steady expansion of social well-being, and that a rising G.N.P. is only a means to this end. G.N.P. is simply a measure of the aggregate output of the economy, whereas social well-being is also directly related to the composition of output, its full costs, and the uses to which it is put. If, as has been true during the past twenty years, much production included in the G.N.P. has been associated with national defense and environmental degradation, growth of the G.N.P. can be a highly misleading index of gains in social well-being. Indices of well-being should be developed to help guide long-term public policy, and G.N.P. also should be recast to provide a more meaningful measure of total output.

Assuming the existence of a strong effective demand by the public for a better urban environment, it cannot be doubted that a redirection of production to supply that demand will expand the well-being of American society. A better environment would enable people to reduce many other costs they now incur for health, property maintenance, recreation, and travel to leave uncongenial surroundings. Rising social well-being is not in conflict with an expanding G.N.P., provided that the increments of production improve the quality of life. On the contrary, growth of production is needed for that purpose. As President Nixon said in his 1970 State of the Union Message: "The answer is not to abandon growth, but to redirect it."

CATHERINE DRINKER BOWEN

. . . We've Never Asked a Woman Before

For thirty years I have been writing about lawyers and the law. And for almost as many years I have been the recipient of invitations to stand on platforms and address large assemblies of legal experts. I enjoy receiving these invitations; it shows that people are reading my books. Yet I often hesitate; the program means serious preparation. A non-lawyer—and a non-man—cannot stand up and talk drivel for thirty minutes or fifty (as specified) to a hall bristling with five hundred or so hard-minded professional gentlemen. Therefore I hold off, saying into the telephone that I haven't the time; I am writing a new book and must stay home by myself, where writers belong. Perhaps the committee will send a letter, giving details? "Mrs. Bowen!" says an urgent voice from Houston or San Francisco. "This is our law society's big annual celebration. We've had Senator Fulbright as speaker, and Wechsler of Columbia, and the Lord Chief Justice of England [and God and Santa Claus]. But we've never asked a woman before."

At this moment all my latent feminism rises up. Why haven't they asked a woman before—aren't there any women lawyers? Impossible to refuse this challenge! In Washington there exists a prestigious group called the American Law Institute. The cream of the profession belongs to it; the work they do is significant to the country at large. After I spoke at the Institute's annual dinner, women lawyers crowded to shake my hand. They said they had sat for years watching those men at the head table; they wanted me to know what it meant to see a woman sitting there. It made me very glad that I had come.

The word feminism is outmoded. "The movement," young women call it today. We know of the ferocity with which the goal is pursued. We have heard of the extremists—ten thousand strong—called Women's Liberation, how they crop their hair short, wear baggy trousers and loose sweaters to conceal the more notable evidences of sex. "Abolish sexism!" is their slogan. Brassieres must go, and beauty contests. "Miss America!" say their banners. "Men make money off *your* body too. Pornography, Bunnies, Playboy Magazine are as degrading to women as racism is to blacks."

But of course! And why, one asks oneself, has it taken the sisters so long to find this out, so long to proclaim that for women sex is neither

cute nor funny and can result in pain, disgrace, or years of virtual—
though respectable—servitude? Sex jokes are a male invention. It is indeed
a naïve girl who grows up in our society unaware of what her world
considers the primary function of women. To suggest that women don't
have to be beautiful is the worst kind of heresy; it means women have
more important functions than pleasing men.

How does all this affect women writers? The answer is, profoundly.
Nobody writes from a vacuum; writers compose from their life experience. They use what they know and feel in the environment round about,
the stuff of life as it has been handed out or as they have been able to
grasp it, hold it up and look at it with courage and with truth. For many
centuries girls have been told that their business is wifehood, motherhood
—and nothing else. "When children cease to be altogether desirable,
women cease to be altogether necessary," said John Langdon Davis in
A Short History of Women. I once had a husband who liked to say that
nothing is expected of a wife-and-mother but respectability. Yet writers,
male and female, belong in the category artist. (Muriel Rukeyser, the
poet, puts women into four classes: whores, saints, wives, and artists.)
No artist can operate lacking belief in his mission. *His* mission; the very
pronoun confesses an age-old situation. I hope the young activists in the
movement wipe out that generalized pronoun, so bland, so denigrating
to the woman professional in any field.

Without a clear view of their capabilities, men and women cannot
function. Convince a two-legged man that he has but one leg, and he will
not be able to walk. A writer must know her horizon, how wide is the
circle within which she, as artist, extends. The world still professes to
wonder why there has been no female Shakespeare or Dante, no woman
Plato or Isaiah. Yet people do what society looks for them to do. The
Quaker Meeting House has existed for centuries, but it has produced no
Bach and no B Minor Mass. Music was not desired by Quakers, it was
frowned on. Poetry, fiction, playwriting have been expected from women
only recently, as history counts time. Of the brilliant, erratic Margaret
Cavendish, her husband, the Duke of Newcastle, remarked, circa 1660,
"A very wise woman is a very foolish thing." As lately as 1922, Christina
Rossetti's biographer wrote of her, that "like most poetesses, she was
purely subjective, and in no sense creative." What a beautiful triple sneer,
and how it encompasses the entire second sex! One recalls the fiery poet*ess,*
Lady Winchelsea, born 1661, said to be "lost in melancholy"—and small
wonder:

> Debarred from all improvements of the mind [she wrote],
> And to be dull, expected and designed. . . .
> Alas! a woman that attempts the pen,
> Such a presumptuous creature is esteemed,
> The fault can by no virtue be redeemed.
> Good breeding, fashion, dancing, dressing, play,

Are the accomplishments we should desire;
To write, or read, or think, or to enquire,
Would cloud our beauty, and exhaust our time,
And interrupt the conquests of our prime,
Whilst the dull manage of a servile house
Is held by some our utmost art and use.

Because I write about the law and the Constitution I am often asked why I entered "a man's field." Men tell me I write like a man. "Mrs. Bowen," they say with pleased smiles, "you *think* like a man." No, gentlemen, thank you, I do not, I write like a woman. I enjoy being a woman and thinking like a woman, which means using my mind and using it hard. Women have an advantage as writers because they are trained from childhood to notice the relationships between people. Upon such perceptions all their later welfare can depend. Is it not a mother's business, a wife's business to soothe hurt feelings, pacify the male, keep peace within her household? She is vitally concerned therefore with human motivation, what trial lawyers call *intent*. In my own field, intent lies at the base of the entire structure; the motivation of mankind makes up the plot of every biography that is written.

Women writers do not think like men. It is when I am told so that I remember Lady Winchelsea, remember also the ladies who had to use men's names on their books: George Eliot, George Sand, Currer Bell and her sisters, the Brontës.

I have used the word ladies in speaking of artists. I ask their forgiveness. No writer, no artist, is a lady. She can't afford to be. The novelist, biographer, historian, looks bleakly at life, lingers to squint at its sorrier aspects, reaches out to touch the dirty places, and raises the hand to the nostrils to make sure. Charles Beard once told me, "You have to have a strong stomach to study history." Happily, I was early indoctrinated against being a lady. At sixteen, the family decided to send me to boarding school, in order to correct certain provincialisms of speech and deportment picked up from schoolmates in the Lehigh Valley town where we lived. I didn't want to go, and protested furiously. A brother, Cecil, ten years my senior, protested also. "That place," he told me morosely, "is called a finishing school. They want to make a lady of you, Katz. But you're born for something better, and don't you ever forget it."

I did not forget it. I was the youngest of six; the four brothers were considerably older. They taught me their skills; in fact, they insisted that I learn. "Push out, Katz, with that right skate. *Don't be scared!* Get your whole body into it." I grew up believing that girls were supposed to compete with boys, not just compete *for* boys. Our mother devoted herself wholly to domesticity. Yet she told my sister and me that a girl could be just as independent and well educated as a boy, there was no reason not. My Aunt Cecilia Beaux was earning a living painting portraits by the time she was twenty-five, though Cecilia, my mother said, resented being referred to in the newspapers as a woman painter. "They don't talk about a *man* painter," Cecilia Beaux said. Aunt Beaux made money enough to buy six acres in Gloucester, Massachusetts, and build a house and studio there called Green Alley.

It would be hard to exaggerate the effect this had on a girl of twelve, fourteen, eighteen. I have been told that women feel guilty competing intellectually with men. Anaïs Nin, the writer, so confesses in her diary, and I have seen graphs drawn by psychologists, showing that girls do badly in what the professors call "achievement-oriented situations vis-à-vis boys." Guilt at competing? To me it is a contradiction in terms. I would have thought myself guilty in *not* competing. My parents expected high marks at school examinations, and if I brought home a bad paper, "What's wrong?" my brother Cecil would ask, "lose your nerve this time, Katz, or just lazy?" As for Beaux's Green Alley, it has become the family summer place. I have written four books there, in Aunt Beaux's studio by the bay; her spirit sustained me while I wrote. "We think back through our mothers if we are women." It was Virginia Woolf who said it.

Nevertheless, the female brain does not reside in the uterus, though women as well as men try their best so to persuade us. A recent newspaper showed Grace Kelly on a platform receiving an award from the YWCA. Glittering in sequins, she announced complacently that today's women, pushing into a man's world, were sacrificing their femininity. (Nothing was said about the twenty-nine million American women who work for their living.) A day or so later, a woman newspaper columnist eagerly affirmed this by recounting at length the joys of motherhood, ending with the dictum that once the children grow up and depart the scene, mothers never again experience a like happiness and sense of fulfillment. Wives too come forward with proud claims: the self-sacrifice, the best years given. "There is no career more exciting or exacting for a woman than marriage to a great man." So writes a recent biographer of Mrs. Gladstone, and a female biographer at that.

Against this flood of bilge water I am fortified by a line in my great-great-grandmother's diary. Elizabeth Drinker, having given birth to nine and reared five, wrote in the year 1790 that she had often thought a woman's best years came after she left off bearing and rearing. I myself happen to be the mother of two and grandmother of four. I always expected to be married and looked forward to it—but not as sole career; never, never as sole career. It is not the maternal chores that oppress but the looming of that altar which has been erected to motherhood, its sacro-sanctity, the assumption that nothing but motherhood is important. For the woman artist this ideal can prove as bewildering as the onset of a national war. Nothing matters but this patriotism, this motherhood. One is praised and petted for being a mother, all other values put in the discard. When the baby comes: "You have joined the human race!" women cry, bringing gifts, adding gleefully that you won't have time *now* for writing (or sculpting or painting or playing the violin). When my two children, a girl and then a boy, came along, I had already published two small books and twelve magazine articles. A local newspaper, the Easton *Daily Express,* paid me a dollar a day for a three-hundred-word column, handsomely boxed in. I looked on the pay as munificent and was terrified that I wouldn't be worth it. When time came for the first baby to be born I wrote two weeks' columns ahead, told the editor, a red-headed Irishman, that I'd be back in a fortnight, received his blessing, and never wrote another line until both children were in nursery school, five years later, and the mornings were once more my own. It was about this time that I came on Katherine Mansfield's thrice-blessed words: "Mothers of children grow on every bush."

A writer's regimen can reduce certain nagging moralisms to dust— the notion, for instance, that housework is ennobling to women, or at least instinctive to them as scuffing leaves to clean his bed is instinctive to a dog. Love of cooking is thought by many to be a secondary female sex characteristic. So is the exercise of following little children interminably about the yard. If I had not been a writer, these moralistic conceptions would have defeated me before I reached the age of thirty. Writing saved me. The housework still had to be done and done cheerfully. The children still had to be followed around the yard. But these activities, repeated day after day for years, were no longer defeating because they were no longer the be-all and end-all of existence.

"How fortunate, dear, that you have this hobby of writing to occupy you while your husband is away!" Thus my mother-in-law in September of the year 1941. I was two years along with *Yankee from Olympus.* My husband, a surgeon and member of the Naval Reserve, had gone to Honolulu on a hospital ship. By this time I had published six books and become inured to married women's attitudes toward the professional writer, so I merely told my mother-in-law, yes, it *was* lucky, and I had better get upstairs to my typewriter. Back and forth in the family the question raged: Should I take our daughter out of college, our son from school, and migrate to Honolulu, Hawaii was paradise! people said. We'd all love it, and what an opportunity! I could do my Holmes research in the Honolulu University's splendid library. Palm trees and warm sea—a paradise!

The notion of Oliver Wendell Holmes of New England revealing himself at the University of Honolulu belonged, of course, in the realms of fantasy. Also, my daughter loved Radcliffe and my son Haverford School. I listened to women spelling out my duty (what today they call a husband-supportive program), and I developed stomachaches, a pain in the lower back. Then one night I had a dream that settled everything, so vivid I can see it today. I sat in a room filled with people; my father, white-haired, white-whiskered, and long since dead, stood across the carpet. He raised an arm and pointed at me. "Thou shalt not go to Paradise!" he said.

Next morning I announced we were staying home, and went on with *Yankee from Olympus.* Nor did I suffer further qualms, Dr. Freud notwithstanding.

Subject A, young women call it today, bringing me the age-old query: How to manage a career, a husband, and children. Despite "the movement" and the liberation fronts, the problem is still here, sharp and demanding. I am likely to give a twofold answer. "You manage it by doing double work, using twice the energy other wives use: housework *and* writing. Or you do what Mrs. Eleanor Roosevelt told me. I quote her, verbatim: 'If a woman wants to pursue her own interests after marriage, she must choose the right husband. Franklin stood back of me in everything I wanted to do.' "

Competition was bred in my bones. Yet I never wrote to rival men; such a thing would not have occurred to me. Actually it was a man—my first husband—who started me writing, in my twenties. And once I saw my product in print, nothing mattered but to get on with the work, get on with studying history and with learning how to write sentences that said what I wanted to say. Many writers hate writing. I happen to love it. With my hands on the typewriter I feel like the war-horse in the Bible that smells the battle far off and saith among the trumpets, Ha, ha. Writers have in them a vast ambition . . . hunger . . . egotism—call it what you will. A writer wants to be read, wants to be known. If there is talent, it must come out or it will choke its host, be she three times wife-and-mother. Scholarship also is a hungry thing, the urge to know. A great legal historian, Maitland, spoke of "the blessing which awaits all those who have honestly taught themselves anything."

A woman biographer must, like anybody else, earn her place in the sun. When I turned from writing about musical subjects to legal subjects, I entered a man's world with a vengeance, though some time passed before I was fully aware of it. The Holmes' Papers were guarded by two literary executors, John Gorham Palfrey (father of the tennis champion) and Felix Frankfurter, of the United States Supreme Court. In the six years since Holmes's death, quite evidently the executors had expected hordes of hungry biographers to descend. It came as a shock that the first to approach was a non-Bostonian, a non-lawyer, and a non-man. Nevertheless, Mr. Palfrey handed me five hundred of Holmes's letters, neatly copied in typescript, saying I could take all the notes I wished. I procured four court stenographers—this was before the days of Xerox—who copied profusely. In Washington I saw Felix Frankfurter, who greeted me jovially (he was an old friend), said of course I didn't plan to present the big cases, the Lochner dissent, Rosika Schwimmer, the Gitlow dissent —the great issues of free speech, the ten-hour day, and so on? I said of course I did, why else would I be writing the book?

I went home and back to work. Two months later a letter came from Mr. Palfrey, enclosing what he called "some of the more unfavorable replies" to his queries among Holmes's legal friends and associates. Nothing in Mrs. Bowen's previous experience, these said, qualified her to write about a lawyer, a New Englander, or indeed an American. In short, the executors had decided to deny access to all unpublished material, even for the purpose of establishing chronology or telling me where Holmes had been at a given time. My work and my Boston visits, Mr. Palfrey said, had spurred the executors to appoint the "definitive biographer," Mark Howe of the Harvard Law School, secretary to the Justice the year before he died.

Plainly, the executors hoped to stop me from writing the book. I let the initial shock wear off and laid plans. Scores of men and women existed who had known Holmes. Whatever I needed from those letters I must get by legwork—even when letters had been sent me by recipients, like Rosika Schwimmer and others. I must persuade the writers to tell me what the Justice had said and done on the occasions their letters described. This exercise took perhaps an added year, but was well worth it. Meanwhile, Frankfurter wrote from time to time. He heard I had been at the Supreme Court building and had left some unsolved questions with the Marshal. Was I actually making an effort to attain accuracy, ceasing to be an artist and becoming merely a thinker? The letters were wonderful and awful. They kindled the anger that sends one on ever harder quests; Frankfurter could be a formidable antagonist. I talked with Irving Olds of United States Steel, Attorney General Francis Biddle, and ten other legal secretaries of Holmes's, choosing them not because of their worldly prominence but because their particular secretarial year coincided with an important Supreme Court case. I think my book benefited from the program, rigorous though it was, and by the denial of those hundreds of letters. A biography can smother under too much quoted material.

When finally the Book-of-the-Month chose my manuscript, Frankfurter sent me a long congratulatory telegram: "I always knew you could do it." I did not see him, however, until ten years and several biographies later. After my book on Sir Edward Coke was published, the director of the Folger Shakespeare Library, Louis Wright, invited me to speak in their Washington theater. He said Justice Frankfurter had telephoned, asking to introduce me, and why was this? Frankfurter never made such requests, Louis said.

On the appointed evening, the Justice sat on the platform with me; I had no notion of his intentions. He got up and told the audience that he had done all he could to stop Mrs. Bowen from writing *Yankee from Olympus,* but there were people who worked better under difficulties and I was one of them. He had not read the book, he would never read it, though he had read my other biographies. But he wished to make public apology, public amends. Then he bowed, grinned at me where I sat, and returned to his chair.

It was handsome of Frankfurter. Yet I had wondered how much of the entire feud, and its climax, could be laid to the fact of my sex. I do not know. But as time passed and I proceeded to other legal biographies—John Adams, Sir Edward Coke, Francis Bacon, *Miracle at Philadelphia*—I know that the rigors I underwent with *Yankee* stood me in good stead, toughened me, made me ready for whatever might come. With John Adams I was again refused unpublished material and again went on my quest, though this time it had to be in research libraries and took five years. Sir Edward Coke's college was Trinity, at Cambridge University. And even Bluebeard did not consider women more expendable than does a Cambridge don. All but one of the law and history professors I met there brushed aside my project and did it smiling, with the careless skill of the knowledgeable Englishman. "Are you planning to write a popular book about Coke?" they asked. I smiled in turn, and said by popular they no doubt meant cheap, and that only the finished manuscript could answer their question. "At least," remarked another, "Mrs. Bowen has been shrewd enough to see that a book about Edward Coke will sell. And a person has to begin to learn *somewhere*." After inquiring how many copies my other biographies had sold, one history professor looked glum. "Someday," he said, snapping his fingers, "I'm going to take a year off and write a popular book."

Seven years later the Acting Master of Trinity wrote to me in Philadelphia, saying he had read the English edition of my Coke biography, *The Lion and the Throne.* Did I recall how he had not, initially, been enthusiastic about the project? He went on to say kind things about the book, acknowledging that he had been mistaken. And next time I was in Cambridge, would I permit him to give a small celebration in my honor?

Again, I cannot know how much of the battle—the defeats and the victories—can be laid to my being a woman. I know only that I spent days of anger, of outrage, and that I enjoyed the challenge. How could one not enjoy it? *"We never invited a woman before. . . ."*

One honors those who march in the streets for a cause; one knows that social liberation does not come peacefully. I have not taken part in the movement, though feminine activists greet me as a sister. I think they know that the woman writer who stays outside the movement by no means dodges the issue. She takes a risk too, though of another kind. Instead of the dangers of marching, she assumes the risks of lifelong dedication to her profession—a program that runs counter to many cherished slogans. As a young woman conversing with young men, I learned to caution myself: "Let him win! When a woman wins she loses." Yet even as I said it I knew that such capitulation was merely for the purposes of flirtation, where a woman can afford the delicious indulgence of yielding. Only when men—or women—block and balk her progress in the professions must a woman strike back, and then she must use every weapon in her artillery.

To bear and rear a child is all that it is said to be; it is joy and sorrow, the very heart of living. There is no comparing it with a woman's profession beyond the home. Simply, the two things do not bear comparison. It is false to say the home comes first, the career second. For the woman writer, there can be no first or second about these matters; even to think it is an offense. For myself I enjoy housekeeping, by which I mean I like living in an attractive house and entertaining my friends. I look on house and garden as the most delightful toys, and take pleasure in every facet. But I know also that if house-and-garden should interfere seriously with work, with writing, house-and-garden would go.

Women in the professions must make their choices. That many refuse, sidestepping to easy pursuits, is a reason why American women have not kept pace with their sisters in India and Russia. The United States Senate of 100 has one woman member.

Perhaps the real turn in the road will come—and I predict it is coming soon—when more than two children to a family will seem bad taste, like wearing mink in a starving village. No woman can devote a life to the rearing of two, she cannot even make a pretense of it. When the mother image loses its sanctity, something will take its place on the altar. And any writer knows that when the image of the heroine changes, the plot changes with her. Such an event could alter, for both men and women, the whole picture of American life.

CHARLES REICH

The Limits of Duty

In Washington, D.C., during the May [1971] anti-war protests, police in automobiles and on scooters aimed their vehicles directly at demonstrators and drove toward them at high speeds in order to herd them off the streets. If one of the protesters had been hit and killed, the police officer driving the vehicle would have been guilty of murder. Not accidental killing or manslaughter but murder. Thus, every one of these officers was potentially guilty of a crime similar to that for which Lieutenant Calley was tried and convicted.

The applicable principle is deeply embedded in our common law. A leading early example is Halloway's Case (King's Bench, 1628). Halloway was the woodward of woods belonging to the Earl of Denbigh. He discovered a boy named Payne in a tree, attempting to steal wood. Payne

THE LIMITS OF DUTY By Charles Reich. Reprinted by permission. © 1971 by The New Yorker Magazine, Inc. From *The New Yorker Magazine,* June 19, 1971.

had a rope tied around his middle, probably to aid him in climbing trees. Halloway ordered the boy down from the tree, and when he descended struck him two blows on his back with a cudgel. Then Halloway tied the other end of the rope to the tail of his horse. The frightened horse dragged Payne three furlongs, killing him. The question was whether this was manslaughter or murder, and the court held it to be murder, for Halloway knew, or should have known, the reckless and wanton risk he was taking with the boy's life. In such a case, the specific intention to kill is not required. The deliberate taking of the risk is enough. Halloway was hanged.

Students at Yale, where I teach in the law school, tell me that District of Columbia bus drivers also aimed their buses toward protesters at high speed and drove ahead without slowing down. How strange that those long-suffering civil servants the bus drivers are now guilty of reckless driving and assault, and, but for the agility of their potential victims, would be guilty of murder. Yet this is not an aberration. It is a pattern that is crucial to understanding what has gone wrong with America. Evil now comes about not necessarily when people violate what they understand to be their duty but, more and more often, when they are conscientiously doing what is expected of them. And for this evil the question of individual blame seems almost irrelevant.

Two oil tankers collide on a foggy morning in San Francisco Bay. The bay and ocean are contaminated, beaches are coated, wildlife is exterminated, a fragile beauty is destroyed for millions of people. Yet the tanker captains were doing their duty to move the oil on time, and behind them were company officials concerned with the maintenance of production schedules. No investigation, no technical fixing of blame would be likely to disclose what we have normally imagined to be the root of crime—a guilty mind or a malign heart. And what is true of the San Francisco oil spill is true of the other major evils that we see around us. From wiretapping to the prosecution of the Vietnam war, our crimes have been started and carried out by men zealously attempting to serve as they have been taught to serve.

It is this altered problem of evil that rightly troubles us in the Calley case. I believe that Calley was properly convicted of murdering Vietnamese civilians, even though the same result produced by different means is officially held to be wholly legal. Yet we must all believe that Calley, in his own wrong and frightened way, was seeking to perform his duty— to do what was expected of him. The enterprise upon which he was engaged is not condemned, only the means he chose to carry it out. Hence the profound disquiet among so many Americans, taught to serve employer or country, who cannot understand why the law apparently no longer cares about goals but only about a nicety of method. Plainly, our long-accepted criminal-law concepts do not fit the crimes of today.

The central reality is that evil today is the product of our system of organization and our technology, and that it occurs because personal responsibility and personal awareness have been obliterated by a system deliberately designed to do just that—eliminate or minimize the human element and insure the supremacy of the system. The whole purpose of this system is to reduce the human component; that is why we have organization charts, a hierarchy of supervision, divided responsibilities, specialization. In the main, it is this rational organization of human effort that has brought us to our present stage of civilization, but we should realize that inherent in the very design of the system is the disappearance of individual blame, and hence the obsolescence of our concepts of individual criminal responsibility.

Let us follow the process of creating an evil more closely. A scientist who is doing his specialized duty to further research and knowledge develops the substance known as napalm. Another specialist makes policy in the field of our nation's foreign affairs. A third is concerned with maintaining the strength of our armed forces with the most modern weaponry. A fourth manufactures what the defense authorities require. A fifth drops napalm from an airplane where he is told to do so. The ultimate evil is the result of carefully segmented acts; the structure itself guarantees an evasion by everyone of responsibility for the full moral act. Indeed, the system, especially when it is combined with advanced technology, makes it unlikely that those who participate in the process will have any real awareness of the ultimate consequences. Neither the scientist nor the man in the State Department nor even the pilot actually sees the horrors of burning napalm on human flesh. The basic result of our system of doing things is to destroy awareness, alienate all of us from the consequences of our actions, and prevent the formation of that very responsibility which has been at the center of our idea of criminal justice.

Our traditional criminal law is based on a standard of conduct that assumes each individual to be a morally responsible human being. A man who runs a speedboat carelessly and kills someone is guilty of manslaughter if his actions fall below the standard. A man who allows his passions or desires to direct his actions so that he harms another person is guilty of assault or murder if, according to the standard, he should have controlled himself. The standard represents an ideal. Sometimes it is a cruel and unreasonable ideal, because the individual defendant lacks the capacity for measuring up to it. But the ideal does have a vital function. It establishes a large, even exalted, concept of man.

In the famous case of The Queen v. Dudley and Stephens, decided in 1884, four English seamen were cast away in an open boat on the high seas sixteen hundred miles from the Cape of Good Hope. After eighteen days, they were reduced to the utmost state of desperation, with neither food nor water. Dudley and Stephens then said that if no hope of rescue appeared one of the four should be sacrificed, so that the others might live. A third man refused to consent to the plan. The fourth, a boy of seventeen or eighteen, was not consulted; he was then in a helpless and weakened state. Dudley and Stephens spoke of their having families, indicating that the boy should be chosen. On the twentieth day, no help appearing, the defendants, after praying for forgiveness, killed the boy, and the three men fed upon his blood and body for four days, after which they were rescued. Dudley and Stephens were brought to England and tried for murder. It was acknowledged that if the boy had not been killed all four would probably have perished before rescue, and the boy would probably have died first. Yet the two men were found guilty.

The opinion of the Queen's Bench was delivered by Lord Coleridge, the Lord Chief Justice of England. Acknowledging that the temptation had been great and the suffering awful, he declared, "We are often compelled to set up standards which we cannot reach ourselves, and to lay down rules which we could not ourselves satisfy." And he went on:

> Though law and morality are not the same, and many things may be immoral which are not necessarily illegal, yet the absolute divorce of law from morality would be of fatal consequence. . . .

Rather than kill the boy, said Lord Coleridge, the men should have been willing to lose their own lives:

> To preserve one's life is generally speaking a duty, but it may be the plainest and the highest duty to sacrifice it. War is full of instances in which it is a man's duty not to live, but to die. The duty, in the case of shipwreck, of a captain to his crew, of the crew to the passengers, of soldiers to women and children, as in the noble case of the *Birkenhead;* these duties impose on men the moral necessity, not of the preservation, but of the sacrifice of their lives for others, from which in no country, least of all, it is to be hoped, in England, will men ever shrink, as indeed, they have not shrunk. . . .

Although the circumstances make this case unique, the basic ideal is found throughout the Anglo-American common law. Commonwealth v. Pierce (1884), a classic American case, written by Mr. Justice Holmes, then a member of the Supreme Judicial Court of Massachusetts, dealt with the problem of a physician whose patient died after he had treated her by keeping her wrapped in flannel saturated with kerosene for three days. Admitting that the physician's intentions were good, Holmes said that if the treatment was morally reckless, judged by the standards of a reasonably prudent man, then the defendant must answer for consequences that he neither intended nor foresaw. If the treatment was dangerous according to common experience, "we cannot recognize a privilege to do acts manifestly endangering human life, on the ground of good intentions alone." Holmes also wrote:

> The very meaning of the fiction of implied malice in such cases at common law was, that a man might have to answer with his life for

consequences which he neither intended nor foresaw . . . his failure or inability to predict them was immaterial if, under the circumstances known to him, the court or jury, as the case might be, thought them obvious.

Recently, I was watching the C.B.S. evening news when a few minutes were devoted to films of one of the favorite antipersonnel weapons used by Americans in Vietnam. It consists of a rocket tightly packed with many ordinary nails. The rocket is fired from a helicopter. The nails scatter widely, propelled with such force that they will go right through the body of anyone in their path. One of the advantages of the weapon, it was explained, is that the gunner doesn't need to see the target at all. The consequences can only be imagined, but what can they be except the reckless maiming of all human beings, old or young, innocent or guilty, who happen to be in the way? Lieutenant Calley is guilty, we are told, but the men who designed these instruments, the men who built them, the men who ordered them to be used, and the men who actually used them were all simply doing their duty. What a diminished view of man this purported version of the law gives us! It tells us that we are all "universal soldiers," in the phrase from one of Donovan Leitch's recordings, morally oblivious of the consequences of our actions. Lord Chief Justice Coleridge completed his argument for full moral responsibility by saying, "It is enough in a Christian country to remind ourselves of the Great Example whom we profess to follow." What has happened when the hard-working, God-fearing people of America are expected to be moral robots, making and firing the nails for mass killings?

Obviously, our thinking has been strained to adapt itself to the realities of technology and organization. That is why all those fixtures of the old criminal law, the guilty mind, the malign heart, actual or presumed malice, the common experience of prudent men, seem so out of place— indeed, ironic—in the Calley case. We all understand that such standards of responsibility are not expected of any of us. Nor would we feel more comfortable about the prosecution of high-ranking generals of political leaders under the Nuremberg theory. They, too, would be found to have been doing their duty.

The Calley case represents a momentary, vestigial reminder of the old law of responsibility. It was unfair to single out one man for such a revival of the old law, to be sure. Still, the reminder sent a shudder of awareness through all of us universal soldiers back home. It was not surprising that President Nixon hastily intervened. What led to his intervention was not just his seeming unconcern for legal processes, or his desire, as the *New Republic* put it, to coddle this particular criminal. The President insists, in every speech he makes, that we should do our small, segmented duties while he—or those in authority—assumes responsibility. The President's intervention was no surprise, because the Calley case confronts us with standards of responsibility that do not fit what the President and others insist are our duties and the limits of our duties. We are all supposed to be motorists on a highway where the maximum speed is sixty and the minimum speed is fifty-nine.

Perhaps the best way to understand those who have resisted the draft —by seeking conscientious-objector status, by going to jail, by fleeing to Canada—is to acknowledge that they are demanding to live and to be judged by the old standards as fully responsible moral beings. They are seeking law, not evading it. Finding no acceptable standard of conduct available in today's organizational society, they have gone to standards that are not their own personal fiat but the old, traditional standards of religion, ethics, and common law. They are saying that they refuse to act in a way that common experience tells them will produce evil—evil that we know about or should know about. Theirs is a revolt for a larger view of man. And for all of us it poses a necessary question: Given that we must all live and work within large organizations, that we must all take only a small part in a large enterprise, how can we restore the awareness, the responsibility, and the law that are the moral essence of free men?

An organization is a hybrid form of machine—one part a tool or system, the other part human. We have made too little use of the human part. We have thought of the humanness as something to be suppressed for efficiency's sake, not something to be valued because it might supply a quality that would otherwise be lacking. All of us who work in organizations should begin to assume a responsibility that is larger than the particular job we do, and this responsibility should ultimately be recognized, protected, and enforced by law. It might take many forms. Perhaps there should be a right—analogous to the long-recognized right to strike for economic objectives—to refuse, on a selective moral basis, to do certain work and perform certain duties. Perhaps this right should be guaranteed to individuals as well as to organized groups. Perhaps the organization should be answerable, on a democratic basis to those who work within it, for its policies and their probable consequences. Surely the present rigid hierarchy of authority must give way to a concept that in an organization all the members have a share of authority.

A corollary to this is that law should be based on the assumption that institutions, far more than individuals, are likely to go astray. Perhaps the primary regulatory work of law should be shifted from that of managing people to that of managing organizations while safeguarding the individuality of the people within them. Because organizations are the most characteristic element of our civilization, the scope of action by the members, employees, or consumers must be widened, and the scope of action by systems and machines must be narrowed and must be supervised by law. In the deepest sense, the purpose of such changes is nothing less than a restoration of one of our richest and most neglected resources— the human potentiality of the great mass of our people. Government by a managerial élite deprives us of the humanity of the many. Policy is made by a few, and the rest are coerced into following by laws that speak in the name of duty. The assumption is made that those who get to the top are naturally qualified to manage and plan for the rest of us, that we must accept what they require of us without allowing our moral knowledge to intervene. Such a neglect of our moral resources is as great a loss as our now well-known neglect of our environmental resources. We need the full participation of each individual. We can no longer afford to be a people who unthinkingly serve.

This brings us back to what happened in Washington. The procedures used against demonstrators who tried to block traffic were flagrantly un-Constitutional. There were arrests without cause—mass roundups, which often included any young person, however innocent, who happened to be visible to the police. Prisoners were not subject to normal arrest procedure. Many were kept at detention centers without being afforded the basic rights of arrested persons. All this, like the murderous driving, was not the product of officers gone berserk but was part of coldly rational plans sanctioned, and later praised, by high authorities. Indeed, the same high authorities have recommended that similar tactics be used again. Can the policemen and bus drivers in question say they are doing all they can to respect the fundamental law of the land if they simply follow orders? Can the civil servants who drove to work that morning, maybe sympathetic to the peace movement but afraid of a demerit, call themselves law-abiding? I am suggesting that following orders is no longer good enough for any of us—not if we want our Constitution preserved. Each of us has a permanent and personal duty to the supreme law of the land. I do not mean the "law" that the Nixon Administration speaks of —something that I would call "force," or "state power." I think the Nixon Administration is deeply contemptuous of law. We cannot count on Attorney General Mitchell to preserve the law, nor, I fear, can we count on the courts. And, from a certain point of view, that is as it should be. It is our Constitution, not theirs.

IVAN ILLICH

The Alternative to Schooling

For generations we have tried to make the world a better place by providing more and more schooling, but so far the endeavor has failed. What we have learned instead is that forcing all children to climb an open-ended education ladder cannot enhance equality but must favor the individual who starts out earlier, healthier, or better prepared; that enforced instruction deadens for most people the will for independent learning; and that knowledge treated as a commodity, delivered in packages, and accepted as private property once it is acquired, must always be scarce.

In response, critics of the educational system are now proposing strong and unorthodox remedies that range from the voucher plan, which would enable each person to buy the education of his choice on an open market, to shifting the responsibility for education from the school to the media and to apprenticeship on the job. Some individuals foresee that the school will have to be disestablished just as the church was disestablished all over the world during the last two centuries. Other reformers propose to replace the universal school with various new systems that would, they claim, better prepare everybody for life in modern society. These proposals for new educational institutions fall into three broad categories: the reformation of the classroom within the school system; the dispersal of free schools throughout society; and the transformation of all society into one huge classroom. But these three approaches—the reformed classroom, the free school, and the worldwide classroom—represent three stages in a proposed escalation of education in which each step threatens more subtle and more pervasive social control than the one it replaces.

I believe that the disestablishment of the school has become inevitable and that this end of an illusion should fill us with hope. But I also believe that the end of the "age of schooling" could usher in the epoch of the global schoolhouse that would be distinguishable only in name from a global madhouse or global prison in which education, correction, and adjustment become synonymous. I therefore believe that the breakdown of the school forces us to look beyond its imminent demise and to face fundamental alternatives in education. Either we can work for fearsome and potent new educational devices that teach about a world which progressively becomes more opaque and forbidding for man, or we can set the conditions for a new era in which technology would be used to

THE ALTERNATIVE TO SCHOOLING By Ivan Illich. From *The Saturday Review,* June 19, 1971. Copyright © 1971 Saturday Review, Inc. Reprinted by permission.

make society more simple and transparent, so that all men can once again know the facts and use the tools that shape their lives. In short, we can disestablish schools or we can deschool culture.

In order to see clearly the alternatives we face, we must first distinguish education from schooling, which means separating the humanistic intent of the teacher from the impact of the invariant structure of the school. This hidden structure constitutes a course of instruction that stays forever beyond the control of the teacher or of his school board: It conveys indelibly the message that only through schooling can an individual prepare himself for adulthood in society, that what is not taught in school is of little value, and that what is learned outside of school is not worth knowing. I call it the hidden curriculum of schooling, because it constitutes the unalterable framework of the system, within which all changes in the curriculum are made.

The hidden curriculum is always the same regardless of school or place. It requires all children of a certain age to assemble in groups of about thirty, under the authority of a certified teacher, for some 500 to 1,000 or more hours each year. It doesn't matter whether the curriculum is designed to teach the principles of fascism, liberalism, Catholicism, or socialism; or whether the purpose of the school is to produce Soviet or United States citizens, mechanics, or doctors. It makes no difference whether the teacher is authoritarian or permissive, whether he imposes his own creed or teaches students to think for themselves. What is important is that students learn that education is valuable when it is acquired in the school through a graded process of consumption; that the degree of success the individual will enjoy in society depends on the amount of learning he consumes; and that learning *about* the world is more valuable than learning *from* the world.

It must be clearly understood that the hidden curriculum translates learning from an activity into a commodity—for which the school monopolizes the market. In all countries knowledge is regarded as the first necessity for survival, but also as a form of currency more liquid than rubles or dollars. We have become accustomed, through Karl Marx's writings, to speak about the alienation of the worker from his work in a class society. We must now recognize the estrangement of man from his learning when it becomes the product of a service profession and he becomes the consumer.

The more learning an individual consumes, the more "knowledge stock" he acquires. The hidden curriculum therefore defines a new class structure for society within which the large consumers of knowledge—those who have acquired large quantities of knowledge stock—enjoy special privileges, high income, and access to the more powerful tools of production. This kind of knowledge-capitalism has been accepted in all industrialized societies and establishes a rationale for the distribution of jobs and income. (This point is especially important in the light of the lack of correspondence between schooling and occupational competence established in studies such as Ivar Berg's *Education and Jobs: The Great Training Robbery.*)

The endeavor to put all men through successive stages of enlightenment is rooted deeply in alchemy, the Great Art of the waning Middle Ages. John Amos Comenius, a Moravian bishop, self-styled Pansophist, and pedagogue, is rightly considered one of the founders of the modern schools. He was among the first to propose seven or twelve grades of compulsory learning. In his *Magna Didactica,* he described schools as devices to "teach everybody everything" and outlined a blueprint for the assembly-line production of knowledge, which according to his method would make education cheaper and better and make growth into full humanity possible for all. But Comenius was not only an early efficiency expert, he was an alchemist who adopted the technical language of his craft to describe the art of rearing children. The alchemist sought to refine base elements by leading their distilled spirits through twelve stages of successive enlightenment, so that for their own and all the world's benefit they might be transmuted into gold. Of course, alchemists failed no matter how often they tried, but each time their "science" yielded new reasons for their failure, and they tried again.

Pedagogy opened a new chapter in the history of Ars Magna. Education became the search for an alchemic process that would bring forth a new type of man, who would fit into an environment created by scientific magic. But, no matter how much each generation spent on its schools, it always turned out that the majority of people were unfit for enlightenment by this process and had to be discarded as unprepared for life in a man-made world.

Educational reformers who accept the idea that schools have failed fall into three groups. The most respectable are certainly the great masters of alchemy who promise better schools. The most seductive are popular magicians, who promise to make every kitchen into an alchemic lab. The most sinister are the new Masons of the Universe, who want to transform the entire world into one huge temple of learning. Notable among today's masters of alchemy are certain research directors employed or sponsored by the large foundations who believe that schools, if they could somehow be improved, could also become economically more feasible than those that are now in trouble, and simultaneously could sell a larger package of services. Those who are concerned primarily with the curriculum claim that it is outdated or irrelevant. So the curriculum is filled with new packaged courses on African Culture, North American Imperialism, Women's Lib, Pollution, or the Consumer Society. Passive learning is wrong—it is indeed—so we graciously allow students to decide what and how they want to be taught. Schools are prison houses. Therefore, principals are authorized to approve teach-outs, moving the school desks to a roped-off Harlem street. Sensitivity training becomes fashionable. So, we import group therapy into the classroom. School, which was supposed to teach everybody everything, now becomes all things to all children.

Other critics emphasize that schools make inefficient use of modern science. Some would administer drugs to make it easier for the instructor to change the child's behavior. Others would transform school into a stadium for educational gaming. Still others would electrify the classroom. If they are simplistic disciples of McLuhan, they replace blackboards and textbooks with multimedia happenings; if they follow Skinner, they claim to be able to modify behavior more efficiently than old-fashioned classroom practitioners can.

Most of these changes have, of course, some good effects. The experimental schools have fewer truants. Parents do have a greater feeling of participation in a decentralized district. Pupils, assigned by their teacher to an apprenticeship, do often turn out more competent than those who stay in the classroom. Some children do improve their knowledge of Spanish in the language lab because they prefer playing with the knobs of a tape recorder to conversations with their Puerto Rican peers. Yet all these improvements operate within predictably narrow limits, since they leave the hidden curriculum of school intact.

Some reformers would like to shake loose from the hidden curriculum, but they rarely succeed. Free schools that lead to further free schools produce a mirage of freedom, even though the chain of attendance is frequently interrupted by long stretches of loafing. Attendance through seduction inculcates the need for educational treatment more persuasively than the reluctant attendance enforced by a truant officer. Permissive teachers in a padded classroom can easily render their pupils impotent to survive once they leave.

Learning in these schools often remains nothing more than the acquisition of socially valued skills defined, in this instance, by the consensus of a commune rather than by the decree of a school board. New presbyter is but old priest writ large.

Free schools, to be truly free, must meet two conditions: First, they must be run in a way to prevent the reintroduction of the hidden curriculum of graded attendance and certified students studying at the feet of certified teachers. And, more importantly, they must provide a framework in which all participants—staff and pupils—can free themselves from the hidden foundations of a schooled society. The first condition is frequently incorporated in the stated aims of a free school. The second condition is only rarely recognized, and is difficult to state as the goal of a free school.

It is useful to distinguish between the hidden curriculum, which I have described, and the occult foundations of schooling. The hidden curriculum is a ritual that can be considered the official initiation into modern society, institutionally established through the school. It is the purpose of this ritual to hide from its participants the contradictions between the myth of an egalitarian society and the class-conscious reality it certifies. Once they are recognized as such, rituals lose their power, and this is what is now beginning to happen to schooling. But there are certain fundamental assumptions about growing up—the occult foundations—which now find their expression in the ceremonial of schooling, and which could easily be reinforced by what free schools do.

Among these assumptions is what Peter Schrag calls the "immigration syndrome," which impels us to treat all people as if they were newcomers who must go through a naturalization process. Only certified consumers of knowledge are admitted to citizenship. Men are not born equal, but are made equal through gestation by Alma Mater.

The rhetoric of all schools states that they form a man for the future, but they do not release him for his task before he has developed a high level of tolerance to the ways of his elders: education *for* life rather than *in* everyday life. Few free schools can avoid doing precisely this. Nevertheless they are among the most important centers from which a new life-style radiates, not because of the effect their graduates will have but, rather, because elders who choose to bring up their children without the benefit of properly ordained teachers frequently belong to a radical minority and because their preoccupation with the rearing of their children sustains them in their new style.

The most dangerous category of educational reformer is one who argues that knowledge can be produced and sold much more effectively on an open market than on one controlled by school. These people argue that most skills can be easily acquired from skill-models if the learner is truly interested in their acquisition; that individual entitlements can provide a more equal purchasing power for education. They demand a careful separation of the process by which knowledge is acquired from the process by which it is measured and certified. These seem to me obvious statements. But it would be a fallacy to believe that the establishment of a free market for knowledge would constitute a radical alternative in education.

The establishment of a free market would indeed abolish what I have previously called the hidden curriculum of present schooling—its age-specific attendance at a graded curriculum. Equally, a free market would at first give the appearance of counteracting what I have called the occult foundations of a schooled society: the "immigration syndrome," the institutional monopoly of teaching, and the ritual of linear initiation. But at the same time a free market in education would provide the alchemist with innumerable hidden hands to fit each man into the multiple, tight little niches a more complex technocracy can provide.

Many decades of reliance on schooling has turned knowledge into a commodity, a marketable staple of a special kind. Knowledge is now regarded simultaneously as a first necessity and also as society's most precious currency. (The transformation of knowledge into a commodity is reflected in a corresponding transformation of language. Words that formerly functioned as verbs are becoming nouns that designate possessions. Until recently dwelling and learning and even healing designated activities. They are now usually conceived as commodities or services to be delivered. We talk about the manufacture of housing or the delivery of medical care. Men are no longer regarded fit to house or heal themselves. In such a society people come to believe that professional services are more valuable than personal care. Instead of learning how to nurse grandmother, the teen-ager learns to picket the hospital that does not admit her.) This attitude could easily survive the disestablishment of school, just as affiliation with a church remained a condition for office long after the adoption of the First Amendment. It is even more evident that test batteries measuring complex knowledge-packages could easily survive the disestablishment of school—and with this would go the compulsion to obligate everybody to acquire a minimum package in the knowledge stock. The scientific measurement of each man's worth and the alchemic dream of each man's "educability to his full humanity" would finally coincide. Under the appearance of a "free" market, the global village would turn into an environmental womb where pedagogic therapists control the complex navel by which each man is nourished.

At present, schools limit the teacher's competence to the classroom. They prevent him from claiming man's whole life as his domain. The demise of school will remove this restriction and give a semblance of legitimacy to the life-long pedagogical invasion of everybody's privacy. It will open the way for a scramble for "knowledge" on a free market, which would lead us toward the paradox of a vulgar, albeit seemingly egalitarian, meritocracy. Unless the concept of knowledge is transformed, the disestablishment of school will lead to a wedding between a growing meritocratic system that separates learning from certification and a society committed to provide therapy for each man until he is ripe for the gilded age.

For those who subscribe to the technocratic ethos, whatever is technically possible must be made available at least to a few whether they want it or not. Neither the privation nor the frustration of the majority counts. If cobalt treatment is possible, then the city of Tegucigalpa needs one apparatus in each of its two major hospitals, at a cost that would free an important part of the population of Honduras from parasites. If supersonic speeds are possible, then it must speed the travel of some. If the flight to Mars can be conceived, then a rationale must be found to make it appear a necessity. In the technocratic ethos poverty is modernized: Not only are old alternatives closed off by new monopolies, but the lack of necessities is also compounded by a growing spread between those services that are technologically feasible and those that are in fact available to the majority.

A teacher turns "educator" when he adopts this technocratic ethos. He then acts as if education were a technological enterprise designed to make man fit into whatever environment the "progress" of science creates. He seems blind to the evidence that constant obsolescence of all commodities comes at a high price: the mounting cost of training people to know about them. He seems to forget that the rising cost of tools is purchased at a high price in education: They decrease the labor intensity of the economy, make learning on the job impossible or, at best, a privilege for a few. All over the world the cost of educating men for society rises faster than the productivity of the entire economy, and fewer people have a sense of intelligent participation in the commonweal.

A revolution against those forms of privilege and power which are based on claims to professional knowledge must start with a transformation of consciousness about the nature of learning. This means, above all, a shift of responsibility for teaching and learning. Knowledge can be defined as a commodity only as long as it is viewed as the result of institutional enterprise or as the fulfillment of institutional objectives. Only when a man recovers the sense of personal responsibility for what he learns and teaches can this spell be broken and the alienation of learning from living be overcome.

The recovery of the power to learn or to teach means that the teacher who takes the risk of interfering in somebody else's private affairs also assumes responsibility for the results. Similarly, the student who exposes himself to the influence of a teacher must take responsibility for his own education. For such purposes educational institutions—if they are at all needed—ideally take the form of facility centers where one can get a roof of the right size over his head, access to a piano or a kiln, and to records, books, or slides. Schools, TV stations, theaters, and the like are designed primarily for use by professionals. Deschooling society means above all the denial of professional status for the second-oldest profession, namely teaching. The certification of teachers now constitutes an undue restriction of the right to free speech: the corporate structure and professional pretensions of journalism an undue restriction on the right to free press. Compulsory attendance rules interfere with free assembly. The deschooling of society is nothing less than a cultural mutation by which a people recovers the effective use of its Constitutional freedoms: learning and teaching by men who know that they are born free rather than treated to freedom. Most people learn most of the time when they do whatever they enjoy; most people are curious and want to give meaning to whatever they come in contact with; and most people are capable of personal intimate intercourse with others unless they are stupefied by inhuman work or turned off by schooling.

The fact that people in rich countries do not learn much on their own constitutes no proof to the contrary. Rather it is a consequence of life in an environment from which, paradoxically, they cannot learn much, precisely because it is so highly programed. They are constantly frustrated by the structure of contemporary society in which the facts on which decisions can be made have become elusive. They live in an environment in which tools that can be used for creative purposes have become luxuries, an environment in which channels of communication serve a few to talk to many.

A modern myth would make us believe that the sense of impotence with which most men live today is a consequence of technology that cannot but create huge systems. But it is not technology that makes systems huge, tools immensely powerful, channels of communication one-directional. Quite the contrary: Properly controlled, technology could provide each man with the ability to understand his environment better, to shape it powerfully with his own hands, and to permit him full intercommunication to a degree never before possible. Such an alternative use of technology constitutes the central alternative in education.

If a person is to grow up he needs, first of all, access to things, to places and to processes, to events and to records. He needs to see, to touch, to tinker with, to grasp whatever there is in a meaningful setting. This access is now largely denied. When knowledge became a commodity, it acquired the protections of private property, and thus a principle designed to guard personal intimacy became a rationale for declaring facts off limits for people without the proper credentials. In schools teachers keep knowledge to themselves unless it fits into the day's program. The media inform, but exclude those things they regard as unfit to print. Information is locked into special languages, and specialized teachers live off its retranslation. Patents are protected by corporations, secrets are guarded by bureaucracies, and the power to keep others out of private preserves—be they cockpits, law offices, junkyards, or clinics—is jealously guarded by professions, institutions, and nations. Neither the political nor the professional structure of our societies, East and West, could withstand the elimination of the power to keep entire classes of people from facts that could serve them. The access to facts that I advocate goes far beyond truth in labeling. Access must be built into reality, while all we ask from advertising is a guarantee that it does not mislead. Access to reality constitutes a fundamental alternative in education to a system that only purports to teach *about* it.

Abolishing the right to corporate secrecy—even when professional opinion holds that this secrecy serves the common good—is, as shall presently appear, a much more radical political goal than the traditional demand for public ownership or control of the tools of production. The socialization of tools without the effective socialization of know-how in their use tends to put the knowledge-capitalist into the position formerly held by the financier. The technocrat's only claim to power is the stock he holds in some class of scarce and secret knowledge, and the best means to protect its value is a large and capital-intensive organization that renders access to know-how formidable and forbidding.

It does not take much time for the interested learner to acquire almost any skill that he wants to use. We tend to forget this in a society where professional teachers monopolize entrance into all fields, and thereby stamp teaching by uncertified individuals as quackery. There are few mechanical skills used in industry or research that are as demanding, complex, and dangerous as driving cars, a skill that most people quickly acquire from a peer. Not all people are suited for advanced logic, yet those who are make rapid progress if they are challenged to play mathematical games at an early age. One out of twenty kids in Cuernavaca can beat me at Wiff 'n' Proof after a couple of weeks' training. In four months all but a small percentage of motivated adults at our CIDOC center learn Spanish well enough to conduct academic business in the new language.

A first step toward opening up access to skills would be to provide various incentives for skilled individuals to share their knowledge. Inevitably, this would run counter to the interest of guilds and professions and unions. Yet, multiple apprenticeship is attractive: It provides everybody with an opportunity to learn something about almost anything. There is no reason why a person should not combine the ability to drive a car, repair telephones and toilets, act as a midwife, and function as an architectural draftsman. Special-interest groups and their disciplined consumers would, of course, claim that the public needs the protection of a professional guarantee. But this argument is now steadily being challenged by consumer protection associations. We have to take much more seriously the objection that economists raise to the radical socialization of skills: that "progress" will be impeded if knowledge—patents, skills, and all the rest—is democratized. Their argument can be faced only if we demonstrate to them the growth rate of futile diseconomies generated by any existing educational system.

Access to people willing to share their skills is no guarantee of learning. Such access is restricted not only by the monopoly of educational programs over learning and of unions over licensing but also by a technology of scarcity. The skills that count today are know-how in the use of highly specialized tools that were designed to be scarce. These tools produce goods or render services that everybody wants but only a few can enjoy, and which only a limited number of people know how to use. Only a few privileged individuals out of the total number of people who have a given disease ever benefit from the results of sophisticated medical technology, and even fewer doctors develop the skill to use it.

The same results of medical research have, however, also been employed to create a basic medical tool kit that permits Army and Navy medics, with only a few months of training, to obtain results, under battlefield conditions, that would have been beyond the expectations of full-fledged doctors during World War II. On an even simpler level any peasant girl could learn how to diagnose and treat most infections if medical scientists prepared dosages and instructions specifically for a given geographic area.

All these examples illustrate the fact that educational considerations alone suffice to demand a radical reduction of the professional structure that now impedes the mutual relationship between the scientist and the majority of people who want access to science. If this demand were heeded, all men could learn to use yesterday's tools, rendered more effective and durable by modern science, to create tomorrow's world.

Unfortunately, precisely the contrary trend prevails at present. I know a coastal area in South America where most people support themselves by fishing from small boats. The outboard motor is certainly the tool that has changed most dramatically the lives of these coastal fishermen. But in the area I have surveyed, half of all outboard motors that were purchased between 1945 and 1950 are still kept running by constant tinkering, while half the motors purchased in 1965 no longer run because they were not built to be repaired. Technological progress provides the majority of people with gadgets they cannot afford and deprives them of the simpler tools they need.

Metals, plastics, and ferro cement used in building have greatly improved since the 1940s and ought to provide more people the opportunity to create their own homes. But while in the United States, in 1948, more than 30 per cent of all one-family homes were owner-built, by the end of the 1960s the percentage of those who acted as their own contractors had dropped to less than 20 per cent.

The lowering of the skill level through so-called economic development becomes even more visible in Latin America. Here most people still build their own homes from floor to roof. Often they use mud, in the form of adobe, and thatchwork of unsurpassed utility in the moist, hot, and windy climate. In other places they make their dwellings out of cardboard, oil-drums, and other industrial refuse. Instead of providing people with simple tools and highly standardized, durable, and easily repaired components, all governments have gone in for the mass production of low-cost buildings. It is clear that not one single country can afford to provide satisfactory modern dwelling units for the majority of its people. Yet, everywhere this policy makes it progressively more difficult for the majority to acquire the knowledge and skills they need to build better houses for themselves.

Educational considerations permit us to formulate a second fundamental characteristic that any post-industrial society must possess: a basic tool kit that by its very nature counteracts technocratic control. For educational reasons we must work toward a society in which scientific knowledge is incorporated in tools and components that can be used meaningfully in units small enough to be within the reach of all. Only such tools can socialize access to skills. Only such tools favor temporary associations among those who want to use them for a specific occasion. Only such tools allow specific goals to emerge in the process of their use, as any tinkerer knows. Only the combination of guaranteed access to facts and of limited power in most tools renders it possible to envisage a subsistence economy capable of incorporating the fruits of modern science.

The development of such a scientific subsistence economy is unquestionably to the advantage of the overwhelming majority of all people in poor countries. It is also the only alternative to progressive pollution, exploitation, and opaqueness in rich countries. But, as we have seen, the dethroning of the GNP cannot be achieved without simultaneously subverting GNE (Gross National Education—usually conceived as manpower capitalization). An egalitarian economy cannot exist in a society in which the right to produce is conferred by schools.

The feasibility of a modern subsistence economy does not depend on new scientific inventions. It depends primarily on the ability of a society to agree on fundamental, self-chosen anti-bureaucratic and anti-technocratic restraints.

These restraints can take many forms, but they will not work unless they touch the basic dimensions of life. (The decision of Congress against development of the supersonic transport plane is one of the most encouraging steps in the right direction.) The substance of these voluntary social restraints would be very simple matters that can be fully understood and judged by any prudent man. The issues at stake in the SST controversy provide a good example. All such restraints would be chosen to promote stable and equal enjoyment of scientific know-how. The French say that it takes a thousand years to educate a peasant to deal with a cow. It would not take two generations to help all people in Latin America or Africa to use and repair outboard motors, simple cars, pumps, medicine kits, and ferro cement machines if their design does not change every few years. And since a joyful life is one of constant meaningful intercourse with others in a meaningful environment, equal enjoyment does translate into equal education.

At present a consensus on austerity is difficult to imagine. The reason usually given for the impotence of the majority is stated in terms of political or economic class. What is not usually understood is that the new class structure of a schooled society is even more powerfully controlled by vested interests. No doubt an imperialist and capitalist organization of society provides the social structure within which a minority can have disproportionate influence over the effective opinion of the majority. But in a technocratic society the power of a minority of knowledge capitalists can prevent the formation of true public opinion through control of scientific know-how and the media of communication. Constitutional guarantees of free speech, free press, and free assembly were meant to ensure government by the people. Modern electronics, photo-offset presses, time-sharing computers, and telephones have in principle provided the hardware that could give an entirely new meaning to these freedoms. Unfortunately, these things are used in modern media to increase the power of knowledge-bankers to funnel their program-packages through international chains to more people, instead of being used to increase true networks that provide equal opportunity for encounter among the members of the majority.

Deschooling the culture and social structure requires the use of technology to make participatory politics possible. Only on the basis of a majority coalition can limits to secrecy and growing power be determined without dictatorship. We need a new environment in which growing up can be classless, or we will get a brave new world in which Big Brother educates us all.

PHILIP D. ORTEGO

Montezuma's Children

The face of Mexico is an Indian face. Traveling the length and width of modern Mexico one is more impressed by the Indian influences on Mexican culture than the European influences. The primitive pyramids of Teotihuacán are more impressive than the elegant facade of Chapultepec Castle. One is more fascinated by the legend of Ixtacihuatl than by the exploits of Cortez. Although the crown and church of Spain almost succeeded in Europeanizing Montezuma's children, they were unable to convert the Indian masses into their own physical image. In our time Indian rather than Spanish blood has become a source of national Mexican pride. To be Spanish is to be a *gapuchin,* a foreigner, an oppressor, a rapist of the ancient Indian culture. To be a Mexican is to be a member of *la raza,* the race of Montezuma's children. More than two-fifths of the Mexican population are pure-blooded Indians, more than half have some Indian blood in them. Yet, despite Indian resilience, the language of the conquerors dominated.

In Mexico, where the Spanish-speaking Indian types have almost no linguistic disadvantage, they have achieved a relatively high degree of equal opportunity. However, the ten million or so of Montezuma's children who live in the United States are still struggling to overcome not only the handicap of speaking a foreign language but the social disadvantage of looking like themselves, that is, Mexicans.

Only recently have Mexican Americans begun to receive significant attention in this country, though they are the second largest minority group in the nation. They constitute the single largest linguistic group. Most Mexican Americans (seven million) live in the five-state area of Texas, New Mexico, Colorado, Arizona, and California. The largest single concentration is in Los Angeles. Just as many black citizens have rejected the description of "Negro" or "Negro-American," many Americans of Mexican ancestry reject the hyphenated Mexican-American description by Anglos and instead prefer to be called Chicanos.

Montezuma's children are not transplanted Americans. Many of their forebears were here before the Puritans, the Pennsylvania Dutch, the Irish of Boston, the Italians of New York, or the Poles of Chicago and Pittsburgh. Yet Mexican Americans subsist on levels far below national norms. The reason for this, many Mexican Americans argue, is that the

MONTEZUMA'S CHILDREN By Philip D. Ortego. Reprinted, with permission, from the November 1970 issue of *The Center Magazine,* a publication of the Center for the Study of Democratic Institutions in Santa Barbara, California.

Treaty of Guadalupe Hidalgo in 1848 classified those who came with the conquered lands of the Southwest as a defeated people. Those who came afterward, in the great migrations of the early nineteen-hundreds, have been similarly victimized as a result of the Mexican-American War. Those who were here before the Mexican-American War have had their land rights usurped and today they have become almost strangers in their own land.

The problems of Mexican Americans relate specifically to American life, not to life in Mexico, just as the problems of Anglo-Americans relate to American life, not to life in England, whatever the linguistic ties. That many Mexican Americans do not speak English does not make them any less American. Their interests, attitudes, and aspirations differ little from those of other Americans. What conspicuously characterizes Mexican Americans is that most of them have an inadequate education, a handicap stemming primarily from socio-economic causes rather than from what educators have called the "language barrier."

The educational statistics on Mexican Americans are shocking. In the Southwest, their dropout rate is more than twice the national average. Estimates of the average number of school years completed by Anglo children in the Southwest is 12.1 years, and by black children, nine years. On the average Mexican Americans there stay in school 7.1 years. Armando Rodriguez, Chief of the Mexican-American Affairs Unit for the U.S. Office of Education, has said that "the rise of cultural militancy among young Chicanos is directly related to the schools' appalling ignorance about the Mexican American and his role in the American democracy."

This ignorance is dramatically manifested in the statistics: in Texas thirty-nine per cent of the Mexican Americans have less than a fifth-grade education; Mexican Americans twenty-five years of age and older have as little as 4.8 years of schooling. Almost half of the Mexican Americans in Texas are still functional illiterates.

The percentage of Mexican-American children entering first grade who know enough English to move forward with their Anglo-American peers is slight. Indeed, many never get to the first grade. Of those who do (especially along the U.S.-Mexican border), according to the first report of the National Advisory Committee on Mexican-American Education, "four out of five . . . fall two grades behind their Anglo classmates by the time they reach the fifth grade." In Texas only about one-third of the five- and six-year-old Mexican Americans are enrolled in school. The National Advisory Committee notes that in some California schools more than fifty per cent of Mexican-American high school students drop out between grades ten and eleven. Moreover, "although Spanish-surnamed students make up more than fourteen per cent of the public school population of California, less than one-half of one per cent of the college students enrolled in the . . . University of California are of this group."

Vicente Ximenes, former chairman of the Inter-Agency for Mexican-

American Affairs, has pointed out that "almost from the very beginning . . . there was prejudice and superiority in the posture of the [Anglo] pioneers from the eastern half of the land." Few Americans are aware that their brown fellow-citizens were segregated in some schools in California until 1947 and in Texas until 1948.

The long, arduous odyssey of Mexican Americans has been given little public attention. In 1940 George I. Sanchez called them "forgotten people," and at the National Educational Association meeting in Tucson in 1966 they were described as "the invisible minority." But the Chicano renaissance is changing this.

The issues in Mexican-American education arise from a complex of psychosocial and cultural linguistic patterns. No one approach to the educational problem of Mexican Americans can achieve significant results. Even the linguistic disadvantages of Mexican-American children are basically the product of a thoroughly lexocentric society: they are in part the result of ignorance about language and its social function, in part they arise from the distortion of Mexican-American culture and history.

Existing educational programs (with the exception of pilot or experimental model programs) make no allowance for the fact that many Mexican-American children come to school either knowing a fair amount of English but psychologically reluctant to use it, or knowing little English, or knowing only Spanish. Whatever the case, Mexican-American children are burdened from the start by an inability to deal with the language of instruction. Often their teachers are Anglo-Americans who are not bilingual and cannot communicate to the children the lessons of first grade. First grade then becomes a sort of language laboratory in which the teacher attempts to create enough English fluency in the pupils to begin with the required instructional materials. But most first-grade teachers are inadequate; untrained in language theory and analysis, they cannot overcome the language barrier. What usually happens is that Spanish-speaking children are seriously traumatized by what too often becomes a demoralizing and degrading experience. Such courses as "Speech X" (Corrective Instruction in English Pronunciation) treat the symptoms rather than the malady.

A third-grade Mexican-American boy, whose parents were born in the eastern part of the United States, was placed in an El Paso public school when his father was assigned to a nearby military base. The parents were soon advised that their son was being recommended for remedial language instruction. An investigation showed that the teacher's recommendation was based on the fact that the boy spoke an eastern dialect of American English rather than the teacher's Texas dialect. She considered the boy's speech atrocious and in need of remediation. This is the kind of "lexotherapy" many Mexican Americans are subjected to.

An editorial in *El Grito: A Journal of Contemporary Mexican-American Thought,* commenting on the linguistic situation of the Southwest, said: "Almost unbelievably, [language] teaching to this day is character-ized by puritanically rigid social sadism and linguistic imperialism."

What is needed—in addition to preparing teachers in linguistic prin-ciples—is training in "lexonomics," the study of linguistic social relations. As a social creature, man is also a creature of words, and therefore a "lexistent." The teacher, as the central figure in the dynamics of social relations in the schools, should comprehend the nature of language and its psychosocial function in human beings, especially children. Failure here is by far the greatest weakness in existing educational programs.

In practice, Spanish-speaking children are frequently relegated to classes for the retarded simply because many teachers equate linguistic ability with intellectual ability. In California, Mexican Americans account for more than forty per cent of the so-called "mentally retarded." This is prima facie evidence of cultural disdain on the part of an Anglo-Amer-ican educational system. Harold Howe, former United States Commis-sioner of Education, pointed out in an address to the National Confer-ence on Educational Opportunities for Mexican Americans that the feeling of Anglo cultural superiority is reflected in hundreds of ways in American society and stated that "until the schools realize how our society projects this conviction of superiority, this cowboy-and-Indians mentality, and takes positive steps to correct it, they will not truly succeed with Mexican-American children."

The schools have to be made aware of the part they play in pro-moting the myth of Anglo cultural superiority. In October of 1969, a group of Mexican Americans took over the boardroom of the Los Angeles City Board of Education to protest the assumption of Anglo cul-tural superiority. Walkouts have occurred in school board meetings in many communities of the Southwest. One of the issues in these walkouts is the custodial notion that emphasizes school attendance and discipline at the expense of learning. Some Mexican Americans, experiencing it, are beginning to suspect that the only reason for keeping Mexican-American students in school is to improve the average daily attendance, the basis of most federal funding and support.

Based on the 1960 census, the estimated number of disadvantaged children in the nation was more than fifteen million, yet the money finally appropriated under the Elementary and Secondary Education Act, Title I, was hardly enough to provide programs for five and a half million of these children. The only thing that most school districts re-ceiving such funds can point to are showcase programs. Some of these showcase programs are so poorly put together that one wonders how they continue to be federally funded. Nowhere among the participants is a Mexican American to be found. The same is true of the Teacher Corps program, which last year recruited sixty Anglo-American interns with only limited fluency in Spanish and not one Mexican American, for a target population of Spanish-speaking Mexican Americans. It then im-mersed these interns in a six-week intensive Spanish-language course.

In most of the schools of education or teachers colleges in the Southwest few, if any, Mexican Americans serve on the teaching faculties. Even fewer are represented in the decision-making for the education of Mexican Americans.

Preschool programs such as Head Start, Follow Through, and other compensatory educational efforts suffer from the assumption that all Spanish-speaking preschoolers in these programs will be fluent in English and ready to begin formal studies in English in the common and traditional education curriculum. Six months of preschool is not enough time to overcome the disadvantage of the Mexican-American child. Herschel T. Manuel, of the University of Texas, one of the long-standing proponents for bilingual education, says: "The special difficulties with which we are struggling are those of children who must learn a second language outside of the home; of children who in addition suffer the disadvantages of poverty; of children who have to adjust to patterns of living in the larger community different from those of the immediate environment; and of children whose migrant parents have no secure place in the community."

Recent advances in applied linguistics have led to a curriculum heavily invested in technological hardware—tape recorders, slide projectors, special typewriters. But gadgets are only as good as the teachers who use them. Thousands of schools which acquired the technological hardware have still not significantly improved the education of Mexican Americans, nor does it appear that they are likely to.

Now there is much talk about English-as-Second-Language programs (E.S.L.) both as compensatory education and as part of experimental bilingual programs. These programs are perhaps the most meritorious effort thus far to meet the language problem. They are marred however by the insistence that to speak English with an accent is unacceptable in the United States. *El Grito* calls this "insidious arrogance," pointing out that such people as Lyndon Baines Johnson, Wernher Von Braun, Edward Kennedy, Otto Preminger, and others speak with colorful accents quite acceptable in the United States. To *El Grito* the conclusion is unequivocal: "In the United States today any accent is acceptable, except that of a Mexican American who speaks English with a Mexican accent."

In many states English is prescribed by law as the official language of instruction. Mexican-American students are expressly forbidden to speak Spanish except in Spanish classes, and even then Anglo teachers of Spanish consider their Spanish tainted. The rationale behind the "no Spanish" rule is that by speaking English the students will learn English. The logic is that once a Spanish-speaking child is forbidden the use of Spanish he will then speak fluent idiomatic English like other Americans. In the *Handbook for Employees* of one Texas school district, the following admonition appears: "USE OF ENGLISH LANGUAGE. Every effort should be made to enforce the rule that English is to be spoken in all schools and on all school grounds by pupils, custodians, lunchroom personnel, and teaching personnel except when they are teaching Spanish as a foreign language or participating in pilot projects as approved by the department of instruction. Written permission from the Texas Education Agency must be secured for any exception to this rule." Note that the "no Spanish" rule applies equally to custodians, lunchroom personnel, and teaching personnel.

Of course, the schools are right in their emphasis on English—it is, after all, the objective in the solution of the language problem of Mexican Americans. But the means used to solve this problem do not justify the ends. American education for the disadvantaged has oftentimes been a degrading experience. In many parts of the Southwest, Mexican-American students are still being punished for breaking the "no Spanish" rules. In Brownsville, Texas, Mexican-American students have been fined for speaking Spanish in the schools. Some Southwest schools have resorted to corporal punishment for students who break the "no Spanish" rules.

Recently the "no Spanish" rules have been challenged by Mexican Americans in San Antonio and El Paso, but only after actual or threatened Mexican-American student uprisings. One San Antonio school official has said that not only should Spanish be allowed in the schools but that Mexican-American pupils should be "motivated to improve their fluency in standard Spanish in such conversation." This is a left-handed concession; the obvious inference is that even the Spanish of Mexican Americans is poor. The Mexican-American border dialect of Spanish is thus reduced to an inferior position on someone's arbitrary linguistic scale. The truth is that there is no "standard" Spanish any more than there is a "standard" English. In Mexico alone there are almost as many dialects of Mexican Spanish as there are dialects of American English in the United States. Yet many Anglo-Americans continue to equate "good" Spanish with Castilian Spanish, lisp and all. In many schools this Castilian Spanish is being taught to Mexican-American students.

In El Paso, only a threatened walkout protesting detention for speaking Spanish on the school grounds forced the school-board trustees to end the practice. Only the threat of massive protest by Mexican Americans forced educational districts of the Southwest into the twentieth century. The proposed action on the part of the National Education Association's West Coast office to decertify one El Paso high school if it continued its policy of Spanish detention helped bring the issue to a head and resolved it in favor of the Spanish-speaking student population of the city.

Though the "no Spanish" rules are slowly being eliminated, the educational systems of the Southwest are still waging a relentless campaign culturally to emasculate Mexican-American youngsters. Jose becomes Joe, and Jesus becomes Jesse because Anglo-Americans find it hard to call someone by that name. Mexican-American students are told they must accept and assimilate quickly into Anglo culture or face economic and financial deprivation later as adults. In effect, this is like telling the Mexican-American child that there is something wrong in being a Mexican American. And though Spanish may no longer be prohibited on some school grounds, Jose has become so self-conscious about his Spanish that he is more and more withdrawn. Harold Howe puts it flatly: "It is time we stopped wasting [our linguistic resources] and instead enabled youngsters to move back and forth from one language to another without any sense of difficulty or strangeness."

About five per cent of American school children score below seventy-five on I.Q. tests and are therefore considered mentally retarded. However, thirteen per cent of Mexican-American youngsters fall below seventy-five when tested. About twenty-five per cent of all children score between seventy-five and ninety on I.Q. tests, but fifty per cent of Mexican Americans fall in this range. Fifty per cent of all children score between ninety and a hundred, but only twenty-five per cent of Mexican-American children score this high. Again, only twelve per cent of Mexican-American children score above a hundred compared to twenty per cent of all others. The percentage of Mexican-American children classified with inferior I.Q.'s is two and a half times the percentage of Mexican Americans in the population.

Those who argue against bilingual education usually point to the results of these questionable tests and measurements to support their contention about the intellectual potential and capability of Spanish-speaking Americans. On the basis of I.Q. tests in the English language (whose culture content has always been drawn from the milieu of the middle-class Anglo-American), Mexican-American youngsters have been considered intellectually inferior. Only recently have educators become aware that they lack the instruments for measuring intelligence and achievement potential of Mexican Americans. Yet as long ago as 1935, Herschel T. Manuel had pointed out the deficiencies of the Stanford-Binet test in assessing the abilities of Spanish-speaking Mexican-American children.

So much stress has been placed on the I.Q. by school administrators, teachers, and the public at large that as a consequence of low I.Q. scores many adult Mexican Americans have accepted and even internalized this negative appraisal. The effect on their children has been devastating. Mexican-American children now face in their homes the same negative valuation they meet in the schools. Anderson and Safar raise this tragic question in presenting their research: "Are we asking too much of a child to continue working toward vague educational goals and gainful employment when most of the significant adults in his life—parents, adult friends, teachers, counselors—all evidence a lack of confidence in his ability to achieve the same goals as his Anglo classmates?" (*Sociology of Education,* Vol. 40, No. 3, Summer, 1967.)

Enlightened educators now see the distinct relationship between "retardation" and the extent to which intelligence tests require a knowledge of English. In *Pygmalion of the Classroom,* for example, authors Robert

Rosenthal and Lenore Jacobson find that the I.Q. is not a true indicator of ability but simply the score of a person's intellectual performance at a given time based on background and experience. They show the nature of self-fulfilling prophecies based on the assumption of innate intellectual inequality.

If a teacher assumes and expects a child to be intelligent, the child will actually perform with greater intellectual capacity. An experiment was conducted in a community of the South San Francisco Unified School District where more than a hundred of the six hundred and fifty students were Mexican Americans. The teachers were told that on the basis of intelligence tests given during the previous year some of the students would probably show significant gain in intellectual ability during the current year. Actually, the names of these "potential gainers" had been chosen so that any difference between the "special" children and the others would be only in the mind of the teacher. The students were tested twice during the year and the "potential gainers" scored significantly higher than the others. Almost twenty-one per cent of them increased their I.Q. scores by thirty points. Almost half increased their I.Q. scores by twenty points. Nearly eighty per cent of the "potential gainers" increased their I.Q. scores by ten points, while only half of the other students experienced a similar increase. It appears, then, that a teacher's perception and expectation of her students demonstrably affect pupil performance.

The effects of environment and culture upon minority students cannot be excluded. A St. Louis cultural enrichment program succeeded in raising the average I.Q. of disadvantaged youngsters by 11.5 points in four years. But I.Q. tests as a measure of intelligence are now highly suspect precisely because of their culture content. They are therefore inconclusive as a measure of innate learning ability.

Adam Yarmolinsky pointed out in *Recognition of Excellence:* "This 'dragnet' function of testing [I.Q.] is almost completely ineffectual in a situation where a child's home and community background has denied him the cultural experience that the test assumes. Intelligence tests are standardized to a native white population. The discrepancy is particularly evident in testing children from disadvantaged ethnic minorities—not only Negroes but Puerto Ricans, American Indians, Japanese and Chinese Americans, persons from U.S. territories, and even Appalachian Mountain whites."

As a result of criticism from the Association of Mexican American Educators, the California State Board of Education created a special advisory committee to investigate charges that I.Q. tests seriously hinder some children—especially minority children—in achieving normal educational goals. (The Los Angeles school system had already banned use of group I.Q. tests in the primary grades.) The findings of the special advisory committee are startling. Mexican-American children, classified as mentally retarded after I.Q. tests in English, have done remarkably better with tests in Spanish. Some of the children had spent as long as three years in special classes for slow learners simply because of low I.Q. scores. The special advisory committee found that the special classes themselves had a retarding influence. After retesting, one Mexican-American student showed an improvement of twenty-eight points while the group's average rose thirteen points. The report of the committee asserts that Mexican-American students are apparently placed in remedial classes "solely on their inability to function in what to them is a foreign language."

If the measure of intelligence is a necessary educational prerequisite, it is clear that Mexican-American children who speak only Spanish or a limited amount of English should be tested for intelligence in Spanish rather than in English and with a test standardized to their population.

Many Mexican-American students find that the only way to get out of a bad educational scene is simply to drop out. There are many individual reasons for dropping out. One of the principal reasons is that Mexican-American youngsters tend to be overage in grade levels; given the linguistic handicaps with which they enter first grade, by the time they are able to do first-grade work, they are old enough to be in second grade. True, almost one-third of the homes and virtually all of the schools in the country are beset by the high-school dropout problem. But Mexican-American children have a higher dropout rate than any comparable group in the nation.

David Gottlieb's study of the Job Corps suggests that most of the youths in the program who dropped out of school did so because they failed to find any relation between their school program and their vocational goals. This can hardly be called a lack of motivation; it is rather a lack of academic relevance.

Martin Deutsch's thesis is that "the lower-class child enters the school situation so poorly prepared to produce what the school demands that initial failures are almost inevitable, and the school experience becomes negatively rather than positively reinforced. Thus the child's experience in school does nothing to counteract the invidious influence to which he is exposed in his slum and, sometimes segregated, neighborhood. . . . The frustration inherent in not understanding, not succeeding, and not being stimulated in the school—although being regulated by it—creates a basis for the further development of negative self-images and low evaluations of individual competencies. . . . No matter how the parents might aspire to a higher achievement level for their child, their lack of knowledge as to the operational implementation, combined with the child's early failure experiences in the school, can so effectively attenuate confidence in his ability ever to handle competently challenge in the academic area that the child loses all motivation."

To keep Mexican-American students in school, federal funds to states and school districts must be increased and the regulations concerning their expenditure must be made explicit. Schools must be encouraged to co-operate in federal programs for Mexican Americans. The programs should relate to the needs of the learners by taking into account their assets, attitudes, skills, personalities, and background. A new breed of teacher is needed, according to Dr. Miguel Montes, member of the California State Board of Education. Montes calls for teachers "sensitive to the many and diverse educational problems of Mexican-American youth."

Finally, every school in a Mexican-American community should have an educatioal coördinating committee composed of Mexican American teachers, parents, and civic leaders who will look into all the problems of Mexican-American students, especially the dropout problem. We know the dropout cycle of Mexican Americans can be broken. "War on poverty" programs like the Youth Training and Employment Project (Y.T.E.P.) of East Los Angeles, whose primary objective is to upgrade disadvantaged Mexican-American dropouts between the ages of sixteen and twenty-one, are steps in the right direction.

Considering the high dropout rate of Mexican-American students, it is not surprising that there are so few Mexican Americans in colleges and universities. Only two per cent of the California state college population is Mexican American. Of these, less than one-half of one per cent go on to graduate. At U.C.L.A., there were only three hundred Mexican-American students last year out of a student population of twenty-nine thousand. Out of approximately twenty-five thousand students at the University of California at Berkeley in 1966 only seventy-eight were Mexican Americans. Yet there are more than a million Mexican Americans in California alone.

Mexican Americans comprise almost half the population of New Mexico, but less than eight per cent of them attend the state universities and colleges. At the University of New Mexico, only ten per cent of the student population is Mexican American, yet they account for fifteen per cent of the freshman dropout rate and only six per cent graduate.

If higher education is to contribute significantly to the upward social mobility of Mexican Americans, then the colleges and universities must be willing to enroll them despite their previous academic records or conditions of poverty. Policies governing college admissions must be tempered with the realities of American socio-economic life. College counseling for high-school students must be strengthened. In a democracy, the university should be the last place for elitist doctrines. The groves of academe must not be allowed to become the Tuileries of an intellectual aristocracy. If a college or university helps Mexican Americans achieve vocational success, then they will have played their part in the fulfillment of the American dream.

The great educational experiment after World War II, the G.I. Bill of Rights, paid off remarkably well. Most of today's professional Mexican Americans are products of that government-financed education program.

A similar program for disadvantaged minorities (in time, perhaps, for all young people) would help overcome the socio-economic plight of Mexican Americans who otherwise are not eligible for government assistance.

Some organizations like the Latin-American Educational Foundation of Colorado, founded in 1949, award grants and loans to Spanish-named students of the state. But the effort is meager compared to the vast numbers of Spanish-speaking Americans who need financial assistance to get to college and to stay there.

With the help of a Ford Foundation grant, La Raza, newly formed organization of Mexican Americans, has so far parceled out money to some Mexican-American students, particularly graduate students interested in going on to law school. With the help of its Legal Defense Fund, La Raza is encouraging Mexican Americans to become civil-rights lawyers; it is also providing a professional pool of Mexican-American lawyers committed to the defense and advancement of Mexican Americans in civil-rights matters.

In California, the Chicano Movement advocates outright elimination of all college entrance requirements for Mexican Americans and the establishment of a Chicano Studies Program better attuned to the needs and necessities of the Chicano community.

Most Mexican Americans see the need for the bilingual-bicultural school as the most pressing issue in Mexican-American education, as well as one of the most challenging. To this end, the Bilingual Education Act, signed in January, 1968, directs the American schools to a new, bold course of education in action—bilingual-bicultural education. But the promise has been more a palliative than a true corrective.

From the beginning, the concept of bilingual-bicultural education has been confused. For example, an article on "Bilingual Education" in the *New Republic* (October 21, 1967) evoked a feedback which simply reflected the lexocentric attitude of most Americans. One response insisted that "segregating children from homes where 'Spanglish' is spoken into classes taught in any other language but English would only widen this barrier of language, not bridge it." Another respondent questioned "whether instruction in Spanish teaches a student more quickly and efficiently than instruction in English." He pointed out the linguistic success in English of Spanish-speakers who came to this country when they were ten or older. The fact is that these Spanish-speakers already had had instruction in the Spanish language, which gave them the necessary kinds of linguistic skills in one language that made the transfer process much less difficult. These are fairly typical reactions to the idea of bilingual-bicultural education, even by educated people.

What is bilingual-bicultural education? Essentially, it is teaching the non-English-speaking (or limited-English-speaking) child in his first language (not his mother tongue as it is so oftentimes erroneously called) at the same time he is introduced, via foreign-language instruction methods, to the target language, in small regulated doses at first, then in increasingly larger time units. Finally the target language becomes the medium of instruction while the child's first language becomes simply a coequal linguistic tool. The effect is to form a truly bilingual individual. Proponents of the bilingual-bicultural school argue that this kind of instruction can also be used to create bilingual Anglo-Americans.

For the first time, bilingual-bicultural education offers a Mexican-American alternative to Mexican-American problems. Mexican Americans are beginning to look for their salvation not in Anglo alternatives but in their own cultural identity and linguistic heritage. Biculturalism stresses the many strands of the American heritage. American history has been distorted to stress the special relationship between Americans and Englishmen. Bicultural education for Mexican Americans will illuminate the dark side of that historical moon by showing the relationship between Spanish-speaking Americans and their Spanish-speaking brethren of Latin America and Spain.

Bilingual-bicultural education is not just foreign-language teaching. It includes the whole range of academic subjects in the child's first language. It also involves acquainting the child not only with the Anglo-American part of his political identity but with the significance of his Spanish-American past.

Some progress has been made in bilingual-bicultural education. In San Antonio, the Horn Project, initiated in 1964, has grown from modest beginnings until it now instructs more than five thousand Mexican-American children in grades one to four. The El Paso bilingual program, though it shows promise, has not yet expanded beyond its initial stage. Bilingual-bicultural education exists at the moment only in fourteen model programs throughout the country. This year, through E.P.D.A. programs, several hundred teachers have been recruited for training in bilingual-bicultural education. Unfortunately the ratio of Mexican-American teachers selected has been small. Bilingual education requires bilingual teachers. Many of the teachers recruited for E.P.D.A. and other bilingual training programs can barely speak Spanish. When they go back to their schools, they do not change their teaching styles. Even on the staffs of many E.P.D.A. institutes, one finds only token Mexican-American educators or workers. The directors of these institutes are almost always Anglos.

Many Mexican Americans see in the current federal programs for Mexican Americans a boondoggle for opportunistic Anglos. They see Anglos controlling the one significant Mexican-American alternative to their problems. It seems strange, for example, that the twenty-eight Mexican-American youngsters from a San Antonio elementary school who were selected for a bilingual demonstration program for the New York City Board of Education in its television studios, were taken to New York by an Anglo teacher. Even stranger, the director of the Bilingual Education Program of the Southwest Education Development Laboratory is an Anglo.

Mexican Americans are not saying that only Mexican Americans can teach Mexican Americans. They are saying that the employment of bilingual Mexican Americans or bilingual Anglo-Americans represents a better approach to bilingual education. However, since Mexican-American children need Mexican-American models in their classrooms, it makes good sense to use bilingual Mexican-American teachers in preference to Anglo teachers in the primary grades.

The success of bilingual education depends upon the teacher. Current estimates place the need at one hundred thousand teachers who will be fluent in both Spanish and English. Bilingual education also calls for new teaching techniques. Language-arts programs must be redesigned for the bilingual-bicultural school.

Of course, money is the key factor. In 1968, Congress authorized thirty million dollars for the first year of the Bilingual Education Act, but it was slow in actually appropriating the money. The Bureau of the Budget recommended only five million dollars for the program. Emergency meetings by the N.E.A., its state affiliates, and concerned Mexican Americans got Congress to appropriate money for bilingual education, and at that far less than authorized or actually required.

The status of bilingual-bicultural education during President Nixon's term of office remains to be seen. Mexican-American leaders hope the project will continue to be funded. In all likelihood the size of the appropriation will be token at best for the next several years. The Chicanos of La Raza are not waiting to see what happens. They are insisting on action now.

Mexican-American educators see the education of Mexican-American children as involving a coalition of the community and the school. Mexican-American parents must be involved in the educational decisions affecting their children. The monocultural grip of school boards must yield. More Mexican Americans must become members of school boards to make the changes needed. If necessary, Chicanos insist that Mexican Americans must take the schools out of the hands of those who are academically suppressing them.

JOSEPH WHITEHILL

The Convict and the Burgher:

A Case Study of Communication and Crime

A writer can live anywhere the rent is low and there is a mailbox—which is why this story starts in Salisbury, Maryland, on the lower Eastern Shore, just over the lip of civilization. Since about half the effort a writer spends is directed toward avoiding writing, I was delighted one day in 1962 to be summoned to serve on the grand jury. Besides routinely handing down indictments of persons accused of serious crimes, members of the grand jury must go gravely about the county inspecting places like the dog pound, the air raid shelter in the basement of City Hall, and the jail. The dog pound was clean enough, but the dogs were rather low class. This was duly noted in our report. The air raid shelter was just full enough of old courthouse files to limit the remaining accommodation to the lawyers, secretaries and judges who populate City Hall, and provide them with racy reading while they were down there being saved.

The jail was god-awful. On the third floor of the courthouse—for the convenience of lawyers and judges—it comprised two bullpens for social life, one for whites and one for Negroes, separated by four-man cells. There was more room per man than in the ordinary submarine, but not a lot. There were two open toilets, one near the center of each bullpen, to assure that everyone knew what everyone else was up to. Male prisoners as well as female were guarded by elderly turnkeys trying not to earn money enough to jeopardize their social security. There was no provision for sunlight, fresh air or exercise. As we made our circuit about the cages, we avoided the eyes of the men locked inside, as if we sensed somehow that the guilt was ours, not theirs. We were right about that, but our report said merely that the jail was very clean.

I went home badly shaken, and next day called the Friends Prison Service Committee, in Philadelphia, to ask what I could do. A bundle of pamphlets arrived in the next mail. (We Quakers print a lot of literature, and it's all free.) Finding nothing in the pamphlets that seemed to apply to me and Salisbury, I invented my own program. Under the tolerance of the sheriff, an excellent man, I began visiting the jail two evenings a week, armed with a yellow tablet and a pencil. Any prisoner who wanted to was allowed to leave the bullpen and go with me into one of the side

THE CONVICT AND THE BURGHER By Joseph Whitehill. Reprinted from *The American Scholar*, Volume 38, Number 3, Summer 1969. Copyright © 1969 by the United Chapters of Phi Beta Kappa. By permission of the publishers and the author.

offices and talk. I made notes as necessary, then spent much of the following day finding lost fathers, looking for jobs for men jailed for nonsupport—jailing for nonsupport is rather like curing asthma with a tourniquet about the neck—persuading lawyers to take profitless cases, and bringing some articulateness to the men who could not explain their own defenses. This was an excellent way, of course, not to write, but I was in despair most of the time. The world of the indigent, the friendless and the ignorant is a very small, bleak place, and it is overcrowded.

There were, however, bright moments. One boy had been arrested for vagrancy. In Salisbury, a vagrant is a young man with long hair, a black leather jacket written on or not, and black leather boots, who is observed to stand on a street corner longer than two full time-cycles of the traffic light. He was just passing through, but he was detained. With pleasure, the arresting officers noted in their report that he had puncture marks on his arms. With equal or perhaps greater pleasure, I demonstrated by affidavit within a week to the state's attorney that the boy had had a job at the time of his arrest, and that his job was that of snake handler in a carnival. The puncture marks were not self-inflicted. The boy was released to catch up with the carnival.

Another man, an illiterate Negro, was arrested for attempted rape of a twelve-year-old girl. In his gentleness, and in his concern for the eight chickens he had left unattended in the dirt yard behind his house, he did not seem to me a likely rapist, even though I did not then nor do I now *know* what a likely rapist looks like. I visited the little girl and found her saucy, jealous and vicious. I visited the doctor who had examined her after the incident, and learned that the blood on her panties had come from a sharp scratch in the groin, as might be got while skinning hurriedly over a barbed wire fence. I visited the man's wife, and learned from her what he had been ashamed to tell me—that because of a chronic genitourinary condition, he had been impotent for more than eight months. Next, I approached the sheriff and told him he had a sick man in his jail among the healthy ones. The sheriff winced, and had the man hospitalized at once. Then I approached the state's attorney and asked him if he would like to go into court to try to prove that a gentle, impotent, sick man had attempted rape on a demonstrably nasty and vengeful little girl. The man was freed immediately, which I protested. I made them keep him in the hospital, at county expense, until he was cured of his difficulty.

I can assure you that something happens to you when you become the accidental instrument of saving a man from life imprisonment or the gas chamber.

About this time I got to know the man really responsible for the rest of this oblique story. He is Kirk Davis, and at the time he seemed remarkably forbearing of me that I, as grand jury member, had lately voted to indict him for second-degree murder. (To jump ahead, he is now coordinator of a new recording for the blind project in Patuxent Institution, and is among my best friends.) We found, during my semiweekly visits with him in the Salisbury jail, that he and I shared many interests—some with agreement and others with heated argument. (It did not hurt, either, that he liked the books I brought him—books I wrote!)

What did hurt, however, was that he interrupted his stay in the Salisbury jail by escaping. The police take that sort of thing very personally; when he was returned, therefore, he was awarded the dubious privacy of the solitary cage-in-a-cage, with the light on all the time. Because the sheriff evidently felt that I had some sort of sedative effect on Kirk, I was invited to visit with him nightly, which I did in the comfort of his quarters.

After he was tried, convicted and sentenced, he was adjudged a defective delinquent, and was committed to Patuxent Institution, at Jessup, Maryland, where all sentences are indeterminate. As nearly as I understand it, a defective delinquent is one who has a more or less recognizable pattern in his criminal behavior, whose crimes have tended to increase in seriousness, and who is thought to be amenable to psychiatric treatment. Patuxent Institution, while still very much a prison, is one of the best. Vocational training, a full high school curriculum, crafts, sports, and group therapy all are provided. It is an experiment, created by an act of the state legislature independent of the rest of the state correctional system, and has to fight hard for its annual budget. Whereas it costs less than $1,500 a year to keep a man vegetating in the penitentiary, it costs over $7,000 a year to keep one doing something in Patuxent.

I continued to correspond with Kirk, wondering all the while what good it was doing—wondering even what the word "good" meant in this context. Sure, I enjoyed his letters and he, I thought, enjoyed mine, but so what? So what beyond simple enjoyment? The more I learned of prisons and the men in them, the more grew my despair. By then I could have told Sisyphus a thing or two. How much could mere letters accomplish?

The first clue was dropped almost by accident. In one letter, Kirk offhandedly mentioned that my letters to him were normally shared by ten to twenty other inmates. I was astonished and a little embarrassed; his letters to me, I discovered when I took trouble to notice, were read by all my family and many of my friends and students. These letters, his and mine, were the sand in the neck of the hourglass.

I fumbled awkwardly with this news. I groped. That seems to be the whole history of this time—fumbling, groping and sensing patterns that vanished when looked at closely.

In another letter, Kirk described the formation, by a small group of inmates, of a Great Books Class loosely organized around Mortimer Adler's Syntopicon. The men did extensive independent reading and met together five nights a week for two hours of talk. (How many of you teachers would dare ask of your students such a seminar and reading load? My own students at Johns Hopkins would flee in a body.) This group was inmate-run and inmate-organized, without the presence of either custodial or school staff. It was something of their own, and they guarded it with an astonishing proprietary jealousy. Admission to the group was carefully controlled, lest incoming opportunists wreck it in some way. The class is now in its third year. A measure of its value to the men is this: Not once since the class began has any member of it received a ticket or incident report because of an infraction of the rules of the institution. No other inmate group has anything like this record.

Still fumbling, still groping for some way to do more, I accepted Kirk's invitation to visit the Great Books Class in session. That was two years ago—a one-time invitation. It grew to my spending every Thursday night of the school year with the men. I had little to teach and much to learn. After getting over the first shock—the sound of these men, none with more than a high school education, moving easily among Kierkegaard, Sartre, Camus, Saint Thomas Aquinas, Hobbes and Saint Augustine—I was able to make a number of curious observations: All these men had I.Q.'s upward of 125; two scored more than 140. All by their histories given to action first and reflection later, they sat in the room with quiet poise, with none of the body movements that normally indicate a restless testing of kinesthesia. They showed acute interest in me—the man with the tie on—studying me carefully for hypocrisy. After all, what was I doing there without getting paid for it? Interestingly, nearly every one of the men in the group was a man of authority in the prison's subgovernment. (Every prison has two governments—the one paid by the state and whose members' names appear on the letterhead, and the other one comprising the bright cons who do all the work in return for status and cumshaw.) One more interesting observation I shall save for a bit.

Now I must digress to pull another thread into the fabric. As you probably know, Mensa is an international group founded in 1945 to bring together the very intelligent. The requirement for membership is the passing of a standardized intelligence test in the top two percent of the population—about 148 on the Cattell Scale. I prefer to call us, instead of "the intelligent," merely those who pass culturally warped intelligence tests very well—a difference, perhaps. In the United States, Mensa's activities are chiefly to argue about its constitution, and to meet monthly in local groups to drink and show off. I joined the way most did—as a blushful joke, to get a number assigned to me, and out of curiosity. I never went to a meeting.

Here is the first of two demonstrations that just because you are intelligent, there is no guarantee that you are not simultaneously pretty stupid. In the Mensa Bulletin for January, last year, appeared a short letter describing a little group of Mensa members calling themselves Mensa Friends, who were engaged in establishing one-to-one correspondence relationships between themselves and high-intelligence felons, to share thinking of a general nature, and to give the men inside some contact with an outside world that would not involve their families.

In all of my years of work in prisons, and in all of my years of membership in Mensa, it had not occurred to me to connect the two.

I went to the next Mensa meeting in Baltimore. I told them of the men in Patuxent, and of Mensa Friends. I asked for volunteers—people to write to prisoners. The response was less than galvanic; three offered, and one of those asked, "Yes, but what happens if we write to one of these men for a year or two, then all of a sudden we find him sitting on our doorstep?" A hard question to answer, especially when fumbling and groping seemed then the mode. I forget what I said. It turns out, however, that the person who asked the question now invites his convict correspondent to Saturday night supper at his house nearly every week, on evening leave. Some questions answer themselves.

Today, thirty members of Baltimore Mensa, out of a total of slightly more than a hundred, are in active correspondence with Patuxent inmates.

Returning now to the Great Books Class in Patuxent, the last important thing I noticed was this: How strange it seemed to me that a man who had well-read a book called *Civilization and Its Discontents* would pronounce the author's name "Sigmund Frood," or that *The Sorrows of Young Werther* was attributed aloud to "Go-ee-the." This despite the solid evidence that the men had read the books, had understood them, and had put them into usable places in their dialogues.

A clear light opened: They had never heard the names pronounced aloud before. While they were quite easy with the use of their mispronounced words in connotation, denotation and context, they had never heard them *said*.

Among the large number of probable reasons that come to mind for this are:

1. Short schooling in dull schools.
2. Family life in which communication is chiefly by grunts, informal white papers of personal displeasure, and physical blows ranging in force from the standard shove to the satisfying knockdown.
3. The mistrust and denigration in those families of anything like smooth talk.
4. The rigidly limiting speech patterns of the peer group. In this group, highest premium of reward is given to conformity, not to variety or invention. There are two contraoperative influences working in this group. While no youth of today would use any other phrase than "Bendix throwout spring" to describe that object, there is a multiplicity of words for "cylinder head," "carburetor," "muffler," "camshaft" and other automobile parts of high cathexis affecting speed, style or owner-image.

    Conversely, it is evident that in this agreed poverty of vocabulary, many code words must carry multiple meanings. Examples are: "dig," "groovy," "boss," "hip," "smack," "bust," "rap" and, of course, the ubiquitous "cool." The intended meaning in each use comes clear, insofar as it really comes clear or really *needs* to at the moment, almost entirely in the bath of context. This is tribalism in its prototypical manifestation—hardly the place to expect to hear Goethe and Freud so pronounced.

5. Television and radio, the chief purveyors of language to the young from "outside," have asymptotic limits to breadth of vocabulary. A recondite word like "recondite" would never make the team, no matter how useful it might be.

The intelligent boy surviving and growing in such a world puts the craft of survival before the risks of disapproved, variant growth. An odd fact for insertion here is that the intelligent boy rarely knows he is intelligent. He knows he is often poor at sports, unlucky with girls, and that his mouth frequently gets him in trouble. He learns to live with the first two, and keeps his mouth shut.

Now, because a man's use of his language is about the last remaining index of his place in society—this since the great fortunes are all either dissipated or discreetly hidden, and cars all look alike, and everybody can dress similarly—it began to seem to me that some means ought to be introduced to enable these men to bring their language facility up to their known intelligence. I cast about—groped is still the word—for some such means. A language laboratory? Reading aloud before a coach? *Something* must be waiting undiscovered.

I had about settled on a kind of combination of both when I discussed the problem with Professor Roger Petersen, who teaches experimental psychology at Washington College in Chestertown, and who has been blind since birth. (Here comes the second pratfall, and surely not the last.) He said, "Whitehill, for an intelligent man, you sure can be stupid at times." That had a familiar ring. "If you're going to have these men reading aloud onto tapes, why in plain hell not have them record books for the blind?"

How simple. . . . But how invisible! We went to the director of Patuxent Institution and got his approval to install there a duplex recording studio, so designed that a monitor can listen to an inmate read aloud, catch his errors, back him up and start him over again. The studio is now in full operation. At the moment there stands a waiting list of fifty inmates wanting to audition for the program. With the possible exception of hunger strikes and riots and things like that, *no* fifty inmates of any place have ever done anything in concert.

A punctuation mark—not a period but a comma—to the recording project for the blind is this: We learned, after our independent invention of the idea, that a small group of inmates of the Massachusetts Correctional Institution at South Walpole has been running such a program for years. (Shades of Darwin and Alfred Russel Wallace!) We immediately asked for an invitation to visit there to learn what we could about planning, equipment and coordination. In a wild spirit of what-the-hell, I asked the director of Patuxent Institution to let us take along two of his inmates—the two men who would head the program in Patuxent—for the three-day trip to South Walpole. As astonishing as a rose in the snow, the permission came at once.

The trip, in all its fun and consequences, is another story. Because I tend to panic immediately in traffic situations involving more than one car besides my own, I used David Hall, a twelve-year veteran of Patuxent, for my navigator. Nearing the Walpole installation. I met a torn-up superhighway intersection presided over by an elderly policeman. Having circled the wreckage three times and found no way out—not even the way I'd come in—I stopped beside the policeman. Rather, he had watched my Skinner box failure and stopped *us*. David Hall handed him the map, and showed him where we were and where we wanted to be. The policeman held the map upside down. This was too much for David. With an insouciance hard to believe in a con of his experience, he asked sweetly, "What's the matter? Didn't they teach you map reading in cop school?"

The rest of the trip was similar in fun, but none of us—my wife, and Professor Petersen and his wife, and the two men of Patuxent—ever forgot for a moment that we all were pioneers. To be permitted to take two felons across five states on an errand unrelated to any court order was, we felt, the headiest of refreshment.

Now we come to the end—the end of the moment. Our groping and fumbling has led us toward some sort of distant light. We have established the triangular symbiosis among the blind, the articulate inmate, and the high-intelligence citizen outside both those prisons who feels inadequately used. What do we know by now?

First, we know a little bit about what is wrong. We know that fixed time sentences for criminals have neither deterrent nor rehabilitative effect. (In eighteenth-century England, when picking pockets was a capital offense, most pockets were picked at public hangings. If the State Highway Department were run on the same principles that the prison system is, we would all still be driving about on cobblestones.)

We know that the *lex talionis* of the Old Testament was wisely refuted by Jesus Christ. We believe, O Lord, but You sure take Your own sweet time in helping us in our unbelief.

We know that the longer a man spends in prison, the less likely is he to rejoin what for some of us is a highly interesting and various society; he rejoins a highly interesting and various contrasociety—and ends up back in the joint.

We know that, besides *out,* the man inside wants, more than anything else but sex, communication with people in square society who are getting away with having fun.

We know that recidivism now stands at sixty to seventy-five percent—a success average that would get any businessman fired in a week.

We know that the proper use of a prison is to detain persons who have committed acts that are called crimes, but which really are mere acts of self-identification of persons needing help. We know that the full battery of psychological diagnostic tests ought to be administered to every entrant.

We know that every sentence, for whatever crime, must be indeterminate; those who can go back quickly ought to be got out as quickly as possible; those whose offenses may be minor but who show the pathology of danger to themselves or others must be detained indefinitely.

We believe that a reduction in recidivism from seventy-five percent to, say, fifteen percent is possible, with a concomitant reduction in street crime.

Last of all, we know that those other things we know all stem from this: Every person taken into custody must be attached as soon as possible to someone of similar makeup on the outside, someone who has a job and perhaps a family and certainly some fun out of life—someone who will demonstrate not by precept but by example that there is a vast congeries of ways of doing things that do not attract the attention of the men in blue.

And we know from that that this office cannot be official. You cannot hire someone to be human.

Our new President said more than he meant to when he said that government cannot do it all. Truthfully, government cannot do anything at all important. It can make war and defend special interests . . . but any of my pathologues can say the same of himself. Government cannot love, and it cannot care.

I thus foresee a time not too far off when taxes are taken not only in money but also in personal involvement.

Else we perish.

MICHAEL NOVAK

White Ethnic

Growing up in America has been an assault upon my sense of worthiness. It has also been a kind of liberation and delight.

There must be countless women in America who have known for years that something is peculiarly unfair, yet who have found it only recently possible, because of Women's Liberation, to give tongue to their pain. In recent months, I have experienced a similar inner thaw, a gradual relaxation, a willingness to think about feelings heretofore shepherded out of sight.

I am born of PIGS—those Poles, Italians, Greeks, and Slavs, non-English-speaking immigrants, numbered so heavily among the working-men of this nation. Not particularly liberal, nor radical, born into a history not white Anglo-Saxon and not Jewish—born outside what in America is considered the intellectual mainstream. And thus privy to neither power nor status nor intellectual voice.

Those Poles of Buffalo and Milwaukee—so notoriously taciturn, sullen, nearly speechless. Who has ever understood them? It is not that Poles do not feel emotion: what is their history if not dark passion, romanticism, betrayal, courage, blood? But where in America is there anywhere a language for voicing what a Christian Pole in this nation feels? He has no Polish culture left him, no Polish tongue. Yet Polish feelings do not go easily into the idiom of happy America, the America of the Anglo-Saxons and, yes, in the arts, the Jews. (The Jews have long been a culture of the word, accustomed to exile, skilled in scholarship and in reflection. The Christian Poles are largely of peasant origin, free men for hardly more than a hundred years.) Of what shall the man of Buffalo think, on his way to work in the mills, departing from his relatively dreary home and street? What roots does he have? What language of the heart is available to him?

The PIGS are not silent willingly. The silence burns like hidden coals in the chest.

All four of my grandparents, unknown to one another, arrived in America from the same country in Slovakia. My grandfather had a small farm in Pennsylvania; his wife died in a wagon accident. Meanwhile, a girl of fifteen arrived on Ellis Island, dizzy, a little ill from witnessing births and deaths and illnesses aboard the crowded ship, with a sign around her neck lettered "PASSAIC." There an aunt told her of the man who had lost his wife in Pennsylvania. She went. They were married. Inheriting his three children, each year for five years she had one of her own; she was among the lucky, only one died. When she was twenty-two, mother of seven, her husband died. And she resumed the work she had begun in Slovakia at the town home of a man known to us now only as "the Professor": she housecleaned and she laundered.

I heard this story only weeks ago. Strange that I had not asked insistently before. Odd that I should have such shallow knowledge of my roots. Amazing to me that I do not know what my family suffered, endured, learned, hoped these past six or seven generations. It is as if there were no project on which we all have been involved. As if history, in some way, began with my father and with me.

Let me hasten to add that the estrangement I have come to feel derives not only from a lack of family history. All my life, I have been made to feel a slight uneasiness when I must say my name. Under challenge in grammar school concerning my nationality, I had been instructed by my father to announce proudly: "American." When my family moved from the Slovak ghetto of Johnstown to the WASP suburb on the hill, my mother impressed upon us how well we must be dressed, and show good manners, and behave—people think of us as "different" and we mustn't give them any cause. "Whatever you do, marry a Slovak girl," was other advice to a similar end: "They cook. They clean. They take good care of you. For your own good."

When it was revealed to me that most movie stars and many other professionals had abandoned European names in order to feed American fantasies, I felt only a little sadness. One of my uncles, for business reasons and rather late in life, changed his name too, to a simple German variant. Not long, either, after World War II.

Nowhere in my schooling do I recall an attempt to put me in touch with my own history. The strategy was clearly to make an American of me. English literature, American literature; and even the history books, as I recall them, were peopled mainly by Anglo-Saxons from Boston (where most historians seemed to live). Not even my native Pennsylvania, let alone my Slovak forebears, counted for very many paragraphs. I don't remember feeling envy or regret: a feeling, perhaps, of unimportance, of remoteness, of not having heft enough to count.

The fact that I was born a Catholic also complicated life. What is a Catholic but what everybody else is in reaction against? Protestants re-formed "the Whore of Babylon," others were "enlightened" from it, and Jews had reason to help Catholicism and the social structures it was rooted in to fall apart. My history books and the whole of education hummed in upon that point (during crucial years I attended a public, not a parochial, school): to be modern is decidedly not to be medieval; to be reasonable is not to be dogmatic; to be free is clearly not to live under ecclesiastical authority; to be scientific is not to attend ancient rituals, cherish irrational symbols, indulge in mythic practices. It is hard to grow up Catholic in America without becoming defensive, perhaps a little paranoid, feeling forced to divide the world between "us" and "them."

We had a special language all our own, our own pronunciation for words we shared in common with others (Augustine, contemplative), sights and sounds and smells in which few others participated (incense at Benediction of the Most Blessed Sacrament, Forty Hours, wakes, and altar bells at the silent consecration of the Host); and we had our own politics and slant on world affairs. Since earliest childhood, I have known about a "power elite" that runs America: the boys from the Ivy League·in the State Department, as opposed to the Catholic boys from Hoover's FBI who, as Daniel Moynihan once put it, keep watch on them. And on a whole host of issues, my people have been, though largely Democratic, conservative: on censorship, on Communism, on abortion, on religious schools . . . Harvard and Yale long meant "them" to us.

The language of Spiro Agnew, the language of George Wallace, ex-

cepting its idiom, awakens childhood memories in me of men arguing in
the barbershop, of my uncle drinking so much beer he threatened to lay
his dick upon the porch rail and wash the whole damn street with steaming piss—while cursing the niggers in the mill, below, and the Yankees in
the mill, above: millstones he felt pressing him. Other relatives were duly
shocked, but everybody loved Uncle George: he said what he thought.

We did not feel this country belonged to us. We felt fierce pride in it,
more loyalty than anyone could know. But we felt blocked at every turn.
There were not many intellectuals among us, not even very many professional men. Laborers mostly. Small businessmen, agents for corporations
perhaps. Content with a little, yes, modest in expectation. But somehow
feeling cheated. For a thousand years the Slovaks survived Hungarian
hegemony, and our strategy here remained the same: endurance and
steady work. Slowly, one day, we would overcome.

A special word is required about a complicated symbol: sex. To this
day my mother finds it hard to spell the word intact, preferring to write
"s--." Not that much was made of sex in our environment. And that's
the point: silence. Demonstrative affection, emotive dances, exuberance
Anglo-Saxons seldom seem to share; but on the realities of sex, discretion.
Reverence, perhaps; seriousness, surely. On intimacies, it is as though our
tongues had been stolen. As though in peasant life for a thousand years
the context had been otherwise. Passion, yes; romance, yes; family and
children, certainly; but sex, rather a minor part of life.

Imagine, then, the conflict in the generation of my brothers, sister, and
myself. (The book critic for the *New York Times* reviews on the same
day two new novels of fantasy: one a pornographic fantasy to end all
such fantasies [he writes], the other about a mad family representing in
some comic way the redemption wrought by Jesus Christ. In language
and verve, the books are rated even. In theme, the reviewer notes his
embarrassment in reporting a religious fantasy, but no embarrassment at
all about the preposterous pornography.) Suddenly, what for a thousand
years was minor becomes an all-absorbing investigation. It is, perhaps,
one drama when the ruling classes (I mean subscribers to *The New
Yorker,* I suppose) move progressively, generation by generation since
Sigmund Freud, toward consciousness-raising sessions in Clit. Lib., but
wholly another when we stumble suddenly upon mores staggering any
expectation our grandparents ever cherished.

Yet more significant in the ethnic experience in America is the intellectual world one meets: the definition of values, ideas, and purposes
emanating from universities, books, magazines, radio, and television.
One hears one's own voice echoed back neither by spokesmen of "Middle
America" (so complacent, smug, nativist, and Protestant), nor by "the
intellectuals." Almost unavoidably, perhaps, education in America leads
the student who entrusts his soul to it in a direction that, lacking a better
word, we might call liberal: respect for individual conscience, a sense of

social responsibility, trust in the free exchange of ideas and procedures of dissent, a certain confidence in the ability of men to "reason together" and to adjudicate their differences, a frank recognition of the vitality of the unconscious, a willingness to protect workers and the poor against the vast economic power of industrial corporations, and the like.

On the other hand, the liberal imagination has appeared to be astonishingly universalist, and relentlessly missionary. Perhaps the metaphor "enlightenment" offers a key. One is initiated into light. Liberal education tends to separate children from their parents, from their roots, from their history, in the cause of a universal and superior religion. One is taught, regarding the unenlightened (even if they be one's Uncles George and Peter, one's parents, one's brothers perhaps), what can only be called a modern equivalent of *odium theologicum.* Richard Hofstadter described anti-intellectualism in America, more accurately in nativist America than in ethnic America, but I have yet to encounter a comparable treatment of anti-unenlightenment among our educated classes.

In particular, I have regretted and keenly felt the absence of that sympathy for PIGS that simple human feeling might have prodded intelligence to muster: that same sympathy that the educated find so easy to conjure up for black culture, Chicano culture, Indian culture, and other cultures of the poor. In such cases, one finds, the universalist pretensions of liberal culture are suspended: some groups, at least, are entitled to be both different and respected. Why do the educated classes find it so difficult to want to understand the man who drives a beer truck, or the fellow with a helmet working on a site across the street with plumbers and electricians, while their sensitivities race easily to Mississippi or even Bedford-Stuyvesant?

There are deep secrets here, no doubt, unvoiced fantasies and scarcely admitted historical resentments. Few persons, in describing "Middle Americans," "the Silent Majority," or Scammon and Wattenberg's "typical American voter," distinguish clearly enough between the nativist American and the ethnic American. The first is likely to be Protestant, the second Catholic. Both may be, in various ways, conservative, loyalist, and unenlightened. Each has his own agonies, fears, betrayed expectations. Neither is ready, quite, to become an ally of the other. Neither has the same history behind him here. Neither has the same hopes. Neither is living out the same psychic voyage. Neither shares the same symbols or has the same sense of reality. The rhetoric and metaphors differ.

There is overlap, of course. But country music is not a polka, a successful politician in a Chicago ward needs a very different "common touch" from the one used by the county clerk in Normal; the urban experience of immigration lacks that mellifluous, optimistic, biblical vision of the good America that springs naturally to the lips of politicians from the Bible Belt. The nativist tends to believe with Richard Nixon that he "knows America and the American heart is good." The ethnic tends to believe that every American who preceded him has an angle, and that he, by God, will one day find one too. (Often, ethnics complain that by working hard, obeying the law, trusting their political leaders, and relying upon the American Dream they now have only their own naïveté to blame for rising no higher than they have.)

It goes without saying that the intellectuals do not love Middle America, and that for all the good warm discovery of America that preoccupied them during the 1950s, no strong tide of respect accumulated in their hearts for the Yahoos, Babbitts, Agnews, and Nixons of the land. Willie Morris, in *North Toward Home,* writes poignantly of the chill, parochial outreach of the liberal sensibility, its failure to engage the humanity of the modest, ordinary little man west of the Hudson. The intellectual's map of the United States is succinct: "Two coasts connected by United Airlines."

Unfortunately, it seems, the ethnics erred in attempting to Americanize themselves, before clearing the project with the educated classes. They learned to wave the flag and to send their sons to war. (The Poles in World War I were 4 per cent of the population but took 12 per cent of the casualties.) They learned to support their President—an easy task, after all, for those accustomed abroad to obeying authority. And where would they have been if Franklin Roosevelt had not sided with them against established interests? They knew a little about Communism, the radicals among them in one way, and by far the larger number of conservatives in another. Not a few exchange letters to this day with cousins and uncles who did not leave for America when they might have, whose lot is demonstrably harder and less than free.

Finally, the ethnics do not like, or trust, or even understand the intellectuals. It is not easy to feel uncomplicated affection for those who call you "pig," "fascist," "racist." One had not yet grown accustomed not to hearing "Hunkie," "Polack," "Spic," "Mick," "Dago," and the rest. At no little sacrifice, one had apologized for foods that smelled too strong for Anglo-Saxon noses, moderated the wide swings of Slavic and Italian emotion, learned decorum, given oneself to education American style, tried to learn tolerance and assimilation. Each generation criticized the earlier for its authoritarian and European and old-fashioned ways. "Up-to-date" was a moral lever. And now when the process nears completion, when a generation appears that speaks without accent and goes to college, still you are considered pigs, fascists, and racists.

Racists? Our ancestors owned no slaves. Most of us ceased being serfs only in the last 200 years—the Russians in 1861. What have we got against blacks or blacks against us? Competition, yes, for jobs and homes and communities; competition, even, for political power. Italians, Lithuanians, Slovaks, Poles are not, in principle, against "community control," or even against ghettos of our own. Whereas the Anglo-Saxon model appears to be a system of atomic individuals and high mobility, our model has tended to stress communities of our own, attachment to family and relatives, stability, and roots. We tend to have a fierce sense of attachment to our homes, having been homeowners less than three generations: a home is almost fulfillment enough for one man's life. We have most ambivalent feelings about suburban assimilation and mobility. The melting pot is a kind of homogenized soup, and its mores only partly appeal to us: to some, yes, and to others, no.

It must be said that we think we are better people than the blacks. Smarter, tougher, harder working, stronger in our families. But maybe many of us are not so sure. Maybe we are uneasy. Emotions here are delicate. One can understand the immensely more difficult circumstances under which the blacks have suffered, and one is not unaware of peculiar forms of fear, envy, and suspicion across color lines. How much of all this we learned in America, by being made conscious of our olive skin, brawny backs, accents, names, and cultural quirks, is not plain to us. Racism is not our invention; we did not bring it with us; we found it here. And should we pay the price for America's guilt? Must all the gains of the blacks, long overdue, be chiefly at our expense? Have we, once again, no defenders but ourselves?

Television announcers and college professors seem so often to us to be speaking in a code. When they say "white racism," it does not seem to be their own traditions they are impugning. Perhaps it is paranoia, but it seems that the affect accompanying such words is directed at steelworkers, auto workers, truck drivers, and police—at us. When they say "humanism" or "progress," it seems to us like moral pressure to abandon our own traditions, our faith, our associations, in order to reap higher rewards in the culture of the national corporations—that culture of quantity, homogeneity, replaceability, and mobility. They want to grind off all the angles, hold us to the lathes, shape us to be objective, meritocratic, orderly, and fully American.

In recent years, of course, a new cleavage has sprung open among the intellectuals. Some seem to speak for technocracy—for that alliance of science, industry, and humanism whose heaven is "progress." Others seem to be taking the view once ascribed to ecclesiastical conservatives and traditionalists: that commitment to enlightenment is narrow, ideological, and hostile to the best interests of mankind. In the past, the great alliance for progress sprang from the conviction that "knowledge is power." Both humanists and scientists could agree on that, and labored in their separate ways to make the institutions of knowledge dominant in society: break the shackles of the Church, extend suffrage to the middle classes and finally to all, win untrammeled liberty for the marketplace of ideas. Today it is no longer plain that the power brought by knowledge is humanistic. Thus the parting of the ways.

Science has ever carried with it the stories and symbols of a major religion. It is ruthlessly universalist. If its participants are not "saved," they are nonetheless "enlightened," which isn't bad. And every single action of the practicing scientist, no matter how humble, could once be understood as a contribution to the welfare of the human race; each smallest gesture was invested with meaning, given a place in a scheme, and weighted with redemptive power. Moreover, the scientist was in possession of "the truth," indeed of the very meaning of and validating procedures for the word. His role was therefore sacred.

Imagine, then, a young strapping Slovak entering an introductory course in the Sociology of Religion at the nearby state university or community college. Is he sent back to his Slovak roots, led to recover paths of experience latent in all his instincts and reflexes, given an image of the life of his grandfather that suddenly, in recognition, brings tears to his eyes? Is he brought to a deeper appreciation of his Lutheran or Catholic heritage and its resonances with other bodies of religious experience? On the contrary, he is secretly taught disdain for what his grandfather *thought* he was doing when he acted or felt or imagined through religious forms. In the boy's psyche, a new religion is implanted: power over others, enlightenment, an atomic (rather than a communitarian) sensibility, a contempt for mystery, ritual, transcendence, soul, absurdity, and tragedy; and deep confidence in the possibilities of building a better world through scientific understanding. He is led to feel ashamed for the statistical portrait of Slovak immigrants which shows them to be conservative, authoritarian, not given to dissent, etc. His teachers instruct him with the purest of intentions, in a way that is value free.

To be sure, certain radical writers in America have begun to bewail "the laying on of culture" and to unmask the cultural religion implicit in the American way of science. Yet radicals, one learns, often have an agenda of their own. What fascinates *them* among working-class ethnics are the traces, now almost lost, of *radical* activities among the working class two or three generations ago. Scratch the resentful boredom of a classroom of working-class youths, we are told, and you will find hidden in their past some formerly imprisoned organizer for the CIO, some Sacco/Vanzetti, some bold pamphleteer for the IWW. All this is true. But supposing that a study of the ethnic past reveals that most ethnics have been, are, and wish to remain, culturally conservative? Suppose, for example, they wish to deepen their religious roots and defend their ethnic enclaves? Must a radical culture be "laid on" them?

America has never confronted squarely the problem of preserving diversity. I can remember hearing in my youth bitter arguments that parochial schools were "divisive." Now the public schools are attacked for their commitment to homogenization. Well, how *does* a nation of no one culture, no one language, no one race, no one history, no one ethnic stock continue to exist as one, while encouraging diversity? How can the rights of all, and particularly of the weak, be defended if power is decentralized and left to local interests? The weak have ever found strength in this country through local chapters of national organizations. But what happens when the national organizations themselves—the schools, the unions, the federal government—become vehicles of a new, universalistic, thoroughly rationalized, technological culture?

Still, it is not that larger question that concerns me here. I am content today to voice the difficulties in the way of saying what I wish to say, when I wish to say it. The tradition of liberalism is a tradition I have had to acquire, despite an innate skepticism about many of its structural metaphors (free marketplace, individual autonomy, reason naked and undisguised, enlightenment). Radicalism, with its bold and simple optimism about human potential and its anarchic tendencies, has been, despite its appeal to me as a vehicle for criticizing liberalism, freighted with emotions, sentiments, and convictions about men that I cannot bring myself to share.

In my guts, I do not feel that institutions are "repressive" in any meaning of the word that leaves it meaningful; the "state of nature" seems to me, emotionally, far less liberating, far more undifferentiated and confining. I have not dwelt for so long in the profession of the intellectual life that I find it easy to be critical and harsh. In almost everything I see or hear or read, I am struck first, rather undiscriminatingly, by all the things I like in it. Only with second effort can I bring myself to discern the flaws. My emotions and values seem to run in affirmative patterns.

My interest is not, in fact, in defining myself over against the American people and the American way of life. I do not expect as much of it as all that. What I should like to do is come to a better and more profound knowledge of who I am, whence my community came, and whither my son and daughter, and their children's children, might wish to head in the future: I want to have a history.

More and more, I think in family terms, less ambitiously, on a less than national scale. The differences implicit in being Slovak, and Catholic, and lower-middle class seem more and more important to me. Perhaps it is too much to try to speak to all peoples in this very various nation of ours. Yet it does not seem evident that by becoming more concrete, accepting one's finite and limited identity, one necessarily becomes parochial. Quite the opposite. It seems more likely that by each of us becoming more profoundly what we are, we shall find greater unity, in those depths in which unity irradiates diversity, than by attempting through the artifices of the American "melting pot" and the cultural religion of science to become what we are not.

There is, I take it, a form of liberalism not wedded to universal Reason, whose ambition is not to homogenize all peoples on this planet, and whose base lies rather in the imagination and in the diversity of human stories: a liberalism I should be happy to have others help me to find.

ALFRED KAZIN

"Oates"

> So the days pass, and I ask myself
> whether one is not hypnotised, as a
> child by a silver globe, by life; and
> whether this is living.
> Virginia Woolf, Diary
> —28 November 1928

Sunday noon on Riverside Drive in Windsor, Ontario, which is not as far away as you would think. Detroit looms up just across the Detroit River—a concentrated industrial silhouette of piers, storage tanks, factory fronts, dead just now in the frosty February stillness. It's certainly quiet, genteel-quiet in the exquisite little house, on the river, of Professor and Mrs. Raymond Smith, Americans who both teach at the University of Windsor. There's peacefully enveloping snow on the ground all around us, Detroit is in front of you but looks far away, and there's a Mozart symphony on the hi-fi just behind the sofa where Mrs. Smith—Joyce Carol Oates—is enduring the interview.

Obviously the Mozart is a help to a very private person who gamely responds to every question put to her, but who volunteers nothing—not even a smile. She sits beside me on the sofa, taking me in with those extraordinary dark eyes that have been described as "burning in a dove's face." In her photographs ("I take terrible pictures, don't I?" she says in her schoolgirl voice) those eyes seem almost too large to be natural. But when you finally see her, you realize that she just freezes up before a camera. Her eyes seem friendly enough, are as inquisitive as the rest of her, and just as timid.

She has not been easy to get hold of; no one I know has even met her! And now that I have jetted to Detroit this Sunday morning, taxied across the International Bridge at Windsor, and am finally sitting with her in her pretty, proper little house, but listening to her with some difficulty through the Mozart, I realize to my dismay that we are soon going to exhaust all biographical items relating to Joyce Carol Oates, and that I will have no excuse not to return to New York this very afternoon.

The problem is not only that she is shy, doesn't drink or smoke, has no small talk, no jokes, no anecdotes, no gossip, no malice, no verbal embroidery of the slightest kind, and is as solemn as a graduate student taking an oral examination, but also that we are free-associating questions and answers so fast that I am rapidly making my way through whatever she *will* talk about. We are getting through this a mile a minute, and while this confirms the sense I get from her fiction of an extraordinary and even tumultuous amount of purely mental existence locked up behind that schoolgirl face, I didn't expect this much of a rush. I had rather looked forward to a leisurely look-around at Windsor, at the university where she is associate professor of English, at "Canada" even if it does look straight at Detroit. But Joyce Carol Oates is shy, *very* reserved, and moves as fast as a writer has to; she also says things like, "I'm not very interesting," "I'm not much," "I'm really not very ambitious." *Herself* is not a big issue with her. She is the most fortunate of writers: she has the instinctive self-confidence of a writer who has been writing stories since she was a child, but no ego, no sense that Joyce Carol Oates is important. In fact, Joyce Carol Oates is not exactly here. When I asked her about her daily routine, what she would do this Sunday, she said with some wonder at my question: "Why, write a story. I have several in my head just now." "And when will you finish it?" "Why, tomorrow morning." She'd also cook dinner. "I do enjoy cooking. Doesn't every woman?"

At thirty-three she looks and sounds like an altogether demure, old-fashioned, altogether proper student intellectual from another generation (or another country) who is dying to get back to her books. Though she is obviously startled by all the attention she has been getting lately, and is absurdly respectful to the middle-aged critic trying to draw her out, the extraordinary *amount* of mental life in her fascinates me. All sorts of filaments are hanging in the air, suggestions for innumerable stories, people, relationships. She obviously can't wait to get back to her desk.

So talking to her everything goes fast-fast-fast—like Oates knocking out one story after another on her electric typewriter. Joyce Carol Oates is a square, a lovely schoolmarm, but her life is in her head; her life is all the stories she carries in her head. And when I say "carry," I do not mean that she is plotting a story there, thinking it out, "working it over," as writers say, against the day when they finally get down to the heart-crushing business of *writing* it, as writers do, with many cigarettes, many cups of coffee, many prayers, shrieks of despair, imprecations, and curses against fate. *Dollars damn me,* said poor old Herman Melville. *Though I wrote the gospels in this century I should die in the gutter.* Poor old Joseph Conrad had positively to be roped into his chair. *Every morning, when I can't put it off any longer,* said a poor old writer of my acquaintance, *I feel I am on trial for my life and will definitely not be acquitted.*

This is not the case with not-poor, not-old Joyce Carol Oates. She writes, she is said to write, the way Mozart wrote down the score already written out in his head. Mozart was just a secretary! And Joyce Carol Oates, who will begin a story on Sunday and finish it on Monday, has four—or is it ten?—stories in her mind just now. Her latest novel (at the time this is written), *them* (1969), was her fourth published novel in the past seven years, during which she also published three collections of short stories; had two plays produced off-Broadway; finished a fifth novel, a book of poems (*Anonymous Sins*), a book on tragedy, and many short essays and reviews. She even has two completed novels in manuscript that she will "probably" not publish, for they may get in the way of the new novels she is planning to write. In the same soft, matter-of-fact, young-girl voice in which she expresses some wonder at the profusion of manuscript in her house (she's had to move some of it to her university office), she says very quietly, without boasting, without any feeling of strangeness, that she's also written stories "taking off" from actual stories by Chekhov and Joyce, and one "taking off" from Thoreau. It is called "Where I Lived and What I Lived For."

In New York, where writers talk about "Oates" without knowledge and without mercy, it is reported that her agent jokingly complained once that as soon as one story went out to a magazine, another came in, thus producing a happy and profitable glut on the literary marketplace. Obviously Joyce Carol Oates leads an altogether austere, hardworking existence straight out of the hard-pressed Thirties in which she was born—a period that haunts her as the great example of the unrelieved social crisis which is her image of America, and which recurs in her novels *A Garden of Earthly Delights* and *them.*

She comes from that colorless, often frozen and inhospitable lonely country in western New York, outside of Lockport, where her father is a tool-and-die designer. It was only with a New York State Regents' Scholarship and a scholarship from Syracuse University that she was able to go to college. Her frugality, simplicity, and even academic solemnity are what you would expect of a scholarship girl whose father is a blue-collar worker, belongs to the United Automobile Workers, and whose family contains recent immigrant strains in addition to the English "Oates" line. She has a Catholic background. She is going to Europe for the very first time this summer. Even her not smoking and drinking, her partiality to soda pop, her belief in the classroom, remind me of the simpler ideals and routines of working-class families during the Thirties. Her biography on book jackets reads like an application for a job:

> . . . received her elementary education in a one-room schoolhouse and then attended city junior and senior high schools . . . majored in English and minored in philosophy . . . class valedictorian . . . Phi Beta Kappa . . . on a fellowship from the University of Wisconsin she earned her master's degree in English . . . at Wisconsin she met her future husband, Raymond Smith, who is a specialist in eighteenth-century literature . . . Miss Oates's love for writing is almost as old as she is. . . .

Since she writes so easily, she probably has more time for reading than many writers do ("I'm just beginning to read D. H. Lawrence!"), even though she has a full teaching schedule and is obviously a dedicated teacher. "I have three geniuses in my writing class this term." She likes every writer you ask her about. Sitting with her, talking to her rush-rush-rush, seeking out a young woman who will not be sought out, I nevertheless find myself happily looking at and listening to her unbelievable "old-fashionedness." Some of her expressions come straight out of the school-room of *my* youth: "And when I have written my story, I copy it out *on good paper.*" Good paper! This is the way good little girls and boys in public school talked in 1929, before Joyce Carol Oates was born!

But perhaps she isn't a good little girl? Though she has so little vanity that you might think writing is her hobby, I am fascinated by the intense dislike she arouses—perhaps especially among women writers, who would like to put her down as a freak. One reviewer pointedly asked her to stop writing. Another, in a general attack called "Violence in the Head," complained of the story "What Death With Love Should Have To Do" (in the collection *Upon the Sweeping Flood*): "The plot crystallizes the motif of sex and death, a sort of lumpen *Liebestod,* that reappears in the novels. There is an authentic feeling in these stories," wrote Elizabeth Dalton, "for the physical ambience of poverty, for the grease stains, the stale smells, the small decorative objects of plastic. What seems less authentic, however, is the violence itself and the rather programmatic way it is used to resolve every situation. . . ." Miss Dalton said of the first novel, *With Shuddering Fall:* "Through the transparent implausibility of the plot there looms a sado-masochistic fantasy which endows the heroine with tremendous power." She complained of *them:* "One reason for the oddly blank effect of all the horror is the lack of structure and internal impetus in the narrative. Events do not build toward a climax, or accumulate tension and meaning, but seem simply to happen in the random and insignificant way of real life." Another woman writer complained that "Oates is entirely undramatic. Dullsville."

These complaints come more often than not from women, I believe, because Joyce Carol Oates is, more than most women writers, entirely open to *social* turmoil, to social havoc and turbulence, to the frighteningly undirected and misapplied force of an American powerhouse like Detroit. It is rare to find a woman writer so externally unconcerned with form. After teaching at the University of Detroit from 1962 to 1967, she remarked that Detroit is a city "so transparent, you can hear it ticking." When publishing *them* (which deals with the 1967 eruption of Detroit's blacks) she described Detroit as "all melodrama." She has an instinct for the social menace packed up in Detroit, waiting to explode, that at the end of the nineteenth century Dreiser felt about Chicago and Stephen Crane about New York. The sheer rich chaos of American life, to say nothing of its staggering armies of poor, desperate, outraged, and by no means peaceful people, presses upon her; her fiction, Robert M. Adams has noticed, takes the form of "retrospective nightmare." What Elizabeth Dalton disapprovingly called "violence in the head" expresses, I suspect, Joyce Carol Oates' inability to blink social violence as the language in which a great many "lower class" Americans naturally deal with each other.

So a writer born in 1938 regularly "returns" to the 1930s in her work. *A Garden of Earthly Delights* begins with the birth on the highway of a migrant worker's child after the truck transporting the workers has been in a collision. I would guess that Joyce Carol Oates' constant sense of *Americans* in collision, not to overlook characters who are obsessed without being able to *talk* freely, perhaps rubs the wrong way critics who like events to "build toward a climax, or accumulate tension and meaning." Oates is unlike many women writers in her feeling for the pressure, mass, density of violent American experience not known to the professional middle class. Praising a little-known social novel by Harriette Arnow, *The Dollmaker,* Oates said:

> It seems to me that the greatest works of literature deal with the human soul caught in the stampede of time, unable to gauge the profundity of what passes over it, like the characters of Yeats who live through terrifying events but who cannot understand them; in this way history passes over most of us. Society is caught in a convulsion, whether of growth or of death, and ordinary people are destroyed. They do not, however, understand that they are "destroyed."

I do not know how applicable this is to *The Dollmaker,* a book I have not read. But this view of "literature" as silent tragedy is a most illuminating description of what interests Oates in fiction and of what she is trying to do in her novels. Her own characters seem to move through a world wholly physical in its detail, yet they touch us and frighten us like disembodied souls calling to us from another world; "they live through terrifying events but cannot understand them." This is what makes Oates a new element in our fiction, involuntarily disturbing. She does not understand why she is disturbing. She is "radical" not programmatically but in her sweetly brutal sense of what American experience is really like. She knows that while "history" is all we save from death, people caught up in the convulsion of society cannot see the meaning to their lives that history will impose. Life as we live it, trying to save ourselves as we go, is really images of other people; hence the many collisions in Oates' work, the couplings that are like collisions, the crash of people against metal and of metal with metal. As Faulkner said, "it's because so much happens. Too much happens." People are literally overpowered by their experience.

Oates is peculiarly and even painfully open to all this, selfless in her imagination, so possessed by other people that in an author's note to *them* she says of the student who became the "Maureen Wendall" of the novel, "Her various problems and complexities overwhelmed me. . . . My initial feeling about her life was, 'This must be fiction, this can't be real!' My more permanent feeling was, 'This is the only kind of fiction that is real.' " This capacity for becoming one's characters (Keats called

it "negative capability") makes Oates a sometimes impenetrably volumi-
nous historian of lives, lives, lives; you feel that you are turning thousands of pages, that her world is as harshly overpopulated as the subway,
that you cannot distinguish the individual sounds within this clamor of
existence.

On the other hand, much contemporary fiction by Americans, women
and men, is not only peculiarly personal, moodily self-assertive, but dominated by a social anxiety that mistakenly traces itself to personal instability.
There are "Danger" signs now posted around every personal landscape.
Much of contemporary American fiction is based not only on the amaz-
ingly expansive sense of self that is the privilege of middle-class society
—"I" means movement, money, the ability to take a chance—but *personal*
vulnerability, the risk we take every day in being exposed, totally, to the
destructiveness of our own power.

The middle-class American, traditionally expansive in his estimate of
life, now feels peculiarly threatened by "history." He is living a life that
is too exceptional to be secure. This expresses itself less as open social
conflict than as individual anxiety; but the anxiety is real enough, and
shows itself in the typically American rhetoric of bitterness—to have
moved up so far, yet no longer to feel safe in anything! This is why so
many women writers now express perfectly the American complaint that
the self, never before so aware of its wants and possibilities, has never
felt so betrayed. Women writers are now the spokesmen for the frustration of the educated, professional middle class.

Oates is feminine all right, and a woman writer whose sensibility can
sometimes detour you through empty country. Her titles—*With Shuddering Fall, By the North Gate, Upon the Sweeping Flood, A Garden of
Earthly Delights, The Wheel of Love*—often taken from English Renaissance poems, are almost comically inappropriate to what she writes about.
She once told an interviewer from *Cosmopolitan* that she is always writing about love. "The emotion of love, probably that's the essence of what
I'm writing about, and it takes many different forms, many different social
levels. . . . I think I write about love in an unconscious way. I look back
upon the novels I've written, and I say, yes, this was my subject. But at
the time I'm writing I'm not really conscious of that. I'm writing about a
certain person who does this and that and comes to a certain end."

What she means by love, you notice, is an attraction of person to
person so violent that it expresses itself as obsession and takes on the
quality of fatality; the emotions of her characters are stark physical truths,
like the strength or weakness of one's body. But she herself is the most
intensely unyielding lover in her books, as witness the force with which
she follows so many people through every trace of their feeling, thinking,
moving. She is herself obsessive in her patience with the sheer factuality
of human existence. This evident love for the "scene" we Americans
make, for the incredible profusion of life in America, also troubles Joyce
Carol Oates, I would guess. Every writer knows himself to be a little

crazy, but her feeling of her own absurdity is probably intensified by
the dreamlike ease with which her works are produced. It must indeed
trouble her that this looks like glibness, when in point of fact her dogged
feeling that she writes out of love is based on the fact that she is utterly
hypnotized, positively drugged, by other people's experiences. The social
violence so marked in her work is like the sheer density of her detail—
this and this and this is what is happening to people. She is attached to
life by well-founded apprehensions that nothing lasts, nothing is safe,
nothing is all around us. In *them,* the best of her novels, Maureen
Wendall thinks:

> Maybe the book with her money in it, and the money so greedily saved,
> and the idea of the money, maybe these things weren't real either. What
> would happen if everything broke into pieces? It was queer how you
> felt, instinctively, that a certain space of time was real and not a dream,
> and you gave your life to it, all your energy and faith, believing it to be
> real. But how could you tell what would last and what wouldn't?
> Marriages ended. Love ended. Money could be stolen, found out and
> taken . . . or it might disappear by itself, like that secretary's notebook.
> Objects disappeared, slipped through cracks, devoured, kicked aside,
> knocked under the bed or into the trash, lost. . . . Her clearest memory
> of the men she'd been with was their moving away from her. They
> were all body then, completed.

The details in Oates' fiction follow each other with a humble truth-
fulness that makes you wonder where she is taking you, that is sometimes
truly disorienting, for she is all attention to the unconscious reactions of
her characters. She needs a lot of space, which is why her short stories
tend to read like scenarios for novels. The amount of concentration this
involves is certainly very singular, and one can well understand the vulnerability, the "reedlike thinness," the face and body tense with listening
that her appearance gives off. My deepest feeling about her is that her
mind is unbelievably crowded with psychic existences, with such a mass
of stories that she lives by being wholly submissive to "them," the others.
She is too burdened by some mysterious clamor to *want* to be an artist,
to make the right and well-fitting structure. "The greatest realities," she
has said, "are physical and economic; all the subtleties of life come afterward. Intellectuals have forgotten, or else they never understood, how
difficult it is to make one's way up from a low economic level, to assert
one's will in a great crude way. It's so difficult. You have to go through
it. You have to be poor."

Yet admiring her sense of reality, so unpresuming, honest, and truly
exceptional, I have to add that the problem of dealing with Oates is that
many of the things she has written are not artistically ambitious enough.
They seem written to relieve her mind of the people who haunt it, not
to create something that will live. So much documentation of the suddenly
frightening American situation is indeed a problem in our fiction just

now; the age of high and proud art has yielded to the climate of crisis. Oates' many stories resemble a card index of situations; they are not the deeply plotted stories that we return to as perfect little dramas; her novels, though they involve the reader because of the author's intense connection with her material, tend, as incident, to fade out of our minds. Too much happens. Indeed, hers are altogether strange books, haunting rather than "successful," because the mind behind them is primarily concerned with a kind of Darwinian struggle for existence between minds, with the truth of the universal human struggle. We miss the perfectly suggestive shapes that modern art and fiction have taught us to venerate. Oates is perhaps a Cassandra bewitched by her private oracle. But it is not disaster that is most on her mind; it is, rather, the recognition of each person as the center of the coming disturbance. And this disturbance, as Pascal said of divinity, has its center everywhere and its circumference nowhere.

So her characters are opaque, ungiving, uncharming; they have the taciturn qualities that come with the kind of people they are—heavy, hallucinated, outside the chatty middle class. Society speaks in them, but *they* are not articulate. They do not yet feel themselves to be emancipated persons. They are caught up in the social convulsion and move unheedingly, compulsively, blindly, through the paces assigned to them by the power god.

That is exactly what Oates' work expresses just now: a sense that American life is taking some of us by the throat. "Too much" is happening: many will disappear. Above all, and most ominously, hers is a world in which our own people, and not just peasants in Vietnam, get "wasted." There is a constant sense of drift, deterioration, the end of things, that contrasts violently with the era of "high art" and the once-fond belief in immortality through art. Oates is someone plainly caught up in this "avalanche" of time.

HAROLD CLURMAN

Reflections on Movies

It is widely held that movies nowadays are much more interesting than the theater. Arithmetically speaking, it is a fact. It should be immediately admitted that a moderately entertaining film is much more attractive than an indifferent play.

The reason for this is simple enough: there are the *pictures.* Most films today are admirably photographed. The pictures' locales are diverse, often exotically fascinating, bold in the maneuvers of their execution. The faces and bodies we see are, with the cameraman's aid, more sensuously gratifying than those beheld at present on the stage. Physical beauty, which should be one of the theater's lures, is now sadly lacking.

While the theater for centuries has been taken as an adjunct of literature, its very name derives from the Greek "theatron," which connotes seeing. In our country at least, the theater has become visually impoverished as well as verbally depleted.

Drama signifies action. In this respect also, the theater has become poor. It is generally deficient in movement. By their very nature, films, even if we think of them only in regard to editing, are all movement. In pictures we are present at the accidents of daily living, the disasters of war, the upheaval and wreckage of nature. Movies act directly on our senses. Because of all this they "grab" us more readily than any other art.

Have I, who began my playgoing career at the age of seven and spent over forty-five years of my professional life in the theater, then turned movie buff? Have I lost my appetite for stage spectacles? The debate over or contrast between the two media is specious . . . I have been going to the movies since the days of Bronco Billy Westerns. I did not give them much thought then, I just went. It never occurred to me, later on, to engage in any argument over the comparative merits of theater and cinema. Such discussion is usually more a matter of pragmatic or commercial than of aesthetic concern. No art replaces another. My addiction to the theater and my growing interest in the movies have never interfered with my reading of poetry and novels, my love of the dance, my attentiveness to painting and sculpture, my enjoyment of old and new music.

Films are a new and exciting mode of expression. They do not, I repeat, render any other medium, however ancient or neglected, obsolete. What we are called upon to enjoy and evaluate in all the arts is the weight and quality of what they express.

REFLECTIONS ON MOVIES By Harold Clurman. Copyright © 1971, by Minneapolis Star and Tribune Co., Inc. Reprinted from the May 1971 issue of *Harper's Magazine* by permission of the author.

The film, I have always believed, is an essentially silent medium. I found myself disturbed at first by the third dimension of speech which intruded on the two dimensionality of the screen image. I held John Ford's *The Informer* in special esteem because he used so little dialogue. (I can remember only two or three lines of the spoken text.) But we have talkies and screenwriters now, and they have added a great deal to the scope of the cinematic form.

Another addition to film vocabulary is color. Its employment has become virtually mandatory not only because of the public's taste for it, but because of the TV companies' insistence upon it. Still, I cannot help but feel that in this way many pictures lose something of their truth. This is a paradox because we do perceive objects in a variety of shades. There are certain films the effects of which are thus enhanced. But the tints employed in most films are more pigment than true color. Faces are too often drenched in an intensity of hue which makes them look glazed in a bath of cosmetics, as if they were on sale.

Many scenes photographed on big-city locations (including the slums) become glamorized to the detriment of the film's artistic intention. Paris in René Clair's *Sous les Toits de Paris* or Agnès Varda's *Cleo from 5 to 7* appears more truly itself than do the usual film images of that town which look like ads for travel agencies. One could hardly believe in the wretched garishness of the dance hall in *They Shoot Horses, Don't They?* because of the chromatic lushness of the photography.

It is possible that, in time, greater delicacy in this regard may be achieved. In any case, except for travelogue enchantment, we have more or less ceased to notice color in films: it is just there. The subliminal effect of its use is to make the world appear opulent, which is perhaps a solace for a fatigued population.

I am now chiefly concerned with the intrinsic content to be found in the films seen in the past two or three years. As I choose only those recommended by people I respect, I can honestly state that I have had a pleasant time at most of them. If I enjoy fifteen or twenty minutes of any film, because of a sequence made exhilarating through an actor's personality, interest in the subject matter, or directorial ingenuity, I do not feel myself cheated.

Though it is entirely proper to speak of the art of films, I find very little art in films except when artists make them—and they are exceedingly rare. I view most films—especially the American—as *documentaries*. They tell us more of the time and place in which we dwell than any of the other media. As fiction, drama, or art, they lie. They are primarily designed as diversions, games, toys; yet they are willy-nilly full of instruction. The response they elicit from their vast audiences is as much part of their message as their material—often more telling than volumes of statistics. Thus, no matter how frivolous they may be, I take them seriously.

Cultured folk, when I began seeing movies, held them in contempt. This was so for many years. Not only were movies primitive in technique, they were also paltry in content. They were kid stuff and as such may have done more harm than good. Even when they became more sophisticated, educated people rarely regarded them worth adult consideration. The big studios made them conform strictly to the myth of America as the land of the pure, the brave, the just, and above all, the happy. There was no ill that our benevolence could not remedy. Love conquered.

All this has changed in the past fifteen years. The increasing interest in foreign pictures plus the breakdown of the old Hollywood system— the dissolution of the monopoly by which producers controlled the industry through ownership of the movie houses—the ensuing financial panic, forced the remaining film entrepreneurs to meet the challenge from Europe and that of the ever increasing number of independent filmmakers and theater proprietors. At last freedom was attained. No holds are now barred. Everything may be shown or said. Should the new films be deemed too licentious, the release may be marked R (restricted) as a warning to parents and a caution to the squeamish.

This newfound freedom has, in my view, opened the way to a new sort of falsity, a fresh factitiousness, a special type of opportunism more dangerous, though more masked, than the old. There is no less distortion and sentimentality in today's daring films than there was when the heinous movie moguls reigned. While the sweet and soupy product of former days was debasing through its avoidance of real issues and facts, the recent spate of knock'em dead or gut movies blows our brains and hearts through benumbing sensationalism. To expose vice and corruption as a spectacle for fun, no matter how well decked out in psychoanalytic hearsay and radical palaver, is just as corrosive of sensibility and intelligence as the indulgence in vacuous daydreams of well-being.

Stag films have become superfluous. Ever since *Hiroshima, Mon Amour,* scenes of nude bodies in tight embrace followed by explicit images of sexual activity have become almost obligatory as emblems of filmic emancipation. But this is a minor matter. The erotic has always occupied an important place in the world's treasury of the arts. There are masterpieces of pornography. I am always gratified by the sight of a beautiful nude body—though such sights are vouchsafed us under much more favorable conditions elsewhere. The issue now is what role such images play in the context of the complete picture.

I do not refer to films primarily intended to arouse desire or to shock or to serve as a come-on to the prurient, although such purposes are by no means overlooked by the film's purveyors. I speak of so-called socially significant films, often praised by film critics in good standing.

Take, for example, *Getting Straight.* It is a picture about the formal education of youth, in other words, about college life. Youth is represented in this movie by a great lummox (supposedly very bright) in the shape of a popular favorite, Elliott Gould, who is probably about thirty. He has great appeal because he is like "everybody": coarse in manner, somewhat thick-tongued in speech, generally crude and blunt. The fellow he plays—like presumably so many of the young—believes our educational institutions to be little more than factories for the production of degrees. (Some of them are just that.) He is, we are to assume, an advanced student, eager for knowledge. His problem is that the college doesn't provide it. What do we get to know of him?

Apparently he spends every night "sexualizing" with his girlfriend, a typical co-ed in the person of Candice Bergen. When he behaves boorishly, she forbids him her bed. This is too great a deprivation for him to bear. He immediately compensates for it by sleeping with a beauteous black girl who asks if he finds this novel experience especially pleasurable.

There are funny scenes—mostly caricatures—showing how dumb the academic doctors are, and there are others in which police brutality on an "epic" scale is photographed: half-measures never suffice in such pictures. Thus the film is not only topical but "revolutionary."

The principal characters in many of these films are shown to be "alienated" when they are not just morons. *Easy Rider,* made at a relatively low cost and so successful that it inspired a "trend" in the big studios, introduces us to several nonconformist youths: which of us is not sympathetic to their like? How do they use their liberty? To profit from their freedom they undertake to transport drugs from Mexico to California.

The best thing in the picture, apart from Jack Nicholson's performance as a drunken dude, is the sight of the landscape. Nicholson is beaten to death because he taunts some red-necks who resent the free life of the long-haired youths. Later the two boys are wantonly shot down by passing red-necks for no reason except that they are hippies. There is a moral to all this: one of the boys, before his death, murmurs "We blew it." In other words, he now realizes that he and his buddy muffed their chance at a good life. Nevertheless they are presented to us as folk heroes of a sort.

The filmmakers are always on the side of the angels. In the supposedly satiric *Bob & Carol & Ted & Alice,* four nitwits experiment in wife-swapping. But they can't make it after all. They are basically "beautiful people." Aside from a few hilarious bits (one of them in a psychoanalyst's office), the picture is a setup for jokes about permissiveness in promiscuity in which little else (children, work) comes into play. One might conclude, then, that this is a picture about sex, but it is really nothing of the sort. Sex is something more than a physical function. Emotions are taken as a matter of course, real sentiment is never suggested, except that the couples do not consummate their cross-copulation. Given the circumstances and the nature of these citizens, this is rather stupid of them.

One of the most engaging among recent films with some truly amusing scenes and several excellent performances is *Five Easy Pieces*. Its central figure is a man who might have been a musician (he was reared in a musical family) and, when we meet him, is a totally disoriented person. He is without any specific direction or impulse, except to drink, fornicate, and run away. He is loyal to pals and is capable of momentary affection but has no regard for women, though he makes passes at all within his reach. At best, he is sorry about his state. He is to be accepted as the maimed hero of our subculture. To see him in this light is surely to indulge in wishy-washiness, a widespread trait in a society in which an understanding of human frailty means to exonerate ourselves from all moral judgment.

There is considerable validity in the theme posited in *Joe*. Racists and reactionaries, the film implies, well-heeled businessmen as well as uncouth hardhats, lacking the sustenance of sound values, are, when balked, impelled toward murderousness. But the plot has it that a "respectable" commercial executive who earns $60,000 a year will go back to the squalid quarters of a vicious drug addict to pick up his daughter's things—she being the fellow's girlfriend—things which consist of a few odd and soiled rags. Here, in his fury at being scoffed at by the derelict youth, he knocks the boy's brains out. Skeptical of the picture's initial steps, we are led from one lurid improbability to another in support of a thesis based on a loosely held ideology which demands proof. Everything finally is made subservient to the fabrication of a bloodcurdling movie replete with thievery, sexual "orgy," drunkenness, playing with pot.

Minute clues reveal the meretriciousness of the whole. Bonnie and Clyde in the picture of that name are played by two spectacularly good-looking actors who needn't have gone hungry even in the darkest days of the Depression. Hollywood was prosperous then; they could have gotten jobs in the movies. More folk heroes? A jolly ballad? Seeing this film and several others less craftily made reminded me of the old cowboy song: "There was blood on the saddle, blood on the ground . . . blood all around." Blood? No, ketchup and Technicolor, as unbelievably fake as the vitals which, along with all manner of high jinks, are supposed to provide a sharply satiric comment in M*A*S*H, a movie practically everyone acclaims because we are all against war and especially ashamed of the Korean and Vietnam adventures, aren't we?

Everything in these films is spelled out. There is, for example, Clyde's impotence and his recovery from it through his loyal and gorgeous mate Bonnie-Dunaway. What a thrill in the mowing down of the two hapless marauders: the girl's body riddled with bullets bounces voluptuously from their impact. When that presumptuous idiot and distinguished novelist in *Diary of a Mad Housewife* disrobes Carrie Snodgress, we observe each separate article of her clothing slowly drop from her body. Then, as a clincher, we are favored in an isolated shot with an ample view of the actress's glowing bottom. If it hadn't actually been shown, we might not have known that she had one. There is more decency in the filth of *Trash*.

Is it really possible to give credence to the extremely pretty and healthy Jane Fonda as the haggard, half-starved, hopelessly beat victim of the dance marathon in *They Shoot Horses, Don't They?* followed by her inviting death at the hands of her sweet partner? For all the degradation through which her miserable life has dragged her, she cannot bear the thought that even such as he may have "deceived" her. Because of this, her contempt for life and love expresses itself by the exercise of fellatio on the master of the sordid ceremonies whose normal approach she refuses in horror with the fierce command, "Don't touch me!"

Our behavioristic flicks tend to assault: they conspire to kick the stuffings out of us. They are unabashed in the use of four-letter words— the more the merrier—though this will soon prove ineffective as an instrument of titillation. The earth shakes, the heavens howl, the beasts yowl and clamor, walls crack and crumble, the world's chaos is magnified tenfold. Calm is unknown, contemplation impossible. For the quiet and calm we find in the films of Bresson, Ozu, Bergman, Satyajit Ray, Olmi, the early Antonioni, Renoir, or the Fellini of *I Vitelloni*—the repose essential to perception—our big audiences have little patience. Truffaut's unemphatically tender *The Wild Child* is a flop. Attention to the little pleasures and the unexplosive dramas of daily life is ignored. The tumult of our civilization has become our films' drug on the market.

Sentimentality may be defined as the disproportion between the reality of feeling and the means employed to convey it. To present reality as a charnel house and a bordello for the sake of arousing superficial shock is as sentimental and as poisonously misleading as to jerk at our tear ducts on behalf of motherhood or the Stars and Stripes. Ugliness, like beauty, is in the eyes of the beholder. The ferocious realism of our tough new pictures is as bogus as the sweetness and light of the old.

No matter how savage their imagery or high-minded their ostensible purpose, most of the new filmmakers treat us as though we were morbidly spoiled children who will heed nothing unless whipped. Their protagonists are themselves nearly always infantile or persons of low-grade mentality. With a slight insinuation from sub-Freudian social psychologists we are, for instance, called upon to understand and therefore to care for and forgive the sadistic hustler of *Midnight Cowboy*. It may be argued against Eric Rohmer's *My Night at Maud's,* or his latest picture, *Claire's Knee,* that they are too verbose and thus insufficiently cinematic. But they are remarkable in one thing at least: they deal with grown-ups whose preoccupations reach beyond the realm of thugs or fatuous slobs.

The rediscovery of sex in recent films—sex without affection, love, or even joyous sensuality—is something more than mere exploitation: it is a sign that we are in doubt about everything else. These films possess one positive asset: they compel a realization that our values are not simply all in question, but that they have never previously been confirmed in us by profound experience or probing inner examination. We have ceased asking ourselves fundamental questions when we satisfy ourselves by pre-digested answers. These are supplied by "those who know," usually members of various Establishments—right and left—whom at the same time we profess to scorn. Those who shout the loudest are the only ones heard. We will not take pains with anything which demands protracted study, concentrated effort, time.

The great mechanism of our society, in which we jiggle and are flung about, wearies us. We do not in consequence demand privacy and peace of mind or socially useful action, but even more of the brutal batter-ing of body and spirit which is driving us senseless.

There is something to ponder on in *Gimme Shelter,* no matter how contrived it may be thought to be. The killers and the victim, lawyers, arrangers, impresarios, agents, publicity men, and crazed acolytes of the Rolling Stones *are* our neighbors and kindred. Little wonder, then, that we accept the roughhouse improvisations of *Husbands* as a huge joke or as a faithful picture of marriage and homelife in America today. Still, a little sober reflection should make us aware that even the stupid and stupefied, the crass and the cruel, the fools and the criminals, are some-thing more than what such films represent them to be.

We shall never be any wiser if we seriously believe that all the new pictures to which we are now asked to pay tribute are truly examples of films coming of age in a new realism. They are the product of gifted, well-intentioned craftsmen in the service of the same old profit-oriented movie industry they and we imagined had been destroyed and abandoned. In the toils of this Moloch, it is all but impossible to preserve genuine thoughtfulness, insight, stouthearted integrity. With the general accep-tance of the platitudinous notions that the modern world is nothing but a stinking stew, an acceptance which has become a complaisance (often disguised as a denunciatory judgment), most filmmakers with the backing of the corporate powers have been sucked into the surrounding bedlam. Their pictures are not antidotes to our diseases; they are both the symp-toms and among the most potent of their conveyors. Hence for me they are eloquent documents and documentaries of our time; they require scrupulous study. One should see them and see them again!

YEVGENY YEVTUSHENKO

Being Famous Isn't Pretty

In taking this line from Pasternak as my title, I've acted without arrogance or self-disparagement, a thing far worse than pride. Let me assure my readers of that. Not that in my poetic adolescence I didn't dream of fame. I did. Nor will I say that now when I write poetry or even this essay I'm indifferent to the opinion of my readers. That would also be a lie. But fame is a far from charming mistress. She demands endless gifts and tokens of affection; she gets hysterical, jealous; she makes me quarrel with my friends, kills my concentration, drags me off on senseless visits, threatens me with abandonment. Many envy me such a spectacular prize. If they lived with her a while they'd change their minds. But then, jealousy never admits to being itself. It hides behind its own suspicions: "What crooked route led that fellow to glory? After all, we're honest and yet, unknown."

And so, legends of suspicion arise with the myths of praise. And when you've heard enough of them about yourself, you're bound to lose your bearings and wonder fearfully who you really are. If you live under the magnifying glass of public curiosity, just as your every honest act seems heroic to some so your every weakness seems criminal to others. Even your honest acts come into question. Of course, where there's smoke there's fire, but the smoke of a myth can sometimes obscure the nature of the fire. Fame is the Medusa's head, horrid and hissing with the snakes of gossip. To look in her face is to turn to stone, even if they call the stone a monument. You need the trusty shield of Perseus to see a safe reflection of your fame. At the start of his journey an artist must struggle for fame; once it's been won, he must learn how to struggle with it.

When I read certain articles about myself in the West, I wonder who in the hell this damned "Y.Y." can be. A movie star, tanned by photographers' flashbulbs? A matador, teasing his red cape in the bull's snout of the age? A tightrope walker, toeing the slack wire between East and West? Or, as one of England's ex-angry-young-men, Kingsley Amis, hinted, an unofficial diplomat, performing certain secret missions for the Kremlin? A rebellious Stenka Razin,[1] as a laureate of the Goncourt Prize,

---

[1] Razin was a leader of a Cossack and peasant rebellion on Russia's southeastern frontier in the late 1660s. He was captured by Cossacks loyal to Moscow and, in 1671, tortured and executed in the capital.

BEING FAMOUS ISN'T PRETTY Translations copyright © 1971 by Doubleday & Company, Inc. From STOLEN APPLES by Yevgeny Yevtushenko. Reprinted by permission of the publisher. First published in *Harper's Magazine*, July 1971.

Armand Lanoux, once wrote? Or maybe a nice, inquisitive traveler, as the magazine *America,* distributed in the USSR, once had it, asking everyone to call him "just Zhenya." A Soviet Beatle? An export item, perhaps, like vodka or black caviar? A conformist masquerading as a champion of liberalization? A radical in moderate's clothing? Or are all these mere ingredients blended in the shaker of the age into a strange cocktail called Yevtushenko?

On the one hand, he's in the fight against anti-Semitism, bureaucratism, etc. You'd like to take the lanky Russian in your arms and whisper to him confidentially, "We're with you in your selfless struggle." On the other hand, he doesn't much care for Western society. In fact, he harshly indicts it for the war in Vietnam, the murders of Martin Luther King and the Kennedys, for bigotry, hypocrisy, and corruption. You get suspicious: if this Russian is really on the side of truth, an honest man in a totalitarian society, what's he doing out of jail? Why does he go abroad from time to time, and then unaccompanied by commissars? Isn't he perhaps a commissar himself?

An aerial diver in a suit, his luggage bulging with hidden microfilms, even went so far as to say that, according to information at his disposal, one out of every two Soviet writers abroad was an agent of the Secret Police, that if one of them traveled alone he was an agent for sure, and that someday Yevtushenko would have to render an account of the reports he wrote on returning home. In his haste he apparently forgot that somewhat earlier in his fascinating confession he admitted informing on that same Yevtushenko as a leader of an intelligentsia underground center. Amazing, isn't it, this charming little contradiction?

But the most amazing thing of all happened in 1967 in Santiago de Chile. There, on the day of my reading, two groups of young people organized demonstrations against me on two different squares. On one, the solemn "ultra-leftists" burned me in effigy as an American spy. On the other the "ultra-rightists" burned me as a Red spy. To be honest, I was pleasantly surprised to find these charming youths rating my services as high as those of some latter-day Mata Hari.

When in 1968 English students supported me as a candidate for the position of Oxford's Professor of Poetry, God! how the aforementioned Amis & Company put me to the knife, calling me a wily propagandist, an official mouthpiece of the Soviet government, and on and on. Again I was pleasantly surprised that my social standing in the USSR seemed so strong. And after all the noise about me as a political agent extraordinaire, there suddenly came the quiet voices of Arthur Miller and William Styron, both of them *obliged to announce that, in their opinion, I was an honest man.* And the voice of my translator, Robin Milner Holland, *compelled to explain that I was a poet,* and not something else.

Even in his own country people not too familiar with this strange fellow, this Yevtushenko, can be found. For the radicals I'm too moderate; for the liberals, too radical; for perfervid dogmatists, almost the devil himself. In a lamentably much-discussed novel, one writer, depicting a traitor to the Motherland, a fascist collaborator now hiding from retribution, even went so far as to put some of my verses on his lips. One poet in his time accused me of being unpatriotic. "What kind of Russian are you," he said, "when you've forgotten your own people?" They've called me a "singer of dirty bedsheets," a "poet of the mod set," and more. To lovers of the philosophical lyric I seem too simplistic; to lovers of the intimate lyric, too rational—a pamphleteer. And to others who interpret poetry only politically, too ambivalent.

Lovers of political poetry, incidentally, are themselves rather sharply split in two. The first group applauds all my lines that condemn Western society and praise the Motherland. "There, that's the way he should always write." But let one line about our ills drop from my pen and they're at me: "There he is, messing around in the wrong country again." They're a suspicious group. Even in my poems about other countries they detect hints directed at our own, and in poems about the pre-Revolutionary past, dangerous allusions to the present.

The second group is the opposite of the first. They take offense at political poems dealing, say, with Vietnam, or the glories of the Motherland, seeing in them no sincere movement of the soul but a political maneuver to gain the favor of those in power. Just as the first group, deaf to their neighber's groan behind the wall, listens only to the bombs in Vietnam, so the second thinks the problems of the world are nothing next to their aching corns. The second group wants only negative poems on domestic problems. Somehow they find it morally questionable to speak of the corruption of the Western world when in the Soviet Union the price of cognac is on the rise, the meat supply uncertain, and the stores, in general, unjust.

When, then, you ask, is Yevtushenko sincere? When writing of Vietnam or Babi Yar? There isn't much profit in defending yourself, but, alas, I must.

It's easy to forget the simple fact that a man can speak sincerely of both Vietnam and Babi Yar, and in both a major and a minor key. Art in general is higher than questions of "for" or "against" alone. Art is a rainbow broad enough even for black. But a rainbow stretched across two shores casts all its colors equally on each. It doesn't leave one side in bright light and the other in the dark.

Injustice is as widely traveled as justice, and a scoundrel with an American passport is no better than a louse with a Soviet one. As Mayakovsky[2] once said, "The widest choice of scoundrels roams through our land and about."

I know, of course, that this one world is really two, even, as they say, three, and tomorrow, maybe four. Still, I think our old, good woman

[2] Vladimir Mayakowski (1893–1930) Russian poet.

Earth, though torn by political conflict, is the only world we have and we're all her tenants, depending in one way or another on each other. A little-known Russian poet, Stefanovich, put it this way:

> All of us share one lot.
> Just sprain your ankle
> And instantly in Addis Ababa
> Someone shrieks in pain.

And so I write poems about Vietnam and Babi Yar and Kent University student Allison Krause and a Siberian concrete-pourer, Nyushka, and a general in the army of freedom, Pancho Villa, and my own mother, who lost her voice singing concerts in snowstorms on the front lines, and a Chilean prostitute who hung a portrait of Leo Tolstoy in her closet, and Sicilian women in black and young girls in white and my own beloved and my son and myself. I want to be a mail boat for everyone divided by the ice of estrangement, a craft before the coming of large navigation, moving through the drifting ice with letters and parcels.

Still, sometimes I deeply resent being discussed as a political personality and not as a poet, and having my poetry examined on the whole from one political standpoint or another. Of course, Heinrich Böll[3] was right when he said that everything published was already committed. Every writer is committed by his conscience and his talent, even if he declares himself "above the fray."

> It's a disgrace to be free of your age.
> A hundred times more shameful than to be its slave.

I don't want to be free from the struggle for freedom. But I do want to be free to determine the forms it will take. Although I once had the indiscretion to say that a poet in Russia is more than a poet, I've never pretended to be a political prophet. In politics I'm undoubtedly a dilettante, even though my loathing for professional politicking prompts me to think it will be a great day for mankind when its politics are in the hands of amateurs rather than professionals.

Compared to the refined, cold master Salieri, who "verified his harmonies with algebra," Mozart must have seemed a dilettante. But it was Mozart, and not Salieri, who advanced the development of the world's music. History flows to the laws of music, and the Mozarts of the world are her masters. Blok's[4] rallying call, "Listen to the music of the Revolution!" is eternal, for revolution is protean and, despite what pessimists may say, the revolution in human consciousness will never end.

You can wave art aside as a weapon in that revolution if you want; it's true, for all the beauty art creates, mankind wallows every day in the filth of its inhumanity. But I'm bold enough to believe that if there

---

[3] Heinrich Böll (b. 1917) German novelist and short-story writer.
[4] Alexander Blok (1880–1921) Russian poet.

is anything exalted in man, if the revolution in consciousness still goes on, by that much is mankind indebted to art.

In the long run I don't much care who picks me to pieces or how, or who puts me in what category. I know that I'm one of the workmen of art, that I toil in her hot, unhealthy shop, poetry, and that this is the meaning of my life. Politically untutored and forever concerned with those little things that so enrich our suffering lives with beauty, I've never formulated any new political concepts. I've only reminded people of the commonplaces of good and evil, justice and injustice. The myths about me spring, of course, not from my "renown" alone, but from my attempts to speak in the same language of justice and injustice, addressing two shores divided by conflict but, like mankind itself, at one in their meaning and destiny.

It does sound suspicious. I'm sometimes guilty of trying to grasp the ungraspable and, as a wise man once said, "When you try to embrace all mankind, you sometimes forget your wife." My strength perhaps, but also my failing, is a greediness for life. My fear of not expressing myself on some topic makes me express myself at times too superficially. Leaping like a seismograph to the quivers of Earth's core, I'm often deaf to the silence. In general, we the poets of the atomic age too often substitute nervousness for spirituality.

I may have won the ear of many nations, but it's a mixed blessing. Readers are too despotic. Once in love with a poet for something, they expect it to appear again and again, forever. They interpret any change in a poet's character, and consequently in his poetry, not as a normal development but as a retreat from principle. There aren't even two readers alike in the world, and if they number in the hundred thousands, how can you please them all? You shouldn't try. A writer who has won the public's interest is misguided if he thinks he'll be free in the end; he'll soon feel its spur and bridle on his flesh.

Not long ago a young teacher from Saratov came to me with this reproach: "All you do now is analyze and analyze," she said, "but you can't uplift the masses with analysis alone. They rally to calls and appeals."

When you're young it's easy enough to streak appeals across the sky like rockets. But as you get older you feel increasingly responsible for those traveling the road your rocket lights. What if you've led them wrong? You grow wary of making reckless appeals, and a sense of responsibility must be tempered above all with analysis and reflection. Relentless analysis alone, not childish shouting, embodies the true appeals.

Once someone lovingly retyped all eight volumes of my collected works as a birthday present. Full of anticipation and delight I lay down on the sofa to read. I was instantly aghast. The lines seemed so naïve and precocious, sometimes criminally so, and congested with slogans. It was too late to do anything. "The word's no sparrow; once it goes, it won't fly back." Since that time my relationship with paper has undergone considerable change. I've begun to fear her, although certainly not enough.

Before judging his age, a writer must find the courage to judge himself. Pushkin was strong enough not only to write poems for the overthrow of autocracy but to say of himself, "And reading my own life with loathing, I tremble and curse." You mustn't be misled by the sins your myth ascribes but look soberly through to the real failings beneath.

Clearly many of my poems have not withstood the test of time, but I secretly believe something of me will survive my stay on Earth. Something at least of my fits of spirit, I hope, even if screened by smoke, may influence the feelings of my descendants, restored to each other at last from the ice of estrangement. That done, it little matters if, hearing the velvety whistles of magnificent ships to come, they don't recall the hoarse voice of the mail boat.

No one can foretell the outcome of our lives. What then must we do?

> Live, and by the smallest measure
> Never step back from oneself,
> But be alive, fully alive,
> Alive and only, to the end.

—*B. Pasternak*

IRVIN STOCK

Black Literature, Relevance, and the New Irrationality

I teach English at an American university, and nowadays—this has, of course, become a familiar plaint—the world I work in is growing increasingly irrational. And it is growing self-righteous about it, too, as if reasoning were for bad guys. Not from students alone, but from colleagues and their articles and books has been coming lately, under the guise of protest against social injustice, a stream of attacks on the human mind—on its freedom, its variousness, its complexity. In a number of highfalutin ways, we are being told that the intellectual life is a battle of self-interest (or class interest or race interest), in which art,

BLACK LITERATURE, RELEVANCE, AND THE NEW IRRATIONALITY By Irvin Stock. From *Change Magazine*, March–April 1971. Reprinted by permission of *Change Magazine* and the author.

reason, principles, intellectual techniques and safeguards are mere ration-
alizations for the brute inner grunt which means "I want it so" or "I
don't want it so," and men can hope to communicate only with those who
are already grunting in unison with them.

Now to anyone who remembers how, in certain quarters, Stalinism
degraded the intellectual life of the thirties such notions—and the answer
they require—are not new. Still, here they are again, and again they have
to be answered. Not only does a generation exist for whom the thirties
are dim or romanticised ancient history; the view of mind they represent
is perennially persuasive, like any half-truth that supports "good" against
"evil." And it seems to me that the answer, as often in the past, must
show both where they are false and where they are true.

The current attack on mind in the universities takes three main forms:
the ethnic approach to literature, the demand for "relevance," and the
denial of the possibility of objectivity. Here, to show exactly what has to
be dealt with, are some examples of each.

A talented black novelist recently told me that our apparent communication was an illusion. The only reality in our relationship was that he
was a victim of colonialism and I was a member of the class of colonialists.
(He, my well-paid colleague, whose novels clearly belong to the Western
tradition of realism; and I, the son of poor Jews who had fled their own
oppressors and slaved to put me through college.) Then, the Afro-American Society of a university sent a memo to its English Department not
long ago explaining that no white teacher should ever be permitted to
teach black literature "because no person has the ability to stand outside
his own conditioning." To communicate with black men at all, the white
man must "recognize that he comes to black literature as an alien and
ultimately as an enemy." (A black teacher of Shakespeare was alarmed
by such "racism" into thoughts of leaving the university. It seemed to
imply no Negro could teach Shakespeare.) This position is carried into
esthetic theory by black Professor Addison Gayle, Jr. In his book *The
Black Situation* we read, "Young black writers for whom the city is
home . . . accept the basic premises of Black Nationalism—that black
people are different from other Americans—and . . . that such differences mandate a different literature." Further: "The theory of the master-
piece," that is, the idea that literature has standards of excellence and
truth not identical with its usefulness to any group ". . . was put forth
by men who sought to erect a barrier between themselves and other
men. . . . However, the black writer can never accept elitism, or a
barrier which separates him from other black men. . . . He replaces the
formula 'art for art's sake' . . . with the humane formula 'art for the
peoples' sake.' "

Nor do such notions come only from black nationalists. The white
critic Richard Gilman, in his book *The Confusion of Realms,* declares
that whites have no right to judge books like Malcolm X's *Autobiography* or Cleaver's *Soul on Ice* because "we whites . . . are, vis-à-vis the

blacks, the imperialists. This is why our vocabularies of rational discourse are so different from black Americans' (when a subject people finds its voice at last, it has to be different from its masters'). The old Mediterranean values—the belief in the sanctity of the individual soul, the importance of logical clarity, brotherhood, reason as arbiter, political order, community—are dead as *useful* frames of reference or pertinent guides to procedure."

As for the current idea of "relevance," we are helped to understand this by an article in *Change,* May-June, 1970, by Professor Louis Kampf of M.I.T. Kampf says he felt "uneasy" about his work on Pope when he realized that, though himself "a socialist, I was taking a friend of [Tory] Lord Bolingbroke as my model." After calling literature at present "a weapon in the hands of imperialism" ("Whom did the values represented by Homer's Achilles serve? . . . Is the counterrevolutionary acceptance of fate in tragedy something we are supposed to teach as a received value?"), he tells us, with, I suppose, commendable candor, how boring the "Western masterpieces" have become in his own classes. His class in Proust, for instance, took on a little life only after he had transferred it to the M.I.T. student center, which had become a sanctuary for draft resisters. But not enough life, apparently, for he ends the anecdote by doubting that he will teach Proust again. Even more odd, he reports that "after some months of unexciting classes" he and his students woke up only when a young man in one class, in order to make some personal contact with a group of students who were shouting slogans, undressed and then resumed his seat naked. General discussion continued until "a female student shouted, 'Bullshit. There is a naked man sitting next to me. We're all thinking of him, yet no one's saying a word.' So for the next two hours we discussed why he had taken off his clothes, and how that related to our being in class and to the books we were reading. It was the only lively discussion we had all semester." Of course, that he has had some boring classes is not especially to his discredit. What teacher hasn't? The significant thing is where he places the blame.

And in *College English,* March, 1970, Stanford Professor Bruce Franklin goes a bit further. In his opinion, "the scholar-critic-professor of literature" is "an ignorant, self-deceived parasite" who thinks "bourgeois culture . . . superior to proletarian culture" because in him "bourgeois criteria are completely internalized" by graduate school indoctrination. This parasite regards as "beyond the pale" such works as "folk-songs, mysteries, westerns, science fiction . . . the most influential and the most widely controversial American poet—Bob Dylan," to say nothing of the writings of Mao, "who tells [the people] that they are the real heroes of history, and that it's right to rebel because the earth belongs to the people." Instead, he makes them read T.S. Eliot, "who tells them that they are trash stuffed with straw, or Jonathan

Swift, who tells them that they are shit-smeared monkeys." (Could so perfect an echo of old-time Stalinism be a "put-on"? No matter. We hear the like uttered seriously again all around us.)

Finally, there is the non-literary version of all this, the recent announcements that "objectivity" in history or sociology or even science is an illusion accepted only by the naive or the unscrupulous. Here is Professor Martin Nicolaus, of the Sociology Liberation Group, "telling it like it is" at a Plenary Session of the American Sociological Association in Boston, on August 26, 1968. (His talk is reprinted in *The American Sociologist* of May, 1969.)

> This assembly . . . is a conclave of high and low priests, scribes, intellectual valets, and their innocent victims, engaged in the mutual affirmation of a falsehood, in common consecration of a myth. Sociology is not now and never has been any kind of objective seeking out of social truth or reality. Historically, the profession is an outgrowth of nineteenth-century European traditionalism and conservatism, wedded to twentieth-century corporation liberalism. . . . Sociologists stand guard over the garrison and report to its masters on the movements of the occupied populace.

And again I can show how such stuff filters down to daily university life by quoting from a memo. This one was written by several younger university teachers to "expose" a chairman who had voted against the reappointment of a new teacher he claimed was incompetent. Their charge is that he voted as he did because the teacher in question was an admitted Communist, that it was a "political firing." Not that the chairman knew what he was doing. Rather, like a novelist being seen through by a certain kind of Marxist critic, he was compelled by determining factors of which he was unaware, though his young critics could see them plain.

> Professor ———— contends that his decision to fire ———— was taken solely for professional reasons. In one sense, this is clearly true. We doubt that he deliberately set out to purge the ———— Department of Communists. Nevertheless, we believe that the decision was a political act, a characteristic expression of the liberal point of view prevalent in American universities and in the society as a whole. Given this orientation, ———— was able to arrive at what he felt was an academic evaluation without understanding its fundamentally political nature.

Interestingly enough, while this inability to be objective is injustice in the liberal, it is virtue in the Marxist. For, to the charge that the teacher had imposed an a priori ideological line on the material studied in class, the memo replies, "how can a Marxist scholar, who proceeds systematically from a set of basic assumptions about society, politics, and history, avoid the charge of 'imposing a priori a particular ideological line' on the material in question? How can a scholar who adopts a thoroughly critical view of American society escape the allegation that his perspective is 'closed,' in other words, that he is hopelessly biased?"

Now, if the mind were so reliably dominated by class or race or ideology, it would be hard to understand why liberals, Communists, white men, black men differ among themselves. (Even militant black men—James Baldwin, in spite of the sacrifice of his talent he has made to the cause of black rebellion, is insultingly rejected by Eldridge Cleaver.) The fact is, of course, the automatic recoil of some of us from such views results from our sense that they are distorting the fundamental realities on which the intellectual life is based. It's true, these people tend to make brief parenthetical bows in their direction—for example, that Afro-American Society memo, amid its assertions of white incapacity to understand black writing, actually declares, "We do not intend to argue against the substantial universality of all good literature." But, as we see, "taking for granted" such realities often means, in practice, not only misunderstanding but even contradicting them. Or else it turns out that they are not pertinent *in the present crisis.* Needless to say, the postponing of intellectual—and moral—scrupulousness to a time more convenient is an old story. The time is rarely convenient for those who are avid for chic or simple solutions to complex problems.

The chief error of people like those I've quoted is that they deny to the human mind the autonomy which, in spite of "conditioning," it never ceases to possess. While in the grip of their theories, they don't actually listen to what novelists (or sociologists or teachers) have to say. Instead they eavesdrop on them for a few easily identifiable clues to "real" motives and meanings which are presumed to be consciously or unconsciously concealed. And what is worse, they eavesdrop not in search of the truth, but only to confirm certain theories of what a work *must* be about—because of its author's conditioning—which they had arrived at before looking at it.

Their authorization for assuming such breathtaking superiority to the whole world of gifted people comes first from a simplified idea of science in general (all men are "determined," all acts and thoughts have prior "causes"); and then, in particular, from the guides presumed to be given to those causes by Marx (economic or class interest is the determinant) or Freud (sexual trauma is the determinant) or lately Fanon (men's relation to colonial power is the determinant—a nationalist adaptation of Marx). Armed with those guides, any second-rate would-be critic can dispense with the job of trying to understand the terms and structures of meaning which the writer himself has worked out to express his ideas or to body forth his vision. Brushing these aside, he notes the clues, he applies his ready-made system of interpretation, and he *knows.*

The error here is not in assuming the mind is "determined," but in assuming we can know what determines it and where it must come out. The truth is, of course, the human mind, though no more unconditioned than anything else in the universe, is free at least from the possibility of ever being understood as science understands the motions of physical bodies, understood so as to be predictable. This for two reasons that ought to be obvious, yet somehow keep being forgotten. First, because of the multiplicity, variety, and subtlety of its determining stimuli. Do you think you know what must shape the feelings and ideas of all American Negroes, and that you are entitled to speak of "the" black man and how he must differ from "the" white? Here is a comment on such presumption from Albert Murray, a black critic whose new book *The Omni-Americans* ranks with Ellison's *Shadow and Act* in its liberating common sense on the subject of race and culture. He is responding to Gordon Parks' account of his own life as conditioned by his black background.

> Yes. *Of course,* his actions are conditioned by the experience of his U.S. Negro background. What the hell else he going to operate out of? . . . [But] the background experience of U.S. Negroes is a rich source of many things . . . [not only] frustration and crime, degradation, emasculation, and self-hatred . . . [which may result from] all human circumstances. . . . Nobody who is really and truly interested in the perpetually fascinating mystery of human motive and conduct is ever likely to ignore the fact that many of the non-Negroes who infest Greenwich Village, the Bowery, and the narcotic dens of the Upper West Side often came from a background of freedom and even wealth and power. . . . In spite of all the substandard test scores, anybody who assumes that the average white U.S. schoolboy is really closer to the classics . . . than the average U.S. Negro schoolboy is either talking about the relative percentage of literary snobs or is simply kidding himself. A white schoolboy may be persuaded to bone up and pass a formal exam on, say, metaphysical poetry, but that doesn't actually mean he gives a damn about it. A Negro boy, on the other hand, might well have a genuine feeling for the blues, which certainly represent an indigenous "substitute" for certified high culture poetry.

One can grant—and Murray doesn't fail to insist—that American Negroes suffer "brutal restrictions." Still, after such a glimpse of the real world, of the mysterious, various, *unfashionable* ways conditioning really works, where would be the usefulness in solemnly declaring that "no person has the ability to stand outside his own conditioning"?

The second reason we must regard the human mind as free—free at least of any danger that its operations can be predicted—is that it responds to stimuli in ways that are not to be explained by the nature of the stimuli alone, in ways that grow out of its own nature. This idea, I gather, is at the bottom of the view of mental growth of Jerome Bruner, who speaks of the ability we have "to exercise initiative, turn round on our information, reorder it, and generate hypotheses," an ability that comes from the "productive, generative structures" in our minds. At any rate, it seems clear enough that we have evolved out of the mind's own ways of dealing with the world a number of techniques of guiding and correcting its operations which are, if not wholly, at least to a significant degree independent of social background. We see them in the sciences; we see them in the various artistic media and genres. This is why one who devotes himself to an intellectual discipline finds that the discipline itself leads him to perspectives, discriminations, combinations he could not have foreseen. This is why a novelist often discovers his true subject and theme—and, it may be, even with surprise or dismay— in the process of struggling to turn the raw material of his life into a valid work of art. And here I could of course quote Henry James, for whom "art makes life," but since it may be feared that his views reflect the rotten values of a dying bourgeoisie, I turn instead to that other victim of racist bourgeois culture I've mentioned, Ralph Ellison. He is speaking in *Shadow and Act* of what happened when he began to learn something of "the craft and intention of modern poetry and fiction."

> The more I learned of literature in this conscious way, the more the details of my background became transformed. I heard undertones in remembered conversations which had escaped me before, local customs took on a more universal meaning, values which I hadn't understood were revealed; some of the people whom I had known were diminished while others were elevated in stature. More important, I began to see my own possibilities with more objective, and in a way, more hopeful eyes.

He tells us further that in acquiring technique a novelist is

> learning to conceive of human values in ways which have been established by the great writers who have developed and extended the art. . . . It is technique which transforms the individual before he is able to transform it. And in that personal transformation he discovers something else; he discovers that he has taken on certain obligations, that he must not embarrass his chosen form, and that in order to avoid this, he must develop taste. He learns—and this is most discouraging—that he is involved with values which turn in their own way, and not in the way of politics, upon the central issues affecting his nation and his time.

There is a third fact ignored by those others which I'll come to in a moment. But these first two alone are surely of decisive importance. Isn't it because we are thus "conditioned" by a virtual infinity of factors, inner and outer, and because our minds add to this complexity by reacting in their own way upon these factors, that we can *learn* from each other? Isn't this the reason our men of talent do come up with fresh ideas, just as our good teachers (and students) do teach us things, instead of merely giving out what was put in a class or race or the *Zeitgeist?* Actually, when not defending some theory, we all know this. We all know that each person is a new world of unique experience, or of common experience in unique degrees and combinations, and that it is out of these new worlds that the fountain of human creations issues which forever enriches or confuses our lives.

But to recognize the uniqueness of each man is to be brought up against a question. How can unique beings communicate with each other, and, what is stranger still, communicate across the additional barriers of race, class, nation, and even centuries? Or are the Gilmans and Kampfs right who, for their own reasons, say they have ceased to do so? Well, we have to begin, of course, with the undoubted fact that they do. The ancient Greek Sophocles, the eleventh-century Japanese Lady Murasaki, the Renaissance Englishman Shakespeare, the nineteenth-century Russian Dostoevsky—as well as philosophers and sages similarly remote from mid-twentieth-century Americans—do make sense to us, even to some of us under thirty. Reading them we do understand better our own natures and possibilities. The reason for this—and here is that third fact—was suggested long ago by Montaigne: *Chaque homme port la forme entière de l'humaine condition.* I take this to imply that all, or at least myriads, of human possibilities exist within each of us, waiting to be lifted into consciousness by the precisely appropriate circumstances or suggestions. A seeming paradox follows, which is the basis of art as it is of most human relationships. The only way to get at what a man has in common with others is to be true to what is particular, what seems unique, in his nature. By the same token, if we impose on his uniqueness some group identity, we both falsify him and turn him into a stranger. "Begin with an individual," as Fitzgerald put it, "and before you know it you find that you have created a type; begin with a type, and you find that you have created—nothing."

It is true that each of us will have memories and interests in common with members of his own group which he is less likely to have in common with outsiders. It is also true that one's class, say, or generation will set limits to what he will experience, think and produce. But the interests and limitations one shares with others in a group, however useful to sociology, which deals mainly in generalized images of man, cannot reveal what he is in his own particular being. For, as already implied, each individual is black, white, Jew, WASP, or of the Romantic Period in his own way, never the simple duplicate of his fellow group members. And because it is only in the unique particulars of a man's nature which elude all such wholesale categories that we come close to the man himself, it is only in them—that paradox again—that we touch the common human potentiality which those particulars alone body forth. On the last page of *Mimesis,* his magnificent reading of the central works of the Western tradition of realism, Erich Auerbach explains this paradox in his own way as he tells how mimetic art, precisely because it brings us so close to the actual lives of individuals, has led us more and more to recognize the oneness of man. The purpose of such art became, he says,

> to put the emphasis on the random occurrence, to exploit it not in the service of a planned continuity of action but in itself. And in the process something new and elemental appeared: nothing less than the wealth of reality and depth of life in every moment to which we surrender ourselves without prejudice. To be sure, what happens in that moment—be it outer or inner processes—concerns in a very personal way the individuals who live in it, but it also (and for that very reason) concerns the elementary things which men in general have in common. It is precisely the random moment which is comparatively independent of the controversial and unstable orders over which men fight and despair; it passes unaffected by them, as daily life. The more it is exploited the more the elementary things which our lives have in common come to light.

But I said there was some truth in those misleading and dangerous notions. First—and this may sound for a moment like a contradiction—it does after all make sense to talk of black (or Jewish or Irish) literature as having a character of its own. The author of these lines has himself been known to deny that a non-Jew can ever fully share his pleasure in Sholom Aleichem. Similarly, one must expect that black men, or Irishmen, reading together a work by one of themselves, are likely to exchange pleased glances at times when we others are merely getting the main idea. But this must be understood correctly. If a writer's fidelity to the particulars of his experience will turn up many details and expressions only his kin will enjoyably *remember,* surely any fiction which offers nothing but the pleasure of such literal accuracy, which does not at the same time put its particulars into some illuminating relationship with each other and thus enable us to recognize an underlying truth, is second-rate. (I don't speak of poetry, in which the language itself, and even the reader's memory of its unique history, are central to the experience, and which is simply closed to those who are not intimate with the language.) If Sholom Aleichem is a great writer, it is because his ability to convey the particulars of Jewish experience and modes of response is matched by his power to show them as *ways to be human.* There is, as a matter of fact, a deeper way to understand the ethnic character of a literature. The experience and traditions common to a group may well account for the predominance among them of certain ways of being human rather than others, just as, in the individual writer, illness or wealth or some other personal pressure may account for the kinds of reality he is led to feel most sharply and therefore to make most vivid to us. But the "strangeness" of a foreign culture, like that of a single original writer, is not a barrier. On the contrary, it introduces us, if we have the capacity for deepening self-awareness, to the unexplored possibilities of our own nature. For this reason, first-rate writing by black Americans—for instance, *The Autobiography of Malcolm X*—should be not only intelligible to whites, but a required part of their education. To quote Ellison again, "The small share of reality which each of our diverse groups is able to snatch from the whirling chaos of history belongs not to the group alone, but to all of us. It is a property and a witness which can be ignored only to the danger of the entire nation."

But there is another apparent contradiction to face up to, even more troublesome. It has to be granted that such emphasis on the universal may diminish our power to see and value the particular forms in which it is always expressed, and thus bleach life of its color, its charm. One must go even further. Spinoza says somewhere that God does not generalize—He sees only fact. That is, the particular concrete fact is never wholly expressed except by itself; all generalizations are approximate. And this means that, after all, it would be wrong—it would be a kind of intellectual hubris—to forget that every human being remains in certain ways alone and that no perfect communication is ever possible. Well, yes. But though that is true, it is also true that language and culture exist, and that we have built great cities together, and great literatures. We have had pleasure and solace from friends. The irreducible residue of the inexpressible in men and experience should not lead us to undervalue such communion as is possible. It is with this communion-that-is-possible that all the world's work is done. In any case, it is not by the stereotypes of race or politics that we are led to confront the actual difference and mystery of a man. By those stereotypes the real man is obliterated.

Then we must grant that even for that foolish turning away in colleges from Pope or Proust, the "Western masterpieces" generally, there is a certain justification. It is regrettably true that literary works have been made to *seem* irrelevant because they have been taught in ways that reduce them to less than they are and that inhibit, rather than promote, a genuine experience of them. In this "age of criticism" from which we are now perhaps emerging, too many English teachers, applying mechanically the lore gathered in graduate school, or the hints of gifted critics, have yielded to the temptation to play the expert and to make little experts of their students. The works of literature ostensibly being studied have been replaced by theories, theories oriented toward technique, myth, symbol, "scientific" categories, and the like. Aside from the fact that this turns literature into a bore, there are two unfortunate results of such "pretense of expertise." One is that it often prevents the more accurate knowledge it claims to ensure. For the only reliable method of dealing with literature, as Eliot has said, is to be very intelligent, which I take to mean not to avoid theory—we can't do that—but to hold theories lightly in our hand, like tools that may at any moment, amid the fluid complexities of literature and of our relationship to it, cease to be appropriate; in other words, to stay open to the as yet *unaccredited* responses and insights of fresh experience. But the second result of the pretense of expertise is worse. It is that it usually rules out of order our own and our students' personal relation with the non-literary, the human core of literary works. It thus inhibits that more conscious concern with life which is surely a chief reward of the study of literature.

But even granting that the classroom should be, as too often it has not been, a place where we try to engage in a genuinely living relationship with literature, why does it follow that we have to remove from it all works that come to us from distant times, places, social classes—except as instructive examples of the *other*—and replace them by works that come from or apply directly to our own? Why is it necessary to enliven the class with titillating pseudo-therapy or to borrow excitement for the dull old text from the issues of the hour? Far from making the study of literature more relevant, such tricks simply distract attention from that true relevance—to our humanity—which is precisely what enables certain books to live past their own time, and which they retain long after all local or fashionable reasons for interest in them have disappeared. (Speaking thus to "the more elementary things which men in general have in common," they will apply often enough, of course, to the issues of the hour, though they may not be useful to narrow partisans.) Strange that one should need to say this to English teachers, but our job is surely to help students see and feel that true relevance, that permanent power of first-rate literature to move and liberate us, which makes our "great books" the richest legacy of human history.

As for the denial of the possibility of objectivity, this seems to me, as I have suggested, only another version of the idea that men can't step outside their conditioning. It is a truth, but in its current, mainly political application a useless and misleading truth. For after all, we don't really require any chemical purity from conditioning—or subjectivity—in order to make a distinction between the true and the false, the honest man and the cheat. It is enough to grant first, that some people deliberately lie to gain private ends, while others want no private advantage that is not based on as much truth as possible; and second, that for those who seek the truth there are ways, in art and the other humanities, as well as in science, to increase significantly the reality content of their thought. This being the case, to emphasize our irremediable subjectivity often sounds suspiciously like a useful alibi for liars.

The fact is, for too many of the intellectuals of the New Left the denial of the possibility of objectivity, of a significant, if partial, freedom from the "conditioning" of race or class or generation, is not a reasoned position but a strategy for silencing those who are in danger of thinking for themselves. The argument goes like this: There is a battle in progress for bread and justice. All you writers and teachers, and the works you place before us, must inevitably serve either the oppressors or their victims. Therefore, give up the pretense or illusion that you have anything of your own to say, or that you can lead to insight which men of differing political persuasions can respect. Instead, join us, and in your work openly express those correct ideas which we already possess.

Now obviously, the world we live in is not what it should be, and intelligent social protest is very much in order. There is a battle going on for bread and justice, which are everywhere inequitably distributed. The situation of black Americans is still a disgrace to the nation, in spite of progress. Our brutal intervention in the Vietnamese civil war is a shame and a horror. And though such demands on our conscience may be used as pretexts by the foolish or the unscrupulous, yet the demands have a real basis. For this reason, certain questions are bound to haunt all of us engaged in intellectual work. If we must be left free in order to make the most of the mind's wealth of unpredictable possibilities, and if, in this freedom, the principles and methods of our work must sometimes be permitted to lead us away from the immediate interests of our fellows, may not this truth too be used as a pretext? May it not be used as a cover for the wish to stay safe while others risk their necks? More precisely, since our work requires peace and quiet and regular meals, may not a refusal to join some battle for social justice be motivated by a fear of reprisals from the powers, not always just, which supply them? To such questions one must uncomfortably assent. That can happen. But again we must be careful in seeing what follows. It surely does not follow that intellectual principles and methods—the "Mediterranean" values of reason, and so on—and those who try to live by them have become agents of oppression or obsolete. If some men of mind are venal and cowardly, others are not. Since the time of Socrates, reason and art have also opposed the "establishment" and found for its victims. Indeed, a good case is often made for the view that No! in thunder, or in whispers, is what reason and art usually say to things as they are, and say it on behalf of that better way they ought to be which is the ultimate goal of the social engineers.

The essential difference between those who would remain faithful to the principles and methods of art and thought—say, a university faculty of the kind that used to be admired—and those who join the social or political battle is not that one group is escaping to an ivory tower and serving only themselves (or the "establishment") and the other confronting reality and serving their fellow men. It is that the first wish to remain open to new ideas and to protect the conditions out of which they come, while the "militants" tend to think they have as much truth as they need. It is also that the former, as a class, serve men in the whole range of their needs, serve that Ideal City (never to be reached, though the struggle toward it can enrich our lives) which will be the home of man's fullest development; and the latter serve men in the short run and the pressing needs of the moment. Undoubtedly, both kinds of service have their place, and occasions do arrive when those who are capable of action had better act. But we must all decide for ourselves how much of our time and energy we owe to each. What we must not do, and what the social engineer ought not to demand that we do, is import into the study or classroom attitudes appropriate to the political arena, which too often means simplify or distort the complex truth to attain some "practical" goal. We must try not to sacrifice for immediate ends any power we have to serve the deeper needs of men that go on forever. Those who demand such a sacrifice—imposing the unreal alternatives "with us or against us," prating of "art for the people," and claiming to scorn the "elitism" of intellectual, artistic, and sometimes even moral standards—are not really being practical and honest as against the escapist and hypocritical others. Instead, they are rejecting—with the practicality of Stalinists or Nazis—the habits of mind by which free men will be able to judge and resist them. And sometimes, too, they are taking the revenge of the mediocre on the gifted, and using social crisis as an alibi for rejecting standards they are incapable of meeting.

I conclude by summing up. It is not true that the intellectual life is a battle of brute self-interest, and that men cannot speak to each other over the barriers imposed by their origins. This recurrent idea is contradicted by the nature of the human mind and the fact of the human community. For the mind is not the puppet of a few obvious conditions, but is shaped by unknowable myriads and in some degree selects or makes its own. And our fellowship with men of other races, nations and times is brought home to us by our continual recognition of ourselves in their works. We know what men may and should become in large part because we see what they have been.

Granted that insistence on the human community can be used to stifle legitimate protest ("Though you have nothing, and I everything, don't be rude, we're brothers underneath"). But the denial of it can be used to impose totalitarian despotism ("Men are divided by class or race, to disagree with us is to be our enemy, lock him up!"). In the same way, an exclusive emphasis on the universal will lead us away from reality, as equally will an exclusive emphasis on the particular. And though it is difficult to avoid both kinds of error, that happens to be the necessary job of those of us who would do justice to the works of human intellect, or would serve our fellows in all the variety of their needs, and serve them without making them pay—as certain kinds of "idealists" always do—by giving up their freedom or part of their mind.

NICK AARON FORD

Black Literature and the Problem of Evaluation

The case for black literature in the curriculums of American schools and colleges has won a sympathetic hearing in all sections of the nation. But its effective implementation has been hampered by troublesome problems whose solutions depend upon a greater willingness and determination fundamentally to alter certain deeply rooted attitudes and thought patterns that have produced the current dilemma. Signs of such alterations, however, are not yet visible.

Before proceeding further let us consider a definition of terms as used in this paper. By *black* literature I mean literature concerning "the black experience" by black writers with African ancestry who have spent most of their lives in the United States. By *literature* I mean writing designed primarily for pleasure or contemplation rather than for the presentation of facts for their own sake. *The American College Dictionary* defines *evaluate* as "to ascertain the value . . . of; appraise carefully." Value is defined as "that property of a thing because of which it is esteemed, desirable, or useful . . . ; worth, merit, or importance." I accept the sense of the dictionary definition as basic reference in my use of the term *evaluation*.

I am acutely aware that literary evaluation in this contemporary period is an unpopular concept and that critics who do not wish to place their reputations in jeopardy generally avoid the subject. Emil Staiger suggests, "Every genuine writer, and every reader endowed with some sense of artistic quality, will react to the problem of literary evaluation with intense suspicion."[1] René Wellek, author of the five-volume *History of Modern Criticism,* after condemning recent attempts of some scholars to doubt the whole enterprise of literary theory and to absorb all literary study into history, admits that "any criticism is today on the defensive." There are, of course, distinguished scholars who object to contemporary discussions of literary evaluation not because they are not concerned about values but because for them the case for literary values was settled long ago, and was settled on the basis of one criterion only: the

[1] "The Questionable Nature of Value Problems," *Problems of Literary Evaluation,* edited by Joseph Strelka (University of Pennsylvania Press, 1969), p. 199.

criterion of aestheticism. Others object because they insist that literary evaluation is completely personal and a discussion of general approaches or methods is futile. Still other objections are based on the premise that literature is primarily a report on human experience and that no one has the right to downgrade the value of any human experience.

Despite arguments to the contrary, I believe a satisfactory solution to the problem of evaluation in relation to the effective inclusion of black literature in school and college curriculums is crucial. My conclusion is based on the following considerations:

> (1) Although there may be no public acknowledgement of the involvement of critical standards or guidelines in the selection of literary works for study in English classes, there can be no doubt of such involvement. The mere selection of anthologies to be used in literature classes, as well as the choice of specific works from the adopted anthology, implies the use of the process of evaluation. Since this subterranean process has, with few exceptions, completely ignored from the beginning of American education to the present, the whole corpus of black literature (excluding literature by whites about blacks which my definition does not cover), it is necessary that these time-worn prejudicial bases for evaluation be openly acknowledged and re-examined for the purpose of making fundamental revisions that will include the newly discovered dimensions of black literature.

> (2) Failure to provide revised approaches to evaluation will justify the current demand of some groups for completely separate modes of evaluation for the selection and study of black literature. Such a development would tend to destroy the concept of literature as a legitimate° subdivision of humanistic study with common principles of organization of and insight into the human experience which distinguish it from history, philosophy and sociology. Under such conditions either black literature or non-black literature as now defined would deserve a new nomenclature.

I propose that all literary scholars and critics actively engaged in their professions seriously consider, individually and collectively, the urgent need drastically to revise traditional norms for evaluating literature according to the WASP pattern in order to include such variations as explorations of the "black experience" by black writers, as well as the experiences of other ethnic minorities by their own indigenous writers. To deny that a narrow prejudiced pattern of evaluation has existed in the past, and does still exist, is to compound error with self-righteousness and arrogance and to invite the complete rejection of school and college literature by the brightest and most sensitive youths of this generation. John H. Fisher, Executive Secretary of the Modern Language Association, recognized this threat when he recently stated, "The subject of English in this country has been used to inculcate a white, Anglo-Saxon, Protestant ethic. This was our principal and most valuable inheritance from the mother country. The most important people in 'English' in this country have traditionally been those who outdid the British at their own game—did better scholarship on Chaucer, Shakespeare, or Milton; brought over the most English books to found a Folger or a Huntington, or a University of Illinois library. . . ."[2]

Several years ago Yale University's distinguished historian, C. Van Woodward, president of the American Historical Association, challenged the scholars in his profession to address themselves to a similar problem by ending the South-oriented writing and teaching of American history, particularly in relation to the Negro.

I suggest that the following shifts in emphases will greatly contribute to the realization of my proposal.

First, the overwhelming insistence upon *aestheticism* as the major criterion for literary evaluation must be repudiated. Aestheticism, which concerns us here, is defined in *The American College Dictionary* as follows: 1. *the acceptance of artistic beauty and taste as a fundamental standard, ethical and other standards being secondary. 2. an exaggerated devotion to art, music, or poetry, with indifference to practical matters.* I charge that this kind of aestheticism has been the guiding principle of literary evaluation by American scholars and critics at least since the advent of the "New Criticism" more than thirty years ago, and that if it continues to dominate, there can be no alternative to the demands of the black revolutionists for completely separate standards of evaluation for black literature.

In a significant sense the emphasis on aestheticism is an emphasis on the formal, the non-human, the determination not to become involved in the sordid aspect of the human condition, the preoccupation with contemplating the stars while bogging down in the muck and mire of the terrestrial terrain. It may be more than a coincidence that aestheticism enjoyed its greatest veneration in a period when the unimaginable horrors of the atomic bomb were inflicted upon the unsuspecting civilians of Hiroshima and Nagasaki. If Kipling was right in his prophecy:

> By all ye cry or whisper,
> By all ye leave or do,
> The silent sullen peoples
> Shall weigh your Gods and you

those silent sullen students forced to sit under the tutelage of English professors committed completely to the theory of aestheticism are now giving short weight to the professor's "god" and less than serious attention to the professor himself.

At its worst the glorification of aestheticism can mean the false belief that literature exists in a vacuum or is the special property of

---

[2] "Movement in English," *ADE Bulletin* (September, 1969), p. 46.

aristocrats with extraordinary sensibilities. Commenting on the philosophic tenets of the American apostles of the "New Criticism," Alfred Kazin charges, in *On Native Grounds* (New York, 1956, p. 331), that "on the obvious level this criticism resulted in a literature of aestheticism that was a defense against modern life. . . . Underneath all the trappings of neoclassic snobbery and the obsession with form as an ideal end in itself, it was a profound and impotent disaffection that moved in this criticism." He quotes John Crowe Ransom as insisting that the modern poet is above the sentimental glorification of poetry as a guide of life, though the modern reader has yet "no recognition of the possibility that an aesthetic effect may exist by itself, independent of morality or any other useful set of ideals" (Kazin, p. 334).

Concerning Allen Tate, who occupies a place among the hierarchy of aesthetic critics equal, if not superior, to that of Ransom, Kazin says, "What one saw in Tate's system was a fantastic inversion of the Marxist system. . . . The Marxist critic could study a work of art only in terms of its social relations; Tate would study literature—that is, only poetry of a certain intensity and difficulty—precisely because it had no social relations at all. . . . Tate never admitted specific formal properties of literature and its relation to civilization" (p. 339). In *Reactionary Essays* Tate gave himself away most completely when he wrote that while slavery was wrong, it was wrong because the master gave everything to the slave and got nothing in return; that the "moral" wrong of slavery meant nothing, since "societies can bear an amazing amount of corruption and still produce high cultures" (Kazin, p. 341).

Is it any wonder that a theory of evaluation with a history and operating principles such as the one characterized above can never acknowledge black literature as a legitimate part of the literary spectrum? Is it any wonder that those who are genuinely concerned about securing equal consideration for the place of black literature in American studies must demand the repudiation of aestheticism as the most privileged criterion for literary evaluation?

In an article discussing the current "Black Arts Movement" Larry Neal, black poet and critic, explains his idea of how black literature differs in aims and methods from the standards of White-Anglo-Saxon-Protestant aestheticism. He declares:

> It is radically opposed to any concept of the artist that alienates him from his community. Black art is the aesthetic and spiritual sister of the Black Power concept. As such it envisions an art that speaks directly to the needs and aspirations of Black America. In order to perform this task, the Black Arts Movement proposes a radical reordering of the western cultural aesthetic. It proposes a separate symbolism, mythology, and iconology. . . . The two movements postulate that there are in fact and in spirit two Americas—one black, one white. It is the opinion of many Black writers . . . that the western aesthetic has run its course:

it is impossible to construct anything meaningful written in its decaying structure.[3]

Although I do not subscribe to all of Neal's fears and dire predictions as of this moment, all available evidence points to the conclusion that unless the literary establishment takes seriously the need for a re-ordering of evaluative standards and procedures *now,* without further subterfuge, many of us who still believe in the "humanity" of our discipline and those who practice it will be forced to acknowledge, like Cardinal Wolsey, a great betrayal. An example of the current travesty of literary evaluation on the basis of aestheticism in so far as black literature is concerned can be seen in the ridiculous naiveté of Allen Tate in his Preface to Melvin Tolson's *Libretto for the Republic of Liberia.*

The Republic of Liberia, Africa, founded in 1847, commissioned Melvin B. Tolson, a black American poet whose first volume of poems, *Rendezvous with America* (1944), had demonstrated worthy poetic talent to write a poem in honor of the centennial. In fulfillment of the terms of his commission he wrote a long commemorative poem published in 1953 under the title *Libretto for the Republic of Liberia.* In a Preface to the volume Allen Tate said, among other things equally as naive:

> For the first time, it seems to me, a Negro poet has assimilated completely the full poetic language of his time and, by implication, the language of the Anglo-American tradition. I do not wish to be understood as saying that Negro poets have hitherto been incapable of this assimilation; there has been perhaps rather a resistance to it on the part of those Negroes who supposed that their peculiar genius lay in "folk" idiom or in the romantic creation of a "new" language within the English language. In these directions interesting and even distinguished work has been done, notably by Langston Hughes and Gwendolyn Brooks. But there are two disadvantages to this approach: first, the "folk" and "new" languages are not very different from those that white poets can write; secondly, the distinguishing Negro quality is not in the language but in the subject-matter, which is usually the plight of the Negro in a White culture. The plight is real and often tragic; but I cannot think that, *from the literary point of view,* the tragic aggressiveness of the modern Negro poet offers wider poetic possibilities than the resigned pathos of Paul Laurence Dunbar, who was only a "White *poète manqué.* Both attitudes have limited the Negro poet to a provincial mediocrity in which one's feelings about one's difficulties become more important than poetry itself.
>
> It seems to me only common sense to assume that the main thing is the poetry, if one is a poet, whatever one's color may be. I think Mr.

---

[3] *Black Theatre.* XLI (Summer, 1966), p. 30.

Tolson has assumed this; and the assumption, I gather, has made him not less but more intensely *Negro* in his apprehension of the world than any of his contemporaries, or any that I have read.[4]

I have been content to use the word naiveté in respect to Tate's critical pronouncements in lieu of harsher words such as obtuseness or hypocrisy because it connotes the lesser offense from a critical standpoint. I do not agree with those who say that no white critic is capable of evaluating a literary work by a black writer simply because he has not lived through the black experience. Naturally, such a critic cannot give a perfect evaluation. But neither can any critic give a perfect evaluation of any work. I require only that a white critic approach the evaluation of black literature in the spirit of humility rather than arrogance and only after he has devoted a similar amount of time and careful study to the whole corpus of black writing as he would normally spend in trying to understand any other unfamiliar field of study. Unfortunately, Tate, like the vast majority of white critics, has not done his homework.

Let us see how uninformed and patently false the evaluation is which I have cited. First, the critic says, "For the first time, it seems to me, a Negro poet has assimilated completely the full poetic language of his time and, by implication, the language of the Anglo-American tradition." The facts are that throughout the whole history of American literature the major criticism of black writers from Phillis Wheatley (1773) to Gwendolyn Brooks, who was awarded the Pulitzer prize in 1950, has been that their poetry is the language of the white Anglo-American poetic tradition. Countee Cullen, an acknowledged apostle of John Keats' cult of beauty in language and sentiment, penned a bitter complaint about such critical treatment which ended with the well-known lines: "Yet do I marvel at this curious thing/to make a poet black and bid him sing." Approximately fifty years earlier, Paul Laurence Dunbar, whom Tate accused of "resigned pathos" for his use of the "folk" idiom of Negro dialect, angrily indicted the literary establishment (white publishers, critics, and readers) for ignoring his poems in literary English and praising only those written "in a broken tongue." Although he ascribes the "mediocrity" of Negro poetry to the black poet's false supposition that "their peculiar genius lay in 'folk' idiom or in the romantic creation of a 'new' language within the English language," he says some interesting and even distinguished work has been done in this vein, "notably by Langston Hughes and Gwendolyn Brooks." It is a sad commentary on the state of white-Anglo-Saxon-Protestant criticism in America when a prestigious member of that establishment does not know that scores of black writers of poetry over a period of two hundred years have assimilated "the language of the Anglo-American tradition" as well as, and in some cases better than, M. B. Tolson's demonstration in 1953.

[4] *Libretto for the Republic of Liberia* (New York: Twayne Publishers, 1953).

Furthermore, our critic asserts with evident seriousness that Tolson's assimilation of the language and spirit of the Anglo-American poetic tradition as demonstrated in *Libretto for the Republic of Liberia* "has made him not less but more intensely *Negro* in his apprehension of the world than any of his contemporaries." He makes this judgment despite the fact that the poet himself has felt it necessary to append to his 29-page poem, supposedly written in Anglo-American English, with no Negro idioms and very few African phrases, 16 pages of notes attempting to clarify his meanings which he was unable to do in the poem itself and which with few exceptions have no roots in black culture.

I hesitate to prolong this agony, but in order to illustrate how errors by one prominent critic can be passed on by lesser breeds and even compounded in the process let me cite one such example. Selden Rodman, editor of more than one literary anthology, in his review of Tolson's poem for the New York *Times Book Review* (January 24, 1954), endorsed with enthusiasm Tate's Preface and added the following evaluation:

> It is a reflection on so-called "white" culture that up to now "Negro poetry" in English has had to be considered as such and handled with special care to avoid giving offense. Praised for its moral intentions and excused for its formal shortcomings, it has generally been tolerated as a literary poor relation. The fact of the matter is that most of this poetry has been second rate, and that critics, partaking of the general responsibility for the Negro's unreadiness to take the "Negro problem" in his stride, have hesitated to say so. . . .

Then turning to the weaknesses of this "best" of all Negro poems, Rodman continues:

> This kind of writing becomes at its best academic and at its worst intellectual exhibitionism, throwing at the reader undigested scraps of everything from Bantu to Esperanto in unrelaxed cacophony. Eliot's taste was equal to giving the results of such a method dignity; Tolson's taste is much more uneven.

Although poetry by its very nature suffers most from the application of the canons of aestheticism, the novel has not entirely escaped a similar fate, especially the black variety when being judged by the white critic. Despite the fact that the most significant novels that are still remembered from past ages have dealt with moral and social issues which confront civilized man, any novel by a black writer which deals honestly and effectively with the problems of race without attempting to blunt the cutting edges by sublimating it into the larger context of universality is denied serious critical attention in obedience to the strictures of aestheticism. Examples of this treatment can be seen in the critical pronouncements of Robert Bone, author of *The Negro Novel in America* and generally accepted by white professors as the most respected authority on the subject. Although Bone deserves credit for his pioneering work in the field when other white scholars considered such research beneath contempt and although he has furnished some important new and valid insights in the study of black novelists, he has succumbed in much of his evaluation to the fallacy of aestheticism. At the end of his Epilogue he declares "In exceptional circumstances, then, both the protest novel and the novel of white life are legitimate concerns of the Negro novelist. To restore perspective, however, it is necessary to restate the general rule: a high protest content is not likely to produce good fiction. . . ." He concludes by assuring the reader that notable progress is being made "as more of the younger Negro writers have learned to respect the difference between social controversy and art. In the long run an art-centered Negro fiction will evolve, free from the crude nationalistic propaganda of the past and the subtler assimilationist propaganda of the present."

Of course, when one condemns the propaganda or protest novel, or places one below the other in the scale of his values, much can depend on the definition of terms. According to my definition of propaganda the term not only includes the protest novel but the political, the anti-war, the religious, and any other kind of novel that fights for or against a cause. I, therefore, classify as propagandistic practically all of the novels of Charles Dickens, Sinclair Lewis (Nobel Prize winner), and Norman Mailer, as well as Dreiser's *An American Tragedy,* Hemingway's *A Farewell to Arms,* and Steinbeck's *The Grapes of Wrath.* However, since none of these is directed at the problem of race, Bone and most of the Protestant-Anglo-Saxon oriented critics would disagree. It is this determination to label as propaganda all literary works protesting racism that evidently impelled Bone to evaluate Zora Neal Hurston's *Their Eyes Were Watching God,* reportedly written in seven weeks under the emotional pressure of a recent love affair, as "possibly the best novel of the period (1930–40), excepting *Native Son."* Such a judgment is amazing when one remembers that Arna Bontemps' magnificent *Black Thunder,* an historical novel about an American slave revolt, was published the previous year, a novel that by all fair standards must be considered less propagandistic than William Styron's *The Confessions of Nat Turner,* which adheres more to the superficialities of aestheticism and less to historical and cultural authenticity.

To keep the record straight, let me emphasize that I am not advocating the complete rejection of aestheticism as *one* of the criteria for literary evaluation. I am rejecting it as *the privileged* or principal criterion for such evaluation. If anyone wants to know what privileged criterion I recommend to replace it, I reply, "None!" I suggest that the time has come to deny any *one* standard a privileged place on the scale of literary evaluation. I agree with Donald Hall in his Introduction to the anthology, *Contemporary American Poetry* (Baltimore, 1967, p. 17) when he says:

In modern art anarchy has proved preferable to the restrictions of a benevolent tyranny. It is preferable as a permanent condition. We do not want merely to substitute one orthodoxy for another . . . but we want all possibilities, even contradictory ones, to exist together. The trouble with orthodoxy is that it prescribes the thinkable limits of variation . . . yet typically the modern artist has allowed nothing to be beyond his consideration. He has acted as if restlessness were a conviction and has destroyed his own past in order to create a future.

As one substitute for aestheticism as the exclusive determinant of literary acceptability, I suggest the criterion of *significant human experience,* which may include the tedious, the ugly, or the obscene. Many critics admit that value judgments about events, persons, and artistic creations tell us as much about the evaluators as they do about the thing being evaluated. The greater the range of consciousness or the breadth of experience the evaluator has achieved, either by actual living or by a wide differentiated variety of reading, the more fair and objective his evaluation will be. Only by exposure to a diversity of experiences, actual or vicarious, can a reader or critic acquire sufficient background to evaluate without narrow prejudice a new encounter. No critic, scholar, or reader who wishes to have his evaluations taken seriously can refuse to read any serious literary work simply because its language or style or content is offensive to his taste. For his capacity to evaluate any book is diminished by the extent that his experiences with different kinds of books have been limited. Thus a teacher who refuses to consider for use in the bibliography for his course a book dealing honestly but *exclusively* with the black experience without conscious or overt overtones of universality is deliberately rejecting *significant human experience* as a legitimate criterion for literary acceptability.

LeRoi Jones, who in many instances does not measure up to my idea of an objective critic, speaks wisely when he suggests that "everything is valuable that men have experienced, because posed against that experience . . . there is only darkness, or not even that." Without the basis of such a philosophy it would be rather difficult to justify fully the recent publication of the three-volume edition of *The Diary of Samuel Pepys,* which consists of 942 pages of commonplace minutiae dully recorded over a period of nine years by a colorless middle-class Englishman, with eight additional volumes in the offing.

Northrop Frye insists, "The literary scholar has nothing to do with sifting out what it will be less rewarding to experience. He has value judgments of selectivity, just as any scholar in any field would have, but his canons of greater or lesser importance are related to the conditions of his specific research, not directly to the literary qualities of his material" (in Strelka, p. 15).

Recently I received a long distance telephone call from a black supervisor of English in the public school system of a large northern city. Frustration and bitterness were in his voice. "Pardon me for disturbing you so late at night, especially since you do not know me," he began, "but I just must talk to a person who can understand my problem." After I assured him that I would be glad to listen, he continued. "I have a number of white teachers under my supervision," he confided, "and I have been trying to encourage them to add some significant black literature to their reading lists; but they say they can't do it because the children's parents object."

"On what grounds?" I asked. "Too much obscenity," he snapped. "Do they make the same complaint about literature by white writers?" I asked, knowing that practically all contemporary literature, as well as the poetry of Chaucer, the comedies of Shakespeare, and the essays of Rabelais, is replete with obscenities. "They do not," he replied; "they say white parents accept obscenities from white writers more willingly than they do from black ones." Astounded by such unbelievable nonsense, I suggested that he try to make his teachers understand that four-letter words smell no better or worse because of the race of the users.

But he was not yet finished. Would I advise, he asked, that significant passages from black writings, with obscenities deleted, be reproduced and offered to teachers for class study? At first he was shocked at my opposition to censorship even though it were done in the name of a good cause, but he seemed to understand when I explained that black writers had a more legitimate reason for the use of obscenities than their white counterparts, since the black experience in the ghetto is usually more obscene than any other and that a writer dedicated to the proposition of *seeing all and telling it like it is* would be false to himself and to his readers if he omitted any significant part of what he saw. I suggested that Ralph Ellison's reference to Trueblood's incestuous act with his daughter in *Invisible Man* is obscene, but it illuminates a facet of ghetto life that is too important to be ignored. Likewise, Richard Wright's description of the little black boys peeping at the sexual acts of their elders in *Native Son* is obscene, but it is a part of the overcrowded living conditions of blacks which breed the social crimes and hopeless frustrations that are the inevitable fruits of ghetto living. I explained that uncensored significant experiences such as these presented in literature for the enlightenment of all form the bases for a knowledgeable interracial and intercultural environment. Wright helped to create a new understanding of the problems of black-white relations when he made Bigger's defense attorney charge rich, philanthropic, honorable Mr. Dalton with the murder of his own daughter (whom Bigger had accidentally killed because of fear), because if the father had permitted his daughter to know (through literature or otherwise) the kinds of experiences black ghetto children are forced to suffer in their day to day experiences with a "superior" white society, she would have known better what to expect from a rebel like Bigger.

Another alternative to the aesthetic criterion is *cultural* and *racial significance*. By this approach one assumes that any literary work which offers significant insight into the cultural or racial background of the civilization that produced it is valuable. Consequently, the appropriateness of form, style, and technique to the cultural or racial background of the specific work would be a major factor in determining its acceptability as literature worthy of serious consideration. Thus James Weldon Johnson's "O Black and Unknown Bards," which celebrates the creation of the Negro spiritual, the only serious music of American origin, would rate high on this scale of evaluation. Two significant cultural facts are recognized in the last two stanzas—these black creators were illiterate and theirs were the only folk creations expressing spiritual strivings.

> There is a wide, wide wonder in it all,
> That from degraded rest and servile toil
> The fiery spirit of the seer should call
> These simple children of the sun and soil.
> O black slave singers, gone, forgot, unfamed,
> You—you alone, of all the long, long line
> Of those who've sung untaught, unknown, unnamed,
> Have stretched out upward, seeking the divine.
> You sang not deeds of heroes or of kings;
> No chant of bloody war, no exulting pean
> Of arms-won triumphs; but your humble strings
> You touched in chord with music empyrean.
> You sang far better than you knew; the songs
> That for your listeners' hungry hearts sufficed
> Still live,—but more than this to you belongs:
> You sang a race from wood and stone to Christ.

Since the language and style of "O Black and Unknown Bards" are characteristic of American (white) poetry of the period, the white critic or anthologist would in all probability consider it imitative and consequently unworthy of serious consideration despite its significant racial and cultural references. "The Poet" by Paul Laurence Dunbar would undoubtedly suffer a similar fate, although it is a bitter cry against the racial and cultural discrimination which refuses to accept black creation that rejects an artificial dialect first invented by a Mississippi white poet and later accepted by the white public as the only acceptable medium for genuine Negro creative expression.

> He sang of love when earth was young,
> But ah, the world, it turned to praise
> And love itself was in his lays.
> A jingle in a broken tongue.

This dilemma becomes frustrating almost beyond endurance when respectable, knowledgeable white critics condemn LeRoi Jones for doing in his play *Slave Ship* the very thing that the ruling critical establishment down through the years has condemned black writers for not doing, namely, using language and styles representative of black culture exclusively rather than the American language and literary styles, common to all Americans.

For example, in a review by the New York *Times'* drama critic, Walter Kerr, who is a good representative of the knowledgeable, moderate white critic operating within the tradition of aestheticism, made the following criticisms of *Slave Ship* in his column dated November 23, 1969:

> I am at a loss to know why "Slave Ship," now being performed at the Chelsea Theater Center in Brooklyn, is called LeRoi Jones's "Slave Ship." Mr. Jones is a writer. But "Slave Ship" is not written. "Slave Ship" is an obvious improvisation, possibly from a scenario that can scarcely have covered more than three typewritten pages [reasonable estimate], in which for an hour and 40 minutes without intermission, 15 actors utter groans, gasps and screeches [reasonable reaction of African slaves who know no English]. . . . Apart from a few lame lines of parodied Uncle Tomming, he has provided nothing but an invitation to the players to be as literal as they like for us as long as they like, which only ends in that fake-actuality that kills belief on the spot.

Could it be that Jones has invented a new dramatic style that makes sense to an open-minded critic or play-goer not committed to the dogma of aestheticism? In "Drama Mailbag," New York *Times,* December 14, 1970, a letter appeared, written by a white male English instructor at New York City Community College, Brooklyn, which contained the following reaction:

> I watched my students watching the production of LeRoi Jones's "Slave Ship" the other night and I realized how many ways Walter Kerr and other critics had missed the boat. Toward the end of the play, during the "When we gonna rise . . ." refrain, many of my young black students were on their feet, swaying and clapping to the beat, totally involved; others were seated but obviously entranced; my white students were staggered, stunned, even hurt—but all, *all,* were inspired by art in a way which no amount of classroom intellectualization could hope to have provided.
>
> . . . The fact that it is historical, that it contains little dialogue, that it cannot be measured by conventional standards, does not detract from the impact it has on its audience. We are made to feel African glory as it rises again from the ashes of American brutalization.

A third alternative to the stultifying grip of aestheticism is the criterion of *relevance.* Unless this criterion is accepted there is little hope that the most significant and effective black literature will find a place in school and college curriculums. I disagree with Professor J. Mitchell Morse of Temple University, who stated in a recent article in *College English:*

For many novels, stories, plays and poems that one would think could not be taken seriously by anybody who knows anything about the art are in fact taken seriously by many people—critics, reviewers, teachers— who professionally profess to know quite a bit about it. . . . They are not insensitive to literary values; often they have demonstrated a fine appreciation of nuances in works of the past; but in their belief that literature should speak to the problems of our time they tend to judge current fiction, drama and even poetry by other than literary standards. When they enter the present age they look for "relevance" above all: social relevance, political relevance, ethical relevance; and when they find it their enthusiasm often leads them to mistake it for literary relevance. . . .

. . . They regard with approval and even with perverse pleasure all kinds of commonplace or sub-commonplace novels that attack racism or militarism or the TV industry or bigoted rural school boards. . . .[5]

In a report on a study of the crisis on college and university campuses the editors, who are college professors, point out that standard college courses in all fields have been severely criticized by students for their remoteness from the problems of the world that exist beyond the campus, and that society is already beginning to decay "when education ceases to be concerned with societal problems of the day."[6]

In the Preface to her *The New Novel in America* (Ithaca, 1970, p. ix) Helen Wineberg says, "Reaction against the novel that had turned away from life toward aestheticism brought with it the rebirth of the novel that turned toward life." She concludes with the thought that the American novel in the sixties has renewed and extended inquiry into man's relations with his history, his society, and his politics, and "that it now seems possible to talk once again about a social environment and to take a stand in it and on it, whether the stand be an affirmation or an attack" (p. xvii). If Miss Wineberg's findings are valid, it appears that Professor Morse may have to give up reading contemporary literature because of its concern for what he calls extra-literary values, a concern which denies the privileged position of aestheticism as the chief basis for judging literary quality or validity. Although he professes great concern about civil rights and the war in Vietnam, he seems to believe that novels concerning such subjects are always written with "more heart than art." He says he will not tell his students that James Baldwin's *Another Country* is a good novel, and the tenor of his discussion indicates that he would not suggest to his students that they read it to see whether or not they can find any satisfying literary pleasures in it. He does not hesitate to assume this Olympian wisdom despite the fact that he knows (as all good teachers of literature should know) that "no amount of scholarly rigor or discretion can make any assertion in criticism more than a sub-

[5] "The Case for Irrelevance," *College English,* 30 (December, 1968), pp. 210–11.
[6] Joseph Axelrod et al., *Search for Relevance* (San Francisco: Jossey-Bass, Inc., 1969), p. 66.

jective speculation, yet it is often used to justify massive dogmatism and inflexibility."[7] It seems that William Butler Yeats was right when he said in his poem, "The Second Coming":

> Things fall apart; the center cannot hold. . . .
> The best lack all conviction, while the worst
> Are full of Passionate intensity. . . .

As long as critics, scholars, and teachers with attitudes similar to those of Professor Morse prevail, significant black literature will continue to be excluded from serious consideration in school and college classrooms.

I conclude this discussion with some good advice from the eminent English critic, David Daiches, who warns:

> In the lower ranges of literature are all sorts of mixed kinds, partly documentary, partly sociological, partly historical, and one of the problems of defining the task of the literary critic is precisely that literature is so wide-ranging, often so "impure," with the spectrum ranging from the almost wholly documentary to the wholly imaginative. One must find a technique of description that enables one to do justice to these mixed kinds, to demonstrate the effectiveness of the literary devices which make the documentary element so much more vivid and persuasive. The novel in particular tends to be a mixed form. In calling these mixed forms "lower" I am not so much implying a value judgment as suggesting a scale between the high visionary and the low documentary, with every kind of combination in between. . . . It can be easily argued that the purely visionary is not by any means the greatest and that a grip on contemporary social fact, however indirectly or obliquely demonstrated, is the mark of the greatest writers. (Strelka, pp. 180–181)

---

[7] Peter H. Elbow, "The Definition of Teaching," *College English,* 30 (December, 1968), p. 194.

JACK NEWFIELD

A Populist Manifesto:

The Making of a New Majority

I think of myself as neither a liberal nor a member of the current New Left. I think of myself as a populist, part of a political tradition that stretches back from Dr. Martin Luther King and Ralph Nader to Estes Kefauver, to the early CIO, to the muckrakers, to "prairie avenger" William Jennings Bryan, to Susan Anthony and Thomas Jefferson. I think of myself as part of a political school based on two old and simple goals: the more equal distribution of wealth and income and the decentralization of power to ensure more citizen participation in making decisions.

I guess I have been working toward a populist stance at least since we made "participatory democracy" the central idea of the *Port Huron Statement,* the founding manifesto of Students for a Democratic Society, drafted in 1962. I continued to think of myself as a populist as I followed Robert Kennedy through the steel mills of Gary, Indiana, in 1968, and watched those tough Wallace voters transfer their trust to an earthy enemy of hunger and war. I felt the effort last year to save 69 homes in Corona was a pure populist cause—working-class Italians against Lindsay's experts, the notion of community participation pitted against an abstract conception of progress.

Consensus liberals, the "problem solvers" like Humphrey, Brooke, Javits, Muskie, Tunney, Stevenson, and Rockefeller, seem to me fatally flawed by their lack of nerve and will, by their lingering faith in centralized bureaucracy, by their complicity in the Vietnam holocaust and in the perpetuation of the cold-warrior mentality, by their lack of original ideas, and by their failure to make important headway on any problems when last in power. On issues like the withdrawal of troops from Europe, conspiracy laws, and tax reform, liberalism has become indistinguishable from Nixonian conservatism.

The New Politics constituency appears limited to the white middle class, excessively preoccupied by nuances of style and personality, and uninterested in working-class discontents. They suffer from issue nymphomania, racing from gay liberation one week to fighting over an unimportant district leadership on the West Side of Manhattan the next. They shirk the hard labor of doing coherent institutional and economic analysis without which they cannot get to the root of things.

The New Left, in its Weathermen, Panther and Yippie incarnations, seems anti-democratic, terroristic, dogmatic, stoned on rhetoric and badly disconnected from everyday reality.

Of all the political traditions of redemption available to us, populism seems best to synthesize the root need to redistribute wealth and the commitment to broaden democratic participation, a synthesis that could unite the poor and almost-poor with the young into a new majority for justice.

So the thesis of this essay is that America is ripe for a new urban populist politic, that daily life for millions of white workingmen has become a pain, and that contrary to Kevin Phillips and Richard Scammon, they are now open to anti-establishment alternatives to Wallace and Procaccino.

Since 1952, since Adlai Stevenson's time, the Democratic Party has slowly abandoned the needs of the white working class, the factory worker, the small farmer, the sanitationman, the millions who earn between $6,000 and $10,000 a year with their hands and suffer the boredom of drudgery.

With the honorable exception of Estes Kefauver, who broke his heart trying to teach his party the economic facts of life in the U.S., Democratic politicians aspiring to be President during the 1950s broke with the tradition of Roosevelt and Truman and stopped making bread-and-butter issues—jobs, housing, corporate price-fixing, tax evasion by the rich—the point of their politics. At the same time, academics like professors Daniel Bell and Seymour M. Lipset authored popular obituaries for radicalism. Everything important was solved, they announced, and predicted an optimistic future in which the only disputes would be over means, not ends.

Satisfaction bordering on smugness became the mood of the liberal, middle-class world. The writers and thinkers turned away from the old economic concerns of the 1930s to take up essentially sociological and cultural questions like affluence, suburbia, status anxiety and the role of art in a mass culture. The best-selling books of this period were Daniel Bell's *The End of Ideology,* Vance Packard's *The Status Seekers,* David Riesman's *The Lonely Crowd* and William H. Whyte's *The Organization Man.*

Then came the revival of insurgent politics during the 1960s. But the power-liberals, the Bundys and the McNamaras and the Rostows and the Moynihans, made two large errors. First, accepting the end-of-ideology theory of the fifties, they tended to see social problems in terms of efficient management, rather than as a function of unequal wealth. A technocrat elite from Harvard and RAND were recruited to Camelot as the new "problem solvers." Vietnam is their monument.

The second blunder of the sixties, which I did not fully understand at the time, was the misconception of the domestic crisis as one of color and not of class. Instead of fashioning agencies and programs that helped everyone, black and white, programs like national health insurance, or a $2.50 minimum wage law, or income guarantees, or tax reform that benefited blue-collar families, or creating more jobs . . . instead, the liberals put their energies into marginal programs aimed at blacks and paid for by the middle class; programs like school busing, and civilian review boards, and something LBJ called "an unconditional war to abolish poverty."

But it turned out to be something less. It turned out to be a patronage hustle for sociologists and consultants and a few black political operators. And it did not touch, much less fundamentally change, the lives of the black underclass.

But it did help generate what we would come to call the backlash, because there were no OEO programs in Corona or Bay Ridge, no storefronts offering legal services in Youngstown, no big grants to save decaying white neighborhoods in Hoboken or South Boston.

I cannot recall either Johnson in 1964 or Humphrey in 1968 campaigning on any positive or original ideas that might excite the almost-poor workers, whose votes they took for granted. I can remember LBJ warning that Goldwater would drag us into a war in Asia, and Humphrey talking tough about crime and trying to please everyone on Vietnam. In 1970, the Democrats ran against Herbert Hoover, which was progress.

In contrast, George Wallace recently has been sounding like William Jennings Bryan as he attacks concentrated wealth in his speeches. "The present tax laws," he said in May, "were written to protect the Rockefellers, the Fords, the Carnegies, and the Mellons. The tax-exempt foundations these families have set up are unfair . . . the average workingman is tired of the Internal Revenue Service snooping in every item of his business."

The Kerner Commission Report in 1968 declared "white racism" was the heart of the matter. At the same time the banks and *Fortune* magazine's 500 leading corporations and the utilities and the insurance companies and the oil and pharmaceutical industries continued to make generous profits. But white workers were finding themselves unemployed, laid-off, powerless, worried about crime, unable to pay the hospital bills, unable to send their children to college, breathing poisoned air, working in unsafe and unhealthy conditions in mines, factories and construction sites, and furious about taxes and inflation.

From 1960 to 1968 liberal Democrats governed the country. But nothing basic got done to make life decisively better for the white workingman. When he bitched about street crime, he was called a Goldwaterite by liberals who felt secure in the suburbs behind high fences and expensive locks. When he complained about his daughter being bused, he was called a racist by liberals who could afford to send their own children to private schools. Meanwhile, the liberal elite repeated their little Polish jokes at Yale and on the Vineyard, and they cheered when Eugene McCarthy reminded them in Oregon that the educated people voted for him and the uneducated people voted for Robert Kennedy.

Liberal hypocrisy created a lot of Wallace votes in 1968.

The current economic system in America can fairly be described as socialism for the rich and capitalism for the poor.

There are ample funds for highways, farm subsidies ($10 billion last year), Albany Malls, World Trade Centers, and $80 billion each year for the Pentagon, which, in turn, takes care of the RAND Corporation and the General Dynamics Corporation. There are oil depletion allowances, untaxed Swiss bank accounts, federal regulatory agencies dominated by the corporations they are supposed to watch, and tax-free foundations. Over 300 Americans with incomes of more than $200,000 paid no income tax at all for 1970, according to Congressman Henry Reuss of Wisconsin. Governor Ronald Reagan paid not one cent in state tax last year, although he drew from the state $76,500 in salary and perquisites. This year the Congress voted $200 million in subsidies to shipbuilders, while it refused to appropriate $5 million to prevent and treat lead poisoning in slum children.

Meanwhile, the myth of affluence fostered in the fifties has been shattered. More than 25 million American citizens are living in poverty, according to the Department of Labor's own statistics, and estimates by Michael Harrington and others run as high as 40 million. In New York City alone, more than a million people today live on welfare. More than 60 per cent of white families in New York City earn less than $9,400 a year.

On May 7 of this year the Census Bureau reported that the number of poor people in the nation increased last year for the first time in a decade. Two-thirds of the total are white. Another 7 million white families earn between $5,000 and $7,000 a year, just above the welfare level. And this is before taxes.

(It must be noted, however, that while one in ten whites lived in poverty, one out of every three blacks was below the poverty line of $4,000 a year for a family of four.)

Another recent Census Bureau study showed that the purchasing power of the typical American family did not increase last year, for the first time in a decade.

These two indexes, coupled with the inexorable rise in unemployment, suggest to me that populism is again on the agenda of domestic politics.

(The Harris Poll of July 1, 1971, revealed that 62 per cent of white people held the view that "the rich get richer, and the poor get poorer.")

What might a modern populist movement sound like? What would be its analysis and its priorities? Let's look at a half-dozen issues, six critical domestic problems, and consider specific programs and remedies.

I.   REDISTRIBUTION OF WEALTH AND INCOME

First some boring but obligatory data. According to Gus Tyler's excellent paper "The White Worker," the bottom fifth of the nation's families in 1968 received 5.7 per cent of the country's income; the top fifth received 40.6 per cent.

This maldistribution has been getting worse, not better. In 1949, Tyler says, the richest 1 per cent of the nation owned 21 per cent of the wealth. In 1956, this rose to 26 per cent. Today the top 1 per cent own more than 37 per cent of all the wealth.

So the first plank in my populist platform would be a demand for radical restructuring of all our tax laws. Currently, the poor and the middle class pay a higher percentage of their income in taxes than do the richest 1 per cent of the population. This system not only perpetuates the inequities, but helps make the white middle class conservative, since they are in fact paying more than their fair share of the bill for welfare, open admissions and other programs they oppose.

The super-rich manage to get richer through many complex exemptions, loopholes, and privileges written into the existing tax laws—capital gains, unreported dividends and interest, expense account gimmicks, sacred cow tax shelters for churches and other institutions, depletion allowances and import quotas. Most giant oil companies pay less than 6 per cent in taxes on their billions in profits, thanks to depletion allowances.

The remedies seem self-evident. Close the loopholes, tax church and foundation property and incomes, end the oil and gas depletion allowance, greatly increase the taxes of the super-rich on inheritances, property, estates, stock transfers, bank and insurance company assets. Concentrations of wealth should not be passed along from generation to generation, to people who have never had to work for their millions, but scream about putting the "welfare chiseler" to work.

Again, let me stress I am talking about ending the monopoly the rich have on socialism. The wealthiest citizens, the biggest foundations and the most monopolistic corporations must be made to pay their share. I am in favor of lowering taxes on the policeman from Queens, and the dock worker from Brooklyn, because only on fairness can we build a new majority for justice.

II.   CONTROL OF THE GIANT CORPORATIONS

The biggest corporations have become too powerful, too rich, and are not accountable to anyone. General Motors' annual revenues last year, $18.8 billion, were larger than the budgets of 100 countries in the world. Chase Manhattan Bank has $25 billion in assets. Standard Oil has $19 billion in assets.

The giant corporations help write the tax laws, dominate the regulatory agencies that are supposed to be the independent eyes of the consumers, and they elect senators and make Presidents. Between 1960 and 1970, corporate profits, after taxes, increased by 88 per cent.

These same corporations manufacture unsafe cars that kill people. They also pollute the air and water with carbon monoxide, mercury, lead, and other contaminants. They fix prices, manipulate our appetites, deceive us in their advertisements, put poisonous chemical additives in our foods, ignore antitrust laws with constant mergers that eliminate competition, and continue to sell us badly made and overpriced products. "Crime in the suites," Ralph Nader calls it.

There are various ways to rectify this situation, some sounding conservative, some sounding radical.

First, I would ban all mergers by any of the 500 largest corporations, break up all existing oligopolies, and actually start putting corporate executives in jail whose companies break antitrust laws and pollute the environment.

Second, I would re-invigorate the federal regulatory agencies. I would make Robert Townsend chairman of the SEC, Nicholas Johnson chairman of the FCC, Bess Myerson chairman of the FDA, journalist James Ridgeway chairman of the Federal Trade Commission, and Ralph Nader chief of the Justice Department's antitrust division. I would appoint Richard Ottinger and Pete Hamill to the state Public Service Commission. I'd also create a separate court to try business crimes committed in regulated industries.

Third, a good dose of workers' control is needed to democratize decision-making and make sure profits aren't the only corporate value. The staff of *Le Monde* in France and *Der Spiegel* in Germany now have a voice in editorial policy, and it has made for better publications. Worker councils in Yugoslavia seem to be successful. The only way to stop coal miners from dying of the black lung, and textile workers from suffering brown lung, is to empower them to allocate a certain amount of profit for the protection of their own safety and health.

And last, I would draft legislation to compel all corporations with Defense Department contracts to set aside 25 per cent of all profits for reconversion planning. There is no reason why Republic and Grumman can't build housing. And no reason why aerospace and electronics workers should face unemployment if we finally end the endless war.

III.   A CONSTRUCTIVE EFFORT TO REDUCE CRIME

The right wing has grown fat on this issue. Careers have been made by politicians who act like they are running for sheriff of Tombstone.

This has happened partly because the liberals and the radicals have abdicated. The New Left has no program to combat crime. Students call cops "pigs" while they holler racist at anyone who calls a Vietnamese a "dink" or a "slope."

The liberals ignored the very real problems of street crime. They called it a euphemism for racism, until crime became a menace in their own middle-class neighborhoods. Some ambitious liberal politicians behaved shamelessly, joining the mindless search for scapegoats. Hubert Humphrey came out against strict gun control legislation. So did Frank Church and Eugene McCarthy. Senator Tydings of Maryland introduced a preventive detention bill. Adlai Stevenson II named Thomas Foran, the enthusiastic prosecutor of the Chicago Eight, to be honorary chairman of his Senate campaign. John Tunney praised the FBI and damned permissiveness, pot, and pornography in dozens of campaign speeches in California last autumn. Ed Muskie and Birch Bayh voted for a probably unconstitutional and definitely repressive anti-riot law.

But violent street crime continued to increase in the absence of any constructive legislation. In most places all that was done about crime by those in power was to add more policemen to the force. Policemen, however, do not actually prevent crime, as the "job action" by New York City's police earlier this year helped demonstrate. All they can do, most of the time, is make arrests, after the fact, which in turn only swamp the already inadequate courts and prisons which are underfunded by the law-and-order yahoos and are ignored by the press and reformers.

So the first step I would take to effectively reduce crime (short of eliminating poverty and heroin addiction) would be to give prison reform absolute priority. Eighty per cent of all crimes are committed by recidivists—by men and women who have been arrested before. Jails and penitentiaries are the places where we might actually rehabilitate the individual criminal. But our entire "correction" system is based on the Puritan concept of punishment rather than on rehabilitation. New York City last year spent less than 1 per cent of its $840-million criminal justice budget on rehabilitation programs. Corrections Commissioner George McGrath *requested* less money for rehabilitation this year ($3.2 million) than he asked for last year ($3.5 million). His new budget sought $2,000 for libraries, and $200,000 for consultant fees.

Only through vocational training classes, job training and placement, psychiatric care, half-way houses, reading and writing classes, better probation, parole and work-release programs can we possibly prevent last year's mugger from becoming next week's murderer. We must stop treating criminals like garbage to be dumped as far away as possible, and then forgotten.

IV. DEMOCRATIZE THE CONCENTRATIONS OF POWER IN THE MASS MEDIA

This is a classic populist issue, but, as with crime, the left has abandoned it. Vice President Agnew seized on a legitimate injustice and distorted it, yet his essential point is correct: a handful of rich, white individuals do control all the mass media's outlets.

Among daily newspapers today, 1,483 cities have monopoly ownerships, and only 64 have competing ownerships. Only New York, Wash-

ington and Boston have three competing dailies. All news is transmitted
through national monopolies, the telephone and telegraph systems. There
are two centralized news services, and three television networks. In 90
cities, a single monopoly owns both the daily paper and the local television
station.

Agnew delivered his fiercest attack on the *Times* and the *Washington
Post* in Montgomery, Alabama, where there is a newspaper monopoly
which he did not mention. He did not mention that the Newhouse chain
owns dailies in Mobile and Huntsville, a television station, an FM station
and an AM station in Birmingham, and a CATV franchise in Anniston
(and 22 other papers around the country). Nor did Agnew refer to the
conservative publishing empires of Hearst and Annenberg, or to the
conservative media complex owned by the *Chicago Tribune* that includes
the *Daily News* and WPIX in New York. And he neglected to mention
Robert Wells, the owner of seven newspapers and four television stations,
whom the President has just appointed to the FCC.

The usual liberal criticisms of television tend to concern content
rather than access or ownership: less violence, less censorship, better
children's programming, more muckraking specials like "The Selling of
the Pentagon," fewer reruns, and equal time provisions that help the
Democrats, but not George Wallace or Tom Hayden.

A populist program to redeem television would be based on the
concept that the airwaves are owned by the people, not the corporate
broadcasters or the corporate sponsors, and certainly not the government
in power at the moment. NBC is just a trustee of the airwaves, GM just
a renter of time.

First, we must decentralize ownership by using the antitrust laws to
break up the conglomerates that dominate the media. RCA, a major
Defense Department contractor, owns NBC, and owns Random House,
which owns Pantheon and Knopf. CBS owns Holt, Rinehart and Winston,
Columbia Records, Creative Playthings (toys) and the Yankees. The
Times Mirror Company owns the *Los Angeles Times,* World Publishing
Co., New American Library, *The Dallas Times Herald, Newsday* and
some CATV franchises.

Citizens must have greater access to television. One way to do this
would be to provide a free hour of prime television time every week to
any organization of, say, 10,000 people. This would mean that the
Fortune Society, block associations, women's groups, the PBA, Health-Pac
and community organizations could prepare their own programs.

Other possible reforms: provide federal subsidies for community
newspapers; give cable television franchises to indigenous community
and civic groups, instead of to conglomerates backed by Time Inc. and
Howard Hughes, as Lindsay has done in Manhattan; provide an hour
of free air time each week for viewers to rebut or attack programming;
require all television stations to make available free and equal time to all
candidates during the election season, and refuse to sell time to candi-

dates; develop a television equivalent of WBAI—a nonprofit, listener-owner channel; and perhaps most importantly, give television licenses to local stations owned by blacks, Indians, Eskimos, Polish-Americans, etc., since there are none operating today.

In short, create diversity through competition in programming and broad citizen participation.

V. ESTABLISH A SYSTEM OF NATIONAL HEALTH INSURANCE

Only the very rich can buy satisfactory health care. The poor can't afford doctors, and every working class family knows that one serious illness can wipe out its savings.

New York City has a segregated two-class hospital system: private hospitals with modern technology and excellent care for the affluent, and dirty, rundown municipal hospitals for the poor.

Life should not be for sale. Medicaid and Medicare have failed to remedy the inequities. They don't help the almost-poor, and they have inflated doctor and hospital costs. The chief beneficiaries of these programs have been the big pharmaceutical companies, the insurance companies like Blue Cross, and the hospital-supply companies—the medical-industrial complex. Last year, despite the economic chaos, the drug industry spent $800 million on public relations and advertising and still showed a 10 per cent increase in profits.

The short-run answer is one class of medical care under national health insurance. A Harris poll in April showed that more than 60 per cent of the country wants it. And national health insurance would most directly help those families who are employed but don't qualify for Medicaid and can't afford private insurance.

Ted Kennedy has introduced, with fifteen co-sponsors, the 1971 Health Security Act (S3 and H.R. 22). This legislation would provide comprehensive protection for every citizen, including unlimited hospitalization, surgery, preventive and ambulatory care, unlimited nursing home care, comprehensive dental care for all children under fifteen, and cover the cost of all prescription drugs. These benefits would be financed under Social Security, with the employee contributing 1 per cent out of his salary, and the employer and the federal government each paying 3 per cent. (Nixon's proposals in the field would just amount to a windfall for the insurance industry.)

Until Kennedy's bill is enacted, the poor will get sick, the sick will get poor, and the medical-industrial complex will continue to get rich.

VI. CURB THE POWER OF THE UTILITIES

Con Edison is a monopoly. In exchange for this special privilege the company provides its consumers with blackouts, brownouts, power cutbacks during the summer and pollution of the air and water. (Con Ed is responsible for 40 per cent of the sulphur dioxide we inhale.) It also provides rate increases, exaggerated bills, and shuts off service if you complain.

The New York Telephone Company is also a monopoly. For that special status the company gives consumers no dial tones, wrong numbers, busy signals for information operators, pay phones that don't function and don't return your dime, and exaggerated bills. It also demands cash deposits from poor people, cooperates with the FBI in illegal taps on private citizens, spends millions each year for newspaper ads and public relations, doesn't answer letters of complaint, and bills customers for wrong numbers. The only stockholder in the New York Telephone Company is AT&T, one of the biggest Vietnam war contractors. Last year, despite deteriorating local service, the telephone company paid AT&T $202.7 million in dividends. In February of this year the telephone company asked the PSC to approve a new 29 per cent rate increase.

The usual consumer tactics—writing letters to legislators, trying to reform the PSC, not paying bills—have been ineffective.

So the answer, then, is to go to the root of the problem and end their monopoly status.

The most realistic way to accomplish this would be to municipalize them. This is the way it works in Los Angeles, and their utility rates are about half of New York's. City ownership would also pinpoint accountability. The mayor would feel compelled to improve service because the voters would hold him responsible. With a private monopoly, there is no accountability or retribution for ineptness.

The programs suggested here are not meant as a fixed blueprint. They merely try to suggest redistribution of wealth and power as the pivot of social change.

These ideas will not prevail without considerable social conflict. Their implementation will not be guaranteed merely by electing a Good Guy to the White House in 1972. They can triumph only as part of a larger movement that transcends party and personality and doesn't wait for national elections to energize itself.

The purest avatars of the movement I am talking about are organizers like Ralph Nader, Cesar Chavez, Jesse Jackson and Saul Alinsky. But there are also politicians who have advocated populist programs in the last three years, and who have won elections; Governor Gilligan in Ohio; Senators like McGovern, Harris, Kennedy, Proxmire and Hughes; Congressmen like Wright Patman (when the Republicans are in power), Dellums, Abzug, Reuss, Badillo, Drinan and Conyers; municipal figures like Abrams and Kretchmer.

All I argue is that these ideas are politically feasible, and if translated into policy, they would help a majority of people live a more humane life. That is all politics can do.

ROBERT JAY LIFTON

Beyond Atrocity

The landscape doesn't change much. For days and days you see just about nothing. It's unfamiliar—always unfamiliar. Even when you go back to the same place, it's unfamiliar. And it makes you feel as though, well, there's nothing left in the world but this. . . . You have the illusion of going great distances and traveling, like hundreds of miles . . . and you end up in the same place because you're only a couple of miles away. . . . But you feel like it's not all real. It couldn't possibly be. We couldn't still be in this country. We've been walking for days. You're in Vietnam and they're using real bullets. . . . Here in Vietnam they're actually shooting people for no reason. Any other time you think. It's such an extreme. Here you can go ahead and shoot them for nothing. As a matter of fact it's even . . . smiled upon, you know. Good for you. Everything is backwards. That's part of the kind of unreality of the thing. To the "grunt" [infantryman] this isn't backwards. He doesn't understand. . . . But something [at Mylai 4] was missing. Something you thought was real that would accompany this. It wasn't there. . . . There was something missing in the whole business that made it seem like it really wasn't happening. . . .

—American GI's recollections of Mylai.

When asked to speak on recent occasions, I have announced my title as "On Living in Atrocity." To be sure, neither I nor anyone else lives there all or even most of the time. But at this moment, in early 1971, an American investigator of atrocity finds himself dealing with something that has become, for his countrymen in general, a terrible subterranean image that can be neither fully faced nor wished away. There is virtue in bringing that image to the surface.

In one sense, no matter what happens in the external world, personal atrocity, for everyone, begins at birth. It can also be said that some of us have a special nose for atrocity. Yet I can remember very well, during the early stirrings of the academic peace movement taking place around Harvard University during the mid- and late 1950s—about two hundred years ago, it now seems—how hard it was for us to *feel* what might

BEYOND ATROCITY By Robert J. Lifton. From CRIMES OF WAR, edited by Richard Falk, Gabriel Kolko and Robert Jay Lifton. Copyright © 1971 by Education-Action Conference on American Crimes of War in Vietnam. Reprinted by permission of Random House, Inc. First published in *The Saturday Review*, March 6, 1971.

happen at the other end of a nuclear weapon. Whatever one's nose for atrocities, there are difficulties surrounding the imaginative act of coming to grips with them.

After six months of living and working in Hiroshima, studying the human effects of the first atomic bomb, I found that these difficulties were partly overcome and partly exacerbated. On the one hand, I learned all too well to feel what happened at the other end of an atomic bomb. But on the other hand, I became impressed with the increasing gap we face between our technological capacity for perpetrating atrocities and our imaginative ability to confront their full actuality. Yet the attempt to narrow that gap can be enlightening, even liberating. For me, Hiroshima was a profoundly "radicalizing" experience—not in any strict ideological sense but in terms of fundamental issues of living and dying, of how one lives, of how one may die.

Whatever the contributing wartime pressures, Hiroshima looms as a paradigm of technological atrocity. Each of the major psychological themes discernible in Hiroshima survivors—death immersion, psychic numbing, residual guilt—has direct relationship to the atrocity's hideously cool and vast technological character. The specific technology of the bomb converted the brief moment of exposure into a lifelong encounter with death—through the sequence of the survivor's early immersion in massive and grotesque death and dying, his experiencing or witnessing bizarre and frequently fatal acute radiation effects during the following weeks and months, his knowledge of the increased incidence over the years of various forms (always fatal) of leukemia and cancer, and finally his acquisition of a death-tainted group identity, an "identity of the dead" or shared sense of feeling emotionally bound both to those killed by the bomb and to the continuing worldwide specter of nuclear genocide.

The experience of psychic numbing, or emotional desensitization—what some survivors called "paralysis of the mind"—was a necessary defense against feeling what they clearly knew to be happening. But when one looks further into the matter he discovers that those who made and planned the use of that first nuclear weapon—and those who today make its successors and plan their use—require their own form of psychic numbing. They too cannot afford to feel what they cognitively know would happen.

Victims and victimizers also shared a sense of guilt, expressed partly in a conspiracy of silence, a prolonged absence of any systematic attempt to learn about the combined physical and psychic assaults of the bomb on human beings. Survivors felt guilty about remaining alive while others died, and also experienced an amorphous sense of having been part of, having imbibed, the overall evil of the atrocity. The perpetrators of Hiroshima (and those in various ways associated with them)—American scientists, military and political leaders, and ordinary people—felt their own forms of guilt, though, ironically, in less tangible ways than the victims. Yet one cannot but wonder to what extent Hiroshima produced in

Americans (and others) a guilt-associated sense that if we could do this we could do anything, and that anyone could do anything to us—in other words, an anticipatory sense of unlimited atrocity.

If these are lessons of Hiroshima, one has to learn them personally. My own immersion in massive death during investigations in that city, though much more privileged and infinitely less brutal, will nonetheless be as permanent as that of Hiroshima survivors themselves. As in their case, it has profoundly changed my relationship to my own death as well as to all collective forms of death that stalk us. I had a similarly personal lesson regarding psychic numbing. During my first few interviews in Hiroshima I felt overwhelmed by the grotesque horrors described to me, but within the short space of a week or so this feeling gave way to a much more comfortable sense of myself as a psychological investigator, still deeply troubled by what he heard but undeterred from his investigative commitment. This kind of partial, task-oriented numbing now strikes me as inevitable and, in this situation, useful—yet at the same time potentially malignant in its implications.

By "becoming" a Hiroshima survivor (as anyone who opens himself to the experience must), while at the same time remaining an American, I shared something of both victims' and victimizers' sense of guilt. This kind of guilt by identification has its pitfalls, but I believe it to be one of the few genuine psychological avenues to confrontation of atrocity. For these three psychological themes are hardly confined to Hiroshima: Death immersion, psychic numbing, and guilt are a psychic trinity found in all atrocity.

Hiroshima also taught me the value and appropriateness of what I would call the apocalyptic imagination. The term offends our notions of steadiness and balance. But the technological dimensions of contemporary atrocity seem to me to require that we attune our imaginations to processes that are apocalyptic in the full dictionary meaning of the word—processes that are "wildly unrestrained" and "ultimately decisive," that involve "forecasting or predicting the ultimate destiny of the world in the shape of future events" and "foreboding imminent disaster or final doom."

In the past this kind of imagination has been viewed as no more than the "world-ending" delusion of the psychotic patient. But for the people of Hiroshima the "end of the world"—or something very close to it—became part of the actuality of their experience. Thus one survivor recalled: "My body seemed all black; everything seemed dark, dark all over . . . then I thought, 'The world is ending.' " And another: "The feeling I had was that everyone was dead. . . . I thought this was the end of Hiroshima—of Japan—of humankind." Those witnessing Nazi mass murder—the greatest of all man's atrocities to date—called forth similar images, though they could usually perceive that the annihilating process was in some way selective (affecting mainly Jews or anti-Nazis or other specific groups). As Hiroshima took me to Auschwitz and Treblinka, however, I was struck mostly by the similarities and parallels in the overall psychology of atrocity.

Yet similar end-of-the-world impressions have been recorded in connection with "God-made" atrocities, as in the case of survivors' accounts of the plagues of the Middle Ages:

> How will posterity believe that there has been a time when without the lightings of heaven or the fires of earth, without wars or other visible slaughter, not this or that part of the earth, but well-nigh the whole globe, has remained without inhabitants. . . . We should think we were dreaming if we did not with our eyes, when we walk abroad, see the city in mourning with funerals, and returning to our home, find it empty, and thus know that what we lament is real.

The plagues were God-made not only in the sense of being a mysterious and deadly form of illness outside of man's initiation or control but also because they could be comprehended as part of a God-centered cosmology. To be sure, scenes like the above strained people's belief in an ordered universe and a just God, but their cosmology contained enough devils, enough flexibility, and enough depth of imprint to provide, if not a full "explanation" of holocaust, at least a continuing psychic framework within which to go on living. In contrast, Hiroshima and Auschwitz were carried out by men upon men, and at a time when old cosmologies had already lost much of their hold and could provide little explanatory power. Survivors were left with an overwhelming sense of dislocation and absurdity: Like the GI quoted earlier in relationship to Mylai, something for them was "missing"—namely, meaning, or a sense of reality. With Hiroshima and Auschwitz now part of man's historical experience, it is perilously naïve to insist that our imaginative relationship to world-destruction can remain unchanged—that we can continue to make a simple-minded distinction between psychotic proclivity for, and "normal" avoidance of, that image.

Yet, whatever the force of external events, there is a subjective, imaginative component to the perceived "end of the world." Hiroshima survivors had to call forth early inner images of separation and helplessness, of stasis and annihilation, images available from everyone's infancy and childhood, but with greater force to some than to others. There is, therefore, a danger, not just for Hiroshima survivors but for all of us, of being trapped in such images, bound by a psychic sense of doom to the point of being immobilized and totally unable or unwilling to participate in essential day-by-day struggles to counter atrocity and prevent the collective annihilation imagined.

Psychological wisdom, then, seems to lie in neither wallowing in, nor numbing ourselves to, our imaginings of apocalypse. A simple example of the constructive use of the apocalyptic imagination is recorded by Eugene Rabinowitch, from the beginning an articulate leader in scientists' anti-atomic bomb movements. Rabinowitch describes how, when walking down the streets of Chicago during the summer of 1945, he looked up at the city's great buildings and suddenly imagined a holocaust in which skyscrapers crumbled. He then vowed to redouble his efforts to prevent that kind of event from happening by means of the scientists' petition he and others were drawing up to head off the dropping of an atomic bomb, without warning, on a populated area. The effort, of course, failed, but this kind of apocalyptic imagination—on the part of Rabinowitch, Leo Szilard, and Bertrand Russell, among others—has made it possible for at least a small minority of men and women to name and face the true conditions of our existence. (Bertrand Russell had earlier exhibited the dangers of the apocalyptic imagination when he advocated that we threaten to drop atomic bombs on Russia in order to compel it to agree to a system of international control of nuclear weapons.) For we live in the shadow of the ultimate atrocity, of the potentially terminal revolution—and if that term is itself a contradiction, the same contradicton is the central fact of our relationship to death and life.

We perpetrate and experience the American atrocity at Mylai in the context of these apocalyptic absurdities and dislocations. The GI's quoted description suggests not only that atrocity can be a dreamlike affair (in this sense, resembling the quoted passage about the plague) but that it is committed by men living outside of ordinary human connection, outside of both society and history. Mylai was acted out by men who had lost their bearings, men wandering about in both a military and psychic no man's land. The atrocity itself can be seen as a grotesquely paradoxical effort to put straight this crooked landscape, to find order and significance in disorder and absurdity. There is at the same time an impulse to carry existing absurdity and disorder to their logical extremes as if both to transcend and demonstrate that aberrant existential state.

Atrocities are committed by desperate men—in the case of Mylai, men victimized by the absolute contradictions of the war they were asked to fight, by the murderous illusions of their country's policy. Atrocity, then, is a perverse quest for meaning, the end result of a spurious sense of mission, the product of false witness.

To say that American military involvement in Vietnam is itself a crime is also to say that it is an atrocity-producing situation. Or to put the matter another way, Mylai illuminates, as nothing else has, the essential nature of America's war in Vietnam. The elements of this atrocity-producing situation include an advanced industrial nation engaged in a counter-insurgency action, in an underdeveloped area, against guerrillas who merge with the people—precisely the elements that Jean-Paul Sartre has described as inevitably genocidal. In the starkness of its murders and the extreme dehumanization experienced by victimizers and imposed on victims, Mylai reveals to us how far America has gone along the path of deadly illusion.

Associated with this deadly illusion are three psychological patterns as painful to the sensitized American critic of the war as they are self-evident. The first is the principle of atrocity building upon atrocity, because of the need to deny the atrocity-producing situation. In this sense, Mylai itself was a product of earlier, smaller Mylais; and it was followed not by an ending of the war but by the American extension of the war into Laos and Cambodia.

The second principle involves the system of non-responsibility. One searches in vain for a man or group of men who will come forward to take the blame or even identify a human source or responsibility for what took place—from those who fired the bullets at Mylai (who must bear some responsibility, but were essentially pawns and victims of the atrocity-producing situation, and are now being made scapegoats as well); to the junior-grade officers who gave orders to do the firing and apparently did some of it themselves; to the senior-grade officers who seemed to have ordered the operation; to the highest military and civilian planners in Vietnam, the Pentagon, and the White House who created such things as a *"permanent free-fire zone"* (which, according to Richard Hammer, means "in essence . . . that any Americans operating within it had, basically, a license to kill and any Vietnamese living within it had a license to be killed"), planners who made even more basic decisions about continuing and even extending the war; to the amorphous conglomerate of the American people who, presumably, chose, or at least now tolerate, the aforementioned as their representatives. The atrocity-producing situation, at least in this case, depends upon what Masao Maruyama has called a "system of non-responsibility." Situation and system alike are characterized by a technology and a technicized bureaucracy not checked by sentient human minds.

The third and perhaps most terrible pattern is the psychology of nothing happening. General Westmoreland gives way to General Abrams, President Johnson to President Nixon, a visibly angry student generation to one silent with rage—and the war, the atrocity-producing situation, continues to grind out its thousands of recorded and unrecorded atrocities. To be more accurate, something does happen: The subliminal American perception of atrocity edges toward consciousness, making it more difficult but, unfortunately, not impossible to defend and maintain the atrocity-producing situation. The widespread feeling of being stuck in atrocity contributes, in ways we can now hardly grasp, to a national sense of degradation and a related attraction to violence, for nothing is more conducive to collective rage and totalism than a sense of being bound to a situation perceived to be both suffocating and evil.

Atrocity in general, and Mylai in particular, brings its perpetrators—even a whole nation—into the realm of existential evil. That state is exemplified by what another GI described to me as a working definition of the enemy in Vietnam: "If it's dead, it's VC—because it's dead. If it's dead, it *had* to be VC. And of course, a corpse couldn't defend itself anyhow." When at some future moment, ethically sensitive historians get around to telling the story of the Vietnam War—assuming that there will be ethically sensitive (or, for that matter, any) historians around—I have no doubt that they will select the phenomenon of the "body count" as the perfect symbol of America's descent into evil. What better represents the numbing, brutalization, illusion (most of the bodies, after all, turn out to be those of civilians), grotesque competition (companies and individuals vie for the highest body counts), and equally grotesque technicizing (progress lies in the *count*) characteristic of the overall American crime of the war in Vietnam.

Mylai is rather unusual in one respect. It combines two kinds of atrocity: technological overkill (of unarmed peasants by Americans using automatic weapons) and a more personal, face-to-face gunning-down of victims at point-blank range. This combination lends the incident particular psychic force, however Americans may try to fend off awareness of its implications. A participating GI could characterize Mylai as "just like a Nazi-type thing" (as recorded in Seymour Hersh's book *My Lai 4*), a characterization made by few if any pilots or crewmen participating in the more technologically distanced killings of larger numbers of Vietamese civilians from the air.

The sense of being associated with existential evil is new to Americans. This is so partly because such perceptions have been suppressed in other atrocity-producing situations, but also because of the humane elements of American tradition that contribute to a national self-image of opposing, through use of force if necessary, just this kind of "Nazi-type thing." The full effects of the war in Vietnam upon this self-image are at this point unclear. The returns from Mylai are not yet in. Perhaps they never are for atrocity. But I for one worry about a society that seems to absorb, with some questioning but without fundamental self-examination, first Hiroshima and now Mylai.

For there is always a cost. Atrocities have a way of coming home. The killings by National Guardsmen of Kent State students protesting the extension of the war into Cambodia reflect the use of violence in defense of illusion and denial of evil—and the killings of blacks at Augusta, Georgia, and of black students at Jackson State in Mississippi reflect more indirectly that atmosphere. Indeed there is a real danger that the impulse to preserve illusion and deny evil could carry America beyond Vietnam and Cambodia into some form of world-destroying nuclear confrontation. In this sense, as well as in its relationship to existential evil, Mylai symbolized a shaking of the American foundations—a bitterly mocking perversion of what was left of the American dream. Like Hiroshima and Auschwitz, Mylai is a revolutionary event: Its total inversion of moral standards raises fundamental questions about the institutions and national practices of the nation responsible for it.

The problem facing Americans now is: What do we do with our atrocities? Do we simply try our best to absorb them by a kind of half-admission that denies their implications and prevents genuine confronta-

tion? That is the classical method of governments for dealing with documented atrocities, and it is clearly the method now being used by the
U.S. government and military in holding trials of individuals. Those who
did the shooting and those who covered up the event are being labeled
aberrant and negligent, so that the larger truth of the atrocity-producing
situation can be avoided. The award of a Pulitzer Prize to Seymour Hersh
for his journalistic feat in uncovering the story of Mylai and telling it in
detail would seem to be a step in the direction of that larger truth. Yet
one cannot but fear that such an award—as in the case of the National
Book Award I received for my work on Hiroshima—can serve as a form
of conscience-saving token recognition in place of confrontation. Surely
more must be faced throughout American society, more must be articu-
lated and given form by leaders and ordinary people, if this atrocity is to
contribute to a national process of illumination instead of further degradation.

I am struck by how little my own profession has had to say about the
matter—about the way in which aberrant *situations* can produce collective
disturbance and mass murder. The psychiatry and psychohistory I would
like to envisage for the future would put such matters at its center. It
would also encourage combining ethical involvement with professional
skills in ways that could simultaneously shed light upon such crimes of
war and contribute to the transformation our country so desperately
requires. In dealing with our dislocations, we need to replace the false
witness of atrocity with the genuine witness of new and liberating forms
and directions. The task, then, is to confront atrocity in order to move
beyond it.

JOHN PASSMORE

Paradise Now

THE LOGIC OF THE NEW MYSTICISM

Mystics of the traditional sort, Christian or Hindu or
Buddhist, would for the most part deny, with some acerbity, that there is
any "real" resemblance between direct enjoyment and mystical union. The
sexual language in which mystics delight, they would assure us, is only
"symbolic"—although why the mystic should turn so naturally to the

PARADISE NOW Reprinted by permission of Charles Scribner's Sons from THE PERFECT-
IBILITY OF MAN by John Passmore. Copyright © 1970 by John Passmore. First published in *Encounter*, November 1970.

symbol of the passive bride remains to be explained. Contemporary mysticism—as exemplified in the "body-mysticism" of Norman Brown's *Life Against Death*—is bolder; it deliberately identifies mystical experience and sensual enjoyment. It is not unique in so doing; in some forms of Eastern mysticism, in Tantric Buddhism, for example, the two are also identified. The "new mystics," however, think of themselves as inheriting the tradition of Christian, as well as Buddhist and Hindu, mysticism, even if they are particularly attracted by the religious attitudes of India, Japan, and Tibet.

What happened in the eighteenth century could be described as the Confucianisation of Europe; what is happening now, one might say in the same sense, is the Buddhisation of Europe. In one of his *Letters to Leontine Zanta* Teilhard [de Chardin] remarks: "We could perhaps learn from the mystics of the Far East how to make our religion more 'Buddhist' instead of being over-absorbed by ethics, that is to say too Confucianist. . . ." It never seems to occur to the new mystics to ask themselves whether the societies in which mysticism and drug-taking have flourished are in any sense "more perfect" than Western societies, whether love is more widespread in them, or a sense of community, or compassion, or courage—to say nothing of creative achievements in art and literature. But since a French convert to Buddhism, André Migot, is prepared to argue that Tibet—as it was in the time of the Lamas—and Upper Mongolia are the best governed people in the world, I suppose someone might also claim that they have the best philosophers, the best scientists, and the best artists.

In most respects, certainly, the new mystics enunciate familiar themes, but from a new, bodily, point of view. Take the case of timelessness. Freud once remarked (although without much relying on the doctrine) that "there is nothing in the id which corresponds to the idea of time." And in a sentence he jotted down at the very end of his life he also wrote: "Mysticism is the obscure self-perception of the realm outside the ego, of the id."[1] We might put the same point, thus: in direct enjoyment there is no reference to the past or the future; mysticism is an attempt to go back beyond repression to a state of uncaring enjoyment or "play."

Brown argues, quite specifically, that the very idea of time is a product of repression. "Time," he says, "is . . . neurotic." So, too, he maintains, are such human achievements—or what we should ordinarily take to be achievements—as formal logic, quantified science, industrial production. As against all such "achievements," Brown sets up as his ideal the "insights" of mysticism, Romantic poetry, the childlike, playful attitude to life, direct sensuous enjoyment, unconfined, unrepressed. The traditional mystics, he says, "take seriously, and traditional psycho-analysis does not, the possibility of human perfectibility and the hope of finding a way out

[1] *New Introductory Lectures on Psycho-Analysis,* XXXI (trans. J. Strachey), in *The Standard Edition of the Complete Psychological Works* (London, 1964) Vol. XXII, p. 74; Vol. XXIII, p. 300.

of the human neurosis into that simple health that animals enjoy, but not man." Freud presented a dilemma: either civilisation, which rests on repression, or unrepressed enjoyment. When it came to the point he preferred civilisation, if with some misgivings. Brown, in the typical mystical fashion, chooses the other horn of the dilemma.

Freud's own teachings, Brown argues, are badly affected by repression. This is why—most clearly, perhaps, in his "Analysis Terminable and Interminable"—Freud was led to reject the view that it is ever possible fully to free a person from internal conflicts, to "perfect" him. "Our aim," Freud wrote, "will not be to rub off every peculiarity of human character for the sake of a schematic 'normality,' nor yet to demand that the person who has been 'thoroughly analysed' shall feel no passions and develop no internal conflicts."[2] The object of psycho-analysis, he rather says, is to secure the effective operation of the ego, the "I" of everyday life. Brown, like the classical mystics, is completely dissatisfied with this everyday "I," and, more generally, with Freud's anti-perfectibilist conclusions.

For Freud, although the child is "polymorphously perverse," civilisation rests on genital heterosexuality. So far as this is so, Brown concludes, civilisation is grossly imperfect. The perfected human being will delight "in that full life of all the body which [he] now fears"; his sexual enjoyment will no longer be flawed by an anxiety lest it overstep the permissible limits of sensuality.[3] The concentration on genital sexuality is, Brown says, "unnatural" and constitutes "the bodily base of the neurotic character disorders in the human ego." We need not pause to ask whether this is so: Brown's ideal is what interests us, the ideal of an enjoyment which is immediate and absolute, which refuses nothing in the way of immediate experience.

As for science, that has value (Brown argues) only if it can be transformed into a "non-morbid" form in which it would be "erotic" rather than "sadistic," seeking, that is, "not mastery over but union with nature." It would then be a type of "erotic exuberance," no longer an attempt to replace the world we enjoy by a set of laconic formulae. Goethe's theory of colours, in which, in opposition to Newton's mathematico-physical analysis, colours are objects of immediate enjoyment, is for Brown, as for so many German or German-inspired thinkers, the paradigm of "true," non-morbid, science.

[2] *Analysis Terminable and Interminable* (trans. J. Rivière), in *Standard Edition,* Vol. XXIII, p. 250.
[3] Recent investigations into sexual life in the United States have made it clear that in that country what Brown sets up as an ideal is in fact being largely realised: sexual relationships, to a rapidly increasing degree, are taking an anal or oral form. See the investigations reported in Charles Winick, *The New People: Desexualization in American Life* (New York, 1968; paperback ed., 1969), pp. 319–23. The new mysticism, in this and in other respects, may be responding to a general social change, as distinct from advocating an eccentric ideal.

THE LIBERTINE AS HERO

Doctrines very like Brown's are to be found in much of the literature of the 1960s, especially in novels originating in the United States. In an underground novel first published in 1966, Richard Farina's *Been Down so Long it Looks Like Up to Me,* drug-taking (with its object the destruction of time and care), sexual promiscuity (which does not involve any care for what is enjoyed), and mysticism (which cares nothing for any merely human achievements), run together in harness with nostalgia for the television serials of the children's session and—of all things—the writings of A. A. Milne. Scenes of sexual enjoyment are interlarded with extracts from *Winnie the Pooh;* one of the characters is named "Heffalump"—another, equally characteristically, is called "Gnossos," to suggest gnosticism.

That "Bible of the hippies," Henry Miller's *Tropic of Capricorn,* no less freely deploys all the old mystical themes. "There is only one great adventure," writes Miller, "and that is inward towards the self, and for that, time nor space nor even deeds matter." To embark on that "adventure," men must not go forward but backwards, according to Miller, into a super-infantile realm of being—to that life of early childhood which "seems like a limitless universe." The "hipster," Norman Mailer writes in a similar spirit, lives "in that enormous present which is without past or future, memory or planned intention." The ideal of John Barth's *Giles Goat-Boy,* characteristically, is "only to Be, always to Be, until nothing was . . . but one placeless, timeless, nameless throb of Being"— and "Be" is used as a synonym for sexual enjoyment.

Indeed, the demand for carefree, child-like enjoyment is what, at least in its "Romantic" form, "the revolt of the young" is about. Many of the young revolutionaries—very obviously in Czechoslovakia but, in some degree, also in the democracies—are still working within the liberal tradition. What they are seeking is an extension of democratic rights, greater access to representative institutions, a higher degree of personal freedom. They may be mistaken in believing that a particular right will give them greater freedom; but this is a mistake about the facts. There is certainly nothing undemocratic, for example, in opposing conscription. The "Romantic" rebels, on the contrary, are not interested in democratic institutions or in democratic processes. In the manner of the anarchists before them, they would like to replace institutions by "community."

Although the two types of revolt are, in practice, interconnected in complicated ways, in their pure forms they stand in complete opposition one to another. This is very clearly brought out in Yves Ciampi's semi-documentary film *A Matter of Days* (1969). The young French "Romantic" revolutionary heroine is bored and exasperated by the Czechoslovakian student revolt; to her, it is merely an attempt to set up that sort of bourgeois society against which, in France, she has been rebelling. The contrast between the risk-taking revolution of the young Czechs and the theatrical gestures of the "Romantic" revolutionaries is only too manifest. But that is not to say that the "Romantic" revolutionaries have absolutely no ground for their revolt, however ill-defined may be their objectives and however unpalatably childish some of its manifestations may be. (Violence can be a form of play: and the faecal preoccupations of some of the more depressing American young are typical of childish scatology—although it has to be added that both violence and obscenity can be a reaction of helplessness. It has also to be added that neither violence nor obscenity is peculiar to the young. What their elders see, abstractly, as authority, the young experience concretely as violence.)

The society of their elders—to a degree exaggerated by the Depression and the war which followed—placed its emphasis either on success or on security, and, in either case, looked to the future. "Everything," writes Henry Miller, describing the household of his childhood, "was for tomorrow, but tomorrow never came." In general, modern life is extraordinarily dependent on time. No doubt, there are still areas of freedom. We have not yet reached the point described in J. G. Ballard's story "Chronopolis,"[4] in which, to avoid traffic problems, every detail of everyone's daily life is governed by a rigid time-table. The narrator of Zamyatin's wholly time-dominated *We* can look back with astonishment to our own era as one when men were still free to walk in the streets, or to have sexual intercourse, at times of their own choosing. But the fact remains that whereas not until the late Middle Ages were there town clocks, modern life would be unimaginable without what the English language significantly calls "a wrist*watch*." It is by no means surprising, then, that the ideal of timelessness—of inhabiting a world in which nobody ever says "you'll be late"—should have its appeal.

Nor is it at all surprising that the ideal of pure enjoyment should be resuscitated. For a great many people, life in our society—as, admittedly, in any other society—has been sheer toil, not at all a "game," let alone an exercise of "loves." This is perhaps particularly true of the executive classes, from the ranks of whose children the New Mystics are so largely recruited. As for play, simple carefree enjoyment, that has threatened to vanish. Forced to postpone enjoyment, the middle-aged generation, as the young can see for themselves, find it unattainable when at last they "have time" for it. They seek for enjoyment, no doubt, but what they find, often enough, is only a new form of toil. Even games in the narrower sense of the word have come to be reserved for those who play them well; and merely to play, as distinct from playing games, is thought of as undignified, unworthy of the "serious man." (There is an extraordinary contrast, at this point, between the attitude of the Japanese—in so far as they are

---

[4] Included in J. G. Ballard, *The Four-Dimensional Nightmare* (Penguin, 1965).

still not wholly converted to Western ways—and the attitude of the West; the idea of relaxation as "play" still survives in Japan. But it is conjoined, it would seem, with an attitude of mind for which work is mere toil, not enjoyment with care.) [5]

If the old puritanical attitudes to sexual play have broken down (this has only happend in part) they have often been replaced by new forms of anxiety, deriving from "sex manuals"—anxieties about "sexual adequacy," anxieties about inhibitions. Whole books are now written on "the sexual responsibility" of the man or of the woman. Sex has become almost as serious a matter, as little spontaneous, as business. "Sexual play" is now, at its best, a "game," but at its worst, dutiful toil, no longer the sponta-neous flowering of tender sensuality, but an applied technique. The inten-tions behind such manuals are often humane; they are attempts to turn sexual activity into a form of love which involves the cherishing of each sexual partner by the other. Many of them take as their starting-point a growing concern for women, the refusal to regard them as mere objects of enjoyment. But every "love," like every "game," can easily be con-verted into a form of anxiety-ridden toil. "We turn lovemaking into a compulsory sport," writes the novelist Stephen Vizinczey in his *In Praise of Older Women,* "an etiquette of technique or a therapeutic prescrip-tion." And then in reaction from this, as he goes on to point out, we "haste to succumb to joy"; we take the libertine as our hero. (The libertine lives in an "Everlasting Now" by deliberately refusing to pay any attention to the future of the woman he seduces.) That kind of love which is neither a game nor a form of toil, which rests on enjoyment with care but cherishes its object is what seems to lie beyond our capacities.

PAROXYSMS OF INTOXICATION

One can only too easily understand why, when "loves" are understood as "toil," the new mystics reject every form of care involving cherishing love, in favour of an immediate anxiety-free enjoyment, Paradise Now, to be obtained by drugs, if in no other way. Their spokesmen, for the most part, fail to make the crucial distinctions on which we have been insisting. They distinguish, merely, between "games" and "non-games"—defining games as "behavioural sequences defined by roles, rules, rituals, goals, strategies, values" and counting as non-games only "physiological reflexes, spontaneous play, and transcendental awareness." [6] But role, rules, goals, strategies, values are as characteristic of toil as of games: such a definition entirely overlooks the element of *enjoyment* in games—perhaps because it is being assumed, as it is so often assumed, that "care" and "enjoyment" are incompatible. As a consequence, it is made to appear that man has to choose between toil and play. It may be argued that the best human society can do for most men is to provide for them intervals

[5] David & Evelyn Riesman, *Conversations in Japan* (1967), pp. 188, 195.
[6] Timothy Leary, Richard Alpert, & Ralph Metzner, *The Psychedelic Experience* (1964), p. 13; Lewis Yablonsky, *The Hippie Trip* (1968), pp. 311–12.

of play in a life of toil. In his *Laws* (653) Plato suggests something of this kind. The Gods, he says, out of pity for men's toil have set up festivals, to offer them relief. The "carnival"—a period of irresponsible enjoyment—is a familiar feature of traditional societies and has survived, in a reduced and modified form, into the modern world. Puritanism, with its ideal of a wholly toil-dominated life, sought to destroy festivals; the contemporary fascination with "orgies" reflects, perhaps, a self-conscious attempt to reinstate them. It is worth observing that not only the essentially totalitarian Plato but also Dostoevsky's Grand Inquisitor suggest that a life which alternates between toil and play is the one which makes men easiest to control. When men enjoy their work they also demand the freedom to innovate within it; toil plus play is a recipe for tyranny, enjoyment in work entails freedom.

Closely associated with the rejection of loves as too onerous is the rejection of freedom and responsibility in favour of the mystical ideal of "unity." The young generation respond (so we are told) "to the sense and sound of friendship and community, to the exultation they feel when thousands of people link hands and sing *We Shall Overcome*." They are prepared to sacrifice everything to "that feeling of community, of life;" they are not to be deterred by "19th-century rhetoric about democracy and freedom."[7] This, of course, was the Nazi attitude. If the young have come to mistrust "19th-century rhetoric about freedom and democracy"— not surprisingly when one recalls how often this "rhetoric" is used by those for whom "freedom" means the despoliation of natural resources and "democracy" the use of the State to suppress minorities—they have still not learnt sufficiently to mistrust 20th-century rhetoric about "community and life."

I do not mean to suggest that the "Romantic Rebels" are Nazis in jeans; they have an almost pathological mistrust of the "leader principle." Fundamentally, they are Dionysians, in Nietzsche's sense of the word. Indeed, Nietzsche's description of the Dionysians sums up their ideals admirably:

> Now the slave is free; now all the stubborn, hostile barriers, which necessity, caprice or shameless fashion have erected between man and man, are broken down. Now, with the gospel of universal harmony, each one feels himself not only united, reconciled, blended with his neighbor, but as one with him; he feels as if the veil of Maya had been torn aside and were now merely fluttering in tatters before the mysterious Primordial Unity. In song and dance man expresses himself as a member of a higher community . . . from him emanate supernatural sounds. He feels himself a god, he himself now walks about enchanted, in ecstasy, like to the gods whom he saw walking about in his dreams. He is no longer an artist, he has become a work of art: in these

[7] Jacobs and Landau, *The New Radicals* (1966), p. 15.

JOHN PASSMORE

paroxysms of intoxication, the artistic power of all nature reveals itself
to the highest gratification of the Primordial Unity.

There could be no better description of the world of pure play.
Nietzsche, too, was no Nazi. But the fact is that the attempt to construct
a society wholly based on "play" and "community" leads either to total
collapse or to tyranny. If not the God Dionysus, then an earthly, and
less amiable, surrogate has to sustain it.[8]
The attempt, however, is understandable. Modern democracy, which
pretends to be pluralistic, daily becomes more atomistic. Universities, for
example, threaten to become stock-piles of experts, who in no way cherish
either the traditions of the University to which they belong or, except in
an accidental way, their colleagues and pupils. The Stoical ideal of self-
sufficiency has in part been realised: the effect is that men feel isolated,
powerless against the State, lonely. Often enough, especially in America,
loneliness is described as if it were the human condition. But the themes
of human loneliness, separation, isolation, are typical of the industrial age,
not of literature as a whole, where loneliness is represented, rather, either
as something to be sought—"I wandered lonely as a cloud"—or as a
condition to which a few, but only a few, human beings are subjected by
chance. Adam Ferguson saw this clearly, even in the 18th century. It is, he
suggests, only in the "commercial state"—although he adds "if ever"—

> that man is sometimes found a detached and a solitary being: he has
> found an object which sets him in competition with his fellow-creatures,
> and he deals with them as he does with his cattle and his soil, for the
> sake of the profits they bring.[9]

The young are rebelling, in part, against the atomistic tendencies of
modern society. But they have reacted, in the manner only too typical of
human beings, by reverting to the old perfectibilist—and in the end
tyrannical—ideal of a total unity rather than the admittedly more complex
ideal of a plurality of intersecting communities. It is very natural to argue
thus: the experience of belonging to a community is essential to "humanity," therefore the best of all possible worlds would be a total community
to which everyone would belong. But this conclusion by no means follows.
If communities can be stimulating, encouraging, the source of "graces,"
they can also be stifling, discouraging, destructive of love. A man can be
born into a community which does not suit him, from which he has to
break loose if he is ever to enjoy his particular loves. One great virtue of
democracy, so long as it continues to be a network of communities, is that
it is always possible to leave one community and join another, with
different rules, different habits, devoted to different pursuits.

[8] See *The Birth of Tragedy from the Spirit of Music* (trans. Fadiman) in *The Philosophy
of Nietzsche* (1937). The reference is to pp. 173–4 of the separately paginated text of
Ecce Homo and *The Birth of Tragedy*.
[9] Adam Ferguson, *An Essay on the History of Civil Society* (1767; ed. 1966), p. 19.

This implies, however, that not *everybody* does so; otherwise, there will be no community to join; the value of a community depends on its possessing a degree of stability, of continuity. (Admitting, of course, that the birth of new communities and the death of old communities is also a part of the democratic process.) Too considerable a degree of mobility destroys community; it generates what Durkheim called *anomie*. A university teacher, for example, is unlikely to cherish his university, his colleagues, his students, if he is perpetually poised, ready to move anywhere which offers him more money or a higher status. He may try to substitute his professional associations for his university, but the professional association provides relatively few personal contacts: it cannot serve as a substitute for a face-to-face group. And it leaves his students, not yet "professionals," with no sense of belonging, in their university, to a genuine community.[10]

These are just the circumstances in which one would expect to encounter a sense of loss, issuing in a demand for a total community, in which one would be "at home" wherever one moved. To react thus, however, is to miss the point that a community needs to be small and adapted to the special interests of its members—"available," up to certain limits of size, to those who share these interests, but certainly not providing a suitable "home" for everybody. A "total" community would be so diluted as to be no longer a community. Concretely, indeed, it would coincide with that completely atomistic society which, abstractly, is its opposite extreme.

It is easy enough to see this in the history of universities. The attempt to include all forms of activity within the university destroys the university; it becomes pointless, from the standpoint of "community," to be a member of it. Everyone begins to pursue his work in isolation from his fellows. So the "total" community—the "multiversity"—ceases to be a community at all, and the advantages which previously excluded persons and activities were supposed to gain from membership of it no longer exist—just as when an attempt is made to "let everybody enjoy" the peace and quiet of a mountain valley by opening a four-lane highway to it. The student, often enough, feels that he belongs to a "real community" only when he joins in revolutionary activity; the "sit-in" is a community, as the university itself is not.

Communities differ in character, however. A university is not, and cannot be, anything like a "sit-in." Terrible confusion has been caused by the confluence of a number of factors: the ridiculous habit of describing the university as "a community of scholars" rather than as, at best, a community of scholars and pupils, the educational dogma that education must be "problem-oriented" rather than "subject-oriented," the overemphasis in universities on the contemporary, the breaking up of educa-

---

[10] There is, of course, an enormous literature on this subject. The major lines of controversy are sketched in Ferdinand Tönnies, *Community and Society* (1887, tr. and ed. Loomis, 1957).

tional sequences into disordered "units." (All of these factors have been particularly influential in faculties of arts and social sciences.) Together, they generate the conclusion that the ideal university would be one in which students and teachers, on equal terms, sat around discussing whatever "problems" happened to be currently fashionable. The fact is that students entering a university are ignorant; what they need is to be introduced to consecutive and ordered subjects. As pupils they have rights in the community, and they can reasonably complain when their masters ignore them, teach them badly, or not at all, and refuse to allow them to participate in the university's government. But a university is not, cannot be, and ought not to be, a community of equals. It could become such only by destroying scholarship, abandoning learning, forgetting that its task is to *teach,* which implies that there are learners, and to advance knowledge, which implies that knowledge is something one only gradually acquires.

Once again, the remedy proposed by the "Romantic rebels" is even worse than the disease. The demand that their teachers be constantly at their beck and call, for example, displays a complete incapacity to understand the conditions necessary for scholarly work. But, on the other hand, a pupil needs to do a great deal more than merely to "audit" a course— that revealing American expression; he needs to participate in courses of studies as distinct from simply "hearing" what is said to him.

In Marshall McLuhan's *The Medium is the Massage*—McLuhan, it is worth observing, is a warm admirer of Teilhard de Chardin—the ideas of timelessness and of "community" are explicitly run together.

> Ours is a brand-new world of allatonceness. Time has ceased, space has vanished. We now live in a *global* village . . . a simultaneous happening. . . . We have begun again to structure the primordial feeling, the tribal emotions from which a few centuries of literacy divorced us.

Considered as an account of what is actually the case, this is utter nonsense. Men live as much in time and space as they ever did, and in a manner by no means global. Television, on which McLuhan lays so much stress, does not carry the world to the sitting-room; on the contrary, much more than a book, it carries the sitting-room to the world. Men still judge what they see in the light of where and what they are. They are not brought into human relationship with one another merely by looking at the same television programme. If, however, McLuhan is misreporting what is actually the case, he is not misreporting what a great many of the younger generation like to think is the case: that only the present counts, and that the present is the same everywhere—a belief which is no doubt encouraged by the illusion of "prescience" and "contemporaneity" which television offers its devotees. The "Everlasting Now" is ready at hand for all men. To see, as Angela of Foligno professed to do, "the whole world, both here and beyond the sea" they stand in no need of ascetic disciplines; they need only buy, or rent, a television set.

NAKED UNISEX

Timelessness and community are by no means the only perfectibilist ideals to which the "Romantic" rebels revert. The word "beat" in the phrase "the beat generation" is not, as might easily be supposed, a way of referring to those who have been beaten by life; it is an abbreviation for the "beatific," those who have experienced the beatific vision. The old perfectibilist demand for absolute purity of motive has once more raised its head. So the Californian "Diggers"—a "Hippie" group—will accept gifts "only if they are given with love," as distinct from charity. ("Charity" no longer means the love of God, but, rather, a patronising "handout"; thus, by an interesting twist of language, acting "out of charity" has come to be identified with acting out of impure motives, whereas to Christians charity was the only pure motive.)

Even the most bizarre "Romantic rebel" behaviour can turn out, indeed, to have its roots in a long-standing mystical perfectibilist tradition. Take, for example, unisexuality.[11] According to Genesis, God first of all created Adam; he did not create Eve directly, as a pure expression of his creative power; he made her out of Adam's rib. Man and woman, according to Genesis, are "one flesh." The implication was not lost on mystical perfectibilists. In the state of perfection, they tell us, there will indeed be only one flesh. In the apocryphal Gospel according to the Egyptians, Jesus tells Salome that the final secrets will not be unveiled until "ye have trampled on the garment of shame, and when the two become one, and the male with the female is neither male nor female." In the so-called "Second Epistle of Clement" this becomes: "When the two shall be one and the outside (that which is without) as the inside (that which is within), and the male with the female neither male nor female."

Jacob Boehme, the 16th-century mystic, was convinced that imperfection entered the world with Eve's creation. No longer were all created things direct emanations of God—Eve was the prime exception. The German mystically-inclined poet, Gottfried Benn—at one time an enthusiastic follower of Hitler—took as his ideal that "pre-logical" stage of human consciousness, when religion reflected "the original monosexuality of the primitive organism, which performed seed-formation, copulation and impregnation within itself."[12] In many Indian sects, male

---

[11] On the unisexual tendencies in the United States see, although with considerable reservations, Charles Winick, *The New People.* The themes of nakedness and unisexuality played a prominent part in the Adamite sects, to which Augustine refers, and were also conspicuous in the teachings of certain of the Brethren of the Free Spirit. Sects of this kind have of course—like the "hippies" of our time—always been a small minority. But the reappearance of these ideas at such crucial stages in the history of civilisation is of more than passing interest. See particularly Wilhelm Fränger, *The Millennium of Hieronymus Bosch* (tr. Wilkins and Kaiser, 1962), ch. 2. In the light of recent developments, Fränger's interpretation (p. 121) of Bosch's notorious "anal flower" may have to be reconsidered; the interpretation he rules out, that the Brethren of the Free Spirit thought every erogenous zone permissible, may well be the correct one.
[12] Gottfried Benn, "Provoziertes Leben," in *Ausdruckswelt: Essays und Aphorismen*

and female are but different aspects of the one deity. "Margot"—one of the "hippies" in Lawrence Lipton's *The Holy Barbarians*—has been told by her male associates that "the gods were conceived of in their pure primitive form as androgynous . . . hermaphroditic." To be godlike, it follows, one must first ignore the differences between the sexes. In search of "Paradise Now," men and women must dress alike, act alike, and in their sexual relationships be indifferent to the sex of their partner.

That is one of the striking features of the "tribal-love rock musical" *Hair*. (Note the typical "community" reference to "tribal-love," the young American rebels are "playing Indians," rejecting the traditional view that the true hero was the individualistic, aggressive, tribe-destroyer, pioneering cowboy.) In the sharpest possible contrast to the traditional "musical," which has always emphasised sexual differentiation, *Hair* makes it hard to distinguish which of the characters are men and which women. And the sexual actions which are casually simulated appear to be determined only by proximity, indifferently directed towards male or female. It is women who suffer from this identification, as is very clearly brought out in *Hair*. Women are mere "hangers-on," no longer sexually necessary. Girls are dressed as boys rather than—for all their long hair and decorative garb— boys as girls. The sexual relationships suggested and simulated are not, for the most part, of a genital kind: they are anal and oral relationships, for which women are not necessary. What we are perhaps witnessing, in the name of "community," is a revolt against women—but a revolt in which women themselves participate because it can be represented (as by Simone de Beauvoir) as a revolt against the conception of a "feminine role." It is Eve, not Adam, who must vanish if the "original state" of perfect humanity is to be regained; she must take her old place, in Adam's rib, no longer separate flesh. This is not the first time that a class has participated in a revolution of which, in the end, it is the victim.

Unisexuality is a reversion to early childhood, to a point before sex-roles were made apparent by differentiation in clothing and behaviour. At the same time, it is a special application of the mystical search for total unity, for a total community in which, as in Fichte's and Winwood Reade's dream, all mankind thinks and feels as One. So long as the role of the sexes is sharply distinguished that total community remains inaccessible. It is no accident that in Mao's China, too, differentiation between the sexes is reduced to a minimum.

Hair is notorious for its naked scene rather than for its unisexuality. But the nakedness, also, is presented as a mystical revelation, a revelation which makes unimportant, in the act of revealing, the difference between the sexes. More significantly, it suggests a ritual sloughing-off, a purifica-tion, through the casting away of "inessentials," mystical and perfectibilist

---

(Wiesbaden, 1949); trans. as "Provoked Life: An Essay on the Anthropology of the Ego" in *The Psychedelic Reader* (ed. Weil, Metzner, and Leary, 1965), p. 42.

in its inspiration. Adam and Eve, in the familiar Genesis story, "were both naked, the man and his wife, and were not ashamed." God knew that Adam had sinned, when he saw he had covered his nakedness. Unself-conscious nakedness, an unawareness of sexual difference, belongs in other words, to Paradise; self-consciousness about nakedness only to man after the Fall. Orthodox Christianity took as its point of departure man in his fallen state; in medieval sculpture, therefore, the naked figure is a "huddled body cowering in consciousness of sin."[13] Metaphorically, however, nakedness continued to play its ancient role. The mystic must "strip himself naked" before he can unite himself with God. In the Syrian monasteries, as amongst Eastern mystics, physical nakedness was by no means uncommon as a sign of sanctity.

At the same time—a fact of which the Nazis made full use in their concentration camps—*compulsory* nakedness can be a powerful weapon of humiliation, as also can be that replacement of names by numbers which is a feature of mathematically perfect societies. By making himself naked—as by scourging himself, by starving himself, by prostrating himself, by submitting without question to authority—the ascetic mystic voluntarily makes use of precisely the dehumanising mechanisms the totalitarian state uses to impose its will on its victims.

THE DROPPING OF INHIBITIONS

With the Renaissance painters, nakedness is once more linked with Paradise. Later writers and painters have developed the association between nakedness and perfection still further. In the eighteenth century the conception of the Pacific as an idyllic Paradise inhabited by noble savages was strengthened by the nakedness of those "savages." E. M. Forster's "The Machine Stops" presents the hero, Kuno, as rebelling against the atomistic life of his machine-governed Utopia. Trying to make his way to the outer world, he reflects:

> I felt that humanity existed, and that it existed without clothes. . . .
> Had I been strong, I would have torn off every garment I had, and gone
> out into the outer air unswaddled.[14]

The inhabitants of the most attractive of Wells' Utopias, *Men Like Gods,* go unself-consciously naked; that the visitors from our planet are horrified, or tantalised, by their nakedness is, as Wells represents the situation, the clearest possible sign of their imperfection. So when the cast of the "Living Theatre" strip themselves naked for their performance of *Paradise Now* they are reverting to an ancient theme. (Of course, the desire to shock is also an ancient one; but it would be a mistake to suppose that this is all that is involved in apocalyptic nakedness.)

The road to Paradise, one might conclude, is simple: It does not involve a prolonged agony through a night of the soul; all one need do is

---

[13] Kenneth Clark, *The Nude* (1956), p. 303.
[14] E. M. Forster, "The Machine Stops," in *Collected Tales* (1968), p. 170.

to take off one's pants. That would not be quite fair. The dropping of pants is a symbol for the dropping of inhibitions. The New Mystic, as we have already seen, rejects Freud's own view that inhibitions are essential to civilisation. Man, he believes, is naturally good; and any society which rests on inhibitions is but an artificial civilisation—a "plastic" substitute for a genuine inhibition-less community, in which man's natural goodness will express itself in love and tenderness.

Drug-taking is another instance in which ancient mystical ideals re-appear in a more explicitly physical guise. Again and again, in describing the effects of drugs, addicts use language which compellingly reminds us of mysticism and of Stoicism.

Many drug-takers, in flight from "humanity" and the care inherent in it, turned first to mysticism. So when they took drugs, the language of mysticism was at their disposal to describe their experiences; they taught that language to new converts. But the fact remains that the old language seemed to them to fit their new experiences like a glove. It is very important to recognise that drug-taking has now—as for centuries past in other cultures—taken on the character of a religion: it has zealous converts, who seek to convert others. Like any other religion, of course, it also serves as a source of profit to "drug-pushers." But this should not be allowed to conceal the manifest sincerity of a great many drug-takers and drug-recommenders. "LSD," Marx might now have written, "is the religion of the intellectuals."[15] Hashish, a 19th-century addict wrote, offers to men "a sense of detachment from oneself, of loss of all impulse towards action, and of widespread indifference to other persons as to all worldly ties." Describing his feelings under the influence of mescalin, a contemporary poet uses such expressions as "I know everything"; "there is no Time"; "I am without care, part of all." The resemblances between drug-inspired and mystical experience have been most thoroughly ex-plored by Aldous Huxley and Alan Watts—who first established his reputation as an exponent of Zen Buddhism. Under the influence of mescalin, Huxley reports,

> visual impressions are greatly intensified. . . . Interest in space is di-minished and interest in time falls almost to zero. . . . The mescalin taker sees no reason for doing anything in particular and finds most of the causes for which, at ordinary times, he was prepared to act and suffer, profoundly uninteresting.[16]

In other words, he no longer cares and no longer cherishes.

Watts adds that drugs revive a sense of community. By breaking down

---

[15] On this point see especially Richard Blum and associates, *Utopiates: The use and users of LSD* (London, 1965), p. 134. For a criticism of the attempt to relate drug mysticism to classical mysticism—a criticism directed especially against Huxley, see R. C. Zachner, *Mysticism: Sacred and Profane* (1957), which particularly insists on the point that Christianity stops short of the idea of an *absolute* unity between the mystic and God.
[16] Aldous Huxley, *The Doors of Perception* (1954), p. 23.

that defensiveness which inhibits physical tenderness, they help men and
women to enter into "associations with others based on physical gestures
of affection," associations which take the form of "rites, dances, or forms
of play which clearly symbolise mutual love between the members of the
group."[17] In the normal life of modern industrial societies, men and
women are inhibited from these relationships; they are unable to permit
themselves any erotic contacts—touching, for example—which fall between the extremes of purely verbalised contacts and full genital sexuality.
But, by destroying inhibitions, drugs make such contacts possible, and in
so doing (it is argued) promote community.

To the traditional Christian it is, of course, an intolerable suggestion
that there is any resemblance whatsoever between "spiritual" and drug-
taking mysticism. But, as Huxley points out, the classical mystics did in
fact produce bodily changes in themselves—by starvation, by flagellation,
by the perpetual muttering of prayers. All of these give rise to physical
changes in the body, precisely the sort of changes which from our knowledge of bio-chemistry we should expect to produce "mystical experience."

These observations do not, of course, suffice to demonstrate that the
mystics were mistaken in what they reported, that they were wrong in
supposing that they have been granted a vision of God. Huxley himself
believed that the taking of drugs can now accomplish what it once took
starvation and flagellation to bring about. It so affects the chemistry of
the brain that the brain no longer acts in its normal fashion as an inhibitor,
allowing us to experience only what is practically important, and so
permits what Huxley calls "Mind at large" to flow through its filters.

The title of Huxley's principal book on drug-taking is *The Doors of
Perception.* His epigraph is from Blake: "If the doors of perception were
cleansed everything would appear to man as it is, infinite." (The quotation
is from *The Marriage of Heaven and Hell;* I have corrected Huxley's
version to make it conform to the text in the Oxford Standard Authors
edition of Blake's *Poetical Works,* p. 254.) In Blake, very many of the
themes we have just been developing are clearly announced: the emphasis
on infancy, *"nestling for delight In laps of pleasure"* (p. 290); the attack
on Newtonian-type science and abstract reasoning (p. 381 and *passim*);
the praise of *"the naked Human Form Divine"* (p. 157); the hostility
to *"the two impossibilities, Chastity and Abstinence, Gods of the
Heathen"* (p. 429). Note as well, what is very typical of the "Romantic
Rebels," Blake's Christianity without God—"God is Jesus" (p. 430)—
and his hostility to societies of *"wheel without wheel, with cogs tyrannic
Moving by compulsion each other"* as contrasted with Eden whose *"wheel
within wheel, in freedom; revolve in harmony and peace"* (p. 388). In
short, Blake forcibly reminds us just how much of what the "Romantic
rebels" teach derives from a long tradition.

[17] Alan W. Watts, *The Joyous Cosmology* (1962), p. 92.

THE PLEASURES OF AUSTERITY

The question what we are to make of reports of mystical experience is, of course, a large one, not lightly to be settled. One thing is obvious: whenever the mystics—"spiritual" or "bodily"—make claims which can be empirically tested, they are false. Angela of Foligno tells us that she was lifted up so that she could see all the countries of the world; it follows that in her mystical vision the world was flat. Had we asked her to de-scribe then-undiscovered Australia it is not a mere guess that she could not have done so accurately. If, similarly, a drug-taker tells us that, now he has taken LSD, he "feels like Einstein" it will certainly be pointless to expect from him some new contribution to the unified field theory. He is in exactly the same position as the alcoholic driver who is convinced that he is now in a fit state to win the *Grand Prix*. William James has told us how under the influence of ether he was convinced that he was thinking great thoughts. Writing them down he discovered them, in his waking moments, to be absolute nonsense, of a pseudo-metaphysical kind. Not every drug-mystic, unfortunately, is a William James, capable of recog-nising nonsense when he sees it.

As for the view, again an empirical claim, that drug-taking encourages a "sense of community," no one can read the pitiful story of American "hippie" communities and still believe that drugs encourage "community," as distinct from vague feelings of "togetherness." A genuine community has common interests and is able to work together in a common life. Out of its common interests affection develops. Touching is not a substitute for love—which is not, by any means, to deny that physical contacts of this sort can have their value.

Nor is there any ground for believing that drugs and spiritual exercises "enlarge the consciousness." Science *does* enlarge men's consciousness: it enables human beings to range more freely through space and time; it reveals to them a set of objects about which they would otherwise be entirely ignorant. Art, too, "enlarges the consciousness"; it creates new objects, objects we can enjoy with care; it helps us to appreciate the shapes and forms, the modes of life, which lie around us. Drugs and mystical exercises, on the contrary, deliberately set out to *destroy* consciousness, governed as it is by care; they seek to carry men back to the world as they experienced it before they were capable of thinking, a world without structure and order, in which contours and forms float free, the world of "pure experience" (as Bradley and James described it) in which even the distinction between men and the world around them does not exist. Becoming a human being consists, precisely, in learning how to reduce to order that primitive chaos of experience—to which we sometimes revert under conditions of fever or extreme fatigue. The mystic wants us to forget everything we have learnt: in short, no longer to be human.

Even more obviously is this true of Zen Buddhism. The Zen monk seeks to go back even beyond childhood, to think of himself as if he were a rock or stone. The typical Zen stone-gardens are made of unchanging rocks—the seasonal changes of the Western garden play no part in them. The living is excluded, because the living involves care, change, death. Such gardens undoubtedly have their attractions as a moral holiday, a respite from the attempt to grasp and cope with a changing world—the same sort of respite which can be obtained in a mountain range.

This, it might be argued, is only in order to deal more effectively with the world; mysticism retreats only in order to advance. Classical mystics, it is sometimes said, recognised that "this is the life that counts, and that the state of self-transcendence is a means, not an end in itself." As a generalisation about "spiritual" mystics, this is false. But some mystics, certainly, have sought in transcendent states a form of spiritual refreshment, which would prepare them to live the religious life on earth.

The claim that mystical experience, whatever its origins, makes its devotees better persons is hard to test—if only because there is often very little agreement between the mystics and their critics about what constitutes "a better person." But so far as there is agreement on this point, the evidence suggests that although drug-takers, at least, *feel* they are better men after their drug-taking, independent observers often disagree with them. Eighty per cent of the drug users examined in Blum's *Utopiates* (p. 104) thought their fellow drug-takers had changed for the better: sixty-nine per cent of observers who did not take drugs thought they had either not changed at all or changed for the worse. The fact seems to be that the breaking down of inhibitions by any means improves some people and makes other people worse; no one who has observed the effect of alcohol will be surprised by this observation. As for the view that the taking of LSD improves the functioning of the intellect, I can only beg the reader—to take one case—to read Timothy Leary's "The Religious Experience: Its Production and Interpretation" (in *The Psychedelic Reader,* pp. 191–213). Intellectual irresponsibility is there exhibited at its very worst. Zen Buddhism positively prides itself on its moral and political irresponsibility; a leading representative of the contemporary Zen movement found no difficulty in becoming a convinced Nazi.[18]

Equally, nineteenth-century opium addicts sometimes believed that opium-taking would offer them "spiritual experiences" which would enable them the more effectively to express themselves in poetry—even if the actual effect, in most cases, was to evoke nothing more productive than "the intention but failure to write a great philosophical work." Contemporary mystics, in contrast, often drop out of the world in intention

[18] Compare on this point Arthur Koestler, *Drinkers of Infinity* (London, 1968), pp. 287–91. In his *The Myth of the Twentieth Century* Alfred Rosenberg traced back the ideas of the Nazis to German mystics, especially Eckhart. This, no doubt, is too hard on the mystics, but it is not *entirely* without justification. Contemporary hippy-mystics are often convinced that they are the recipients of a special divine grace. They display that fanaticism, "aristocratic" pride, and antinomianism which Wesley so feared, setting themselves above all kinds of moral restraint.

as well as in effect; they are the modern equivalent of the fourth-century hermits in the Syrian desert—although their desert is not Syria but California and what they are mourning is not so much the worldliness of Christianity as the worldiness of Civilisation.

The fact remains that even when the mystic believes that he has an obligation towards his fellow-men which his temporary retreat from the world will enable him, in the long run, more effectively to perform, he does not find perfection in that human relationship but only in his relationship to the One. And even if it be true that, as a result of mystical withdrawal, he finds it possible to act in ways in which he could not otherwise act, this does nothing to demonstrate that the withdrawal is itself anything but a form of play. Other men feel the need for orgies, whether sexual orgies or orgies of destruction, for bouts of drunkenness, or for violent physical exercise, to achieve the same catharsis.

To speak of the mystical ideal as one of unalloyed enjoyment is, it might be objected, an absurd misinterpretation of the situation. How can it possibly be said that the mystic is longing for a life of unalloyed enjoyment when he endures such austerities? But two points arise here. First, we have come to be somewhat suspicious of austerities. As little as half a century ago Baron von Hügel could relate with every expectation of approval the story of a nun who, on learning that a favourite pupil had become the mistress of a wealthy man, told her that until the relationship was terminated, she would scourge herself daily so that she stood in a pool of her own blood. Such spiritual blackmail has nowadays lost much of its moral appeal. But even apart from that, the nun's motives would now, very commonly, be regarded with suspicion; the sexual complications of such self-scourging are only too familiar. Scourging can be a form of sexual play. The practices of famous medieval ascetics are described in detail in the case-histories of Krafft-Ebing's *Psychopathia Sexualis.*

As well, and more fundamentally, mystical austerities are commonly represented as a "stripping off" to the point of nakedness. It is a constant theme of perfectibilists that men need to return to an earlier state, to become as little children, to find their way back to unity with Nature, to the undifferentiated whole they experienced before they began to think, to primitive community. Difficulty, struggle, toil, are needed only in order to find the way back. That the mystic is forced to toil, to struggle, does nothing to demonstrate that what he is seeking to achieve at the end of his struggle is something other than a state of absolute unalloyed enjoy-ment. The old mystic differs from the new mystic only in believing that to achieve that state he must first toil, not in his definition of what he hopes to achieve. The danger attaching to LSD, the fact that it may, often does, produce suffering—a "dark night" of depression and horror —is part of its attractiveness to some of its devotees; it links them more closely with the mystical tradition.

PSEUDO-LOVES AND LITTLE LOVES

At the opposite extreme from the play-ideal lies Puritanism, that Puritanism, so potent in the United States, but widespread also in Europe, against which the new mystics are reacting and which has to be taken into account if their attitudes are to be comprehensible.

Obscenities are a rebellion against the euphemisms of the "comfort-station" and the "power-room:" nakedness against an extreme body-Puritanism, for which even to show the navel was wicked: unisexuality against a rigid distinction between masculine and feminine roles, panic-stricken by homosexuality; dirtiness and, more particularly, carelessness about faeces against the exaggeration of hygiene and toilet-training; pacifism against the cult of violence and gun-carrying; the ideal of "community" against a viciously competitive individualism; the ideal of play against an intense seriousness of purpose, wholly hostile to wit, irony or any kind of secret smile; the "return to Nature" against savage industrial despoliation; mysticism and ritualism against a moralistic version of Christianity.

> "Play of whatever sort," [a German educator once wrote] "should be forbidden in all evangelical schools, and its vanity and folly should be explained to the children with warnings of how it turns the mind away from God and eternal life, and works destruction on their immortal souls."[19]

"Play," in this context, has of course the widest possible application: any form of enjoyment, whether it be play, game, or love, "turns the mind away from God." Life should be wholly devoted, according to the Puritan, to toil. Secularists have sometimes adopted a not dissimilar attitude. Anxious not to be condemned as pagan hedonists they—some of the Fabians, for example—have so strongly emphasised the importance of duty, of service, of seriousness that, in their practical attitudes to life, they could scarcely be distinguished from the most pious of Puritans. There is certainly nothing playful about George Eliot, or about the Webbs.

Up to a point, in reacting against the Puritan attitude to life the exponents of Paradise Now are saying no more than what is said in those somewhat trite but extremely pertinent lines of the Georgian poet W. H. Davies;

> What is this life, if full of care
> We have no time to stand and stare?

Looking back on his own past life, so serious a philosopher as Herder was led to comment adversely, as many of us might do on looking back

[19] The pietist Töllner, quoted in K. Groos, *The Play of Man* (1901), pp. 398–9.

at our own life, on its absence of play. "The sense of touch and the world of sensuous pleasures," he writes, ". . . these I have not enjoyed. I see and feel *at a distance.*" We have all lost, he goes on to suggest, "the noble sensuality of ancient times, especially in the East." He himself had suffered in later life, he came to think, because he had failed, in his youth, to live the life "of images, of sensations, of upsurging delight."[20]

In so far as contemporary mysticism develops this theme, in so far, that is, as it is a reaction against a life too "full of care," one does not have to be a mystic to appreciate its attractions. J. M. Keynes was certainly no mystic; but even he complained that men have looked too much to the future; in the language of the nursery, they have placed too much stress on jam tomorrow, too little on jam today.[21]

There is certainly room in life for play, room for "moral holidays," more room than our society has permitted. Herbert Marcuse has particularly emphasised that the "scarcity" which is used to justify the postponement of gratification is, in modern industrial societies, largely artificial; ideas like "economic growth" and a "higher standard of living," used to justify more and more toil, have become absurd fetishes. When Freud argued that civilisation can only be founded on repression, because human resources are so limited that immediate gratification would destroy civilisation, he was reflecting the ideas of a pre-technological age. Much human toil, nowadays, is directed towards the obtaining of possessions and status which are simply not worth having—which, having, one does not enjoy; which are possessed only to be cast aside in favor of objects which are more "up-to-date" and can be purchased only by additional toil. If violence increases to a point at which every citizen has to buy a double lock for every door and add a room to his house as an armoury, this will contribute to economic growth. A country may have a high national income only because it is busy producing weapons of war. Its standard of living may be statistically reported as "high" only because unscrupulous salesmen are successful in selling shoddy goods by fradulent methods to customers who get no enjoyment out of what they are persuaded into buying.[22]

[20] J. G. Herder, *Travel Diary* (trans. Barnard), in *J. G. Herder on Social and Political Culture* (1969), pp. 69, 78, 83.
[21] J. M. Keynes, *Essays in Persuasion* (1931), p. 370.
[22] For more on the topic of economic growth see, allowing for his idiosyncrasies, E. J. Mishan, *The Costs of Economic Growth* (London, 1967) and on national income see, for example, C. S. Shoup, *Principles of National Income Analysis* (Boston, 1947), pp. 269–70. It is interesting to note that although he is a fundamentally conservative thinker Mishan agrees with the "Romantic rebels" on at least two crucial points: the need for recreating a sense of community and the need for living more fully in the present. The conventional "Left" and the conventional "Right" are still squabbling about who is to get what, and by what means; the Soviet Union and the United States are equally committed to the fetish of economic growth. That is one major reason why the conventional divisions between political parties now seem to many people quite irrelevant: the basic conflict, only gradually emerging, is between those who are still wholly committed to the ideal of economic growth and those who are uninterested in economic growth, except

But this is not to say that we should take as our ideal a world which is without past and future or entirely devoid of care. Brown is certainly right. If men were not "full of care," they would have no sense of time—as children at first have not, or that kind of adult who is ordinarily condemned as "irresponsible." They would have no logic, no history, no quantified science, no technology, no system of production. One can go much further than this. They would have no art, no friendship, no stable human relationships. No doubt, these points are disputable. The attempt to turn art into a "happening" is, one might say, precisely the attempt to create an art without "care," which is to be enjoyed once and for all as it happens and which is to be in its creation entirely spontaneous, the expression of an immediate enjoyment.[23] And this is only the Romantic conception of art carried to its extremes; in a fashion characteristic of Romanticism it encourages Pelagian pride, pride in one's "creativity" or originality, discourages pride in work.

Art, however, is not simply play, it is a form of love—enjoyment with care, cherishing an object. So is science. A "science" which was "erotic exuberance," which did not try to generalise, to economise, which sought only to enjoy each individual object for itself as distinct from cherishing the growth of knowledge would simply not *be* science. What we may question, indeed, is whether the ideal of a life wholly devoted to enjoyment is even conceivable. The baby must, eventually, withdraw its lips from its mother's breast; the sexual embrace cannot last forever. Only if the mystic is right, only if there is an "Everlasting Now" to which one can be eternally attached, is perpetual enjoyment possible. And the idea of such an "Everlasting Now" to which a temporal being can somehow attach himself cannot stand up to philosophical criticism. It "saves" itself only by retreating into unintelligibility, as the doctrines of the pseudo-Dionysus will sufficiently illustrate.

For all its virtues, then, play is not enough. Theatrical "happenings" —except when they are interspersed, as they so often are, with boring, sentimental and witless dialogue—can be exciting, in their primitive way; they may represent the return of a not-undesirable Dionysian element into our art. To suppose, however, that a society would be more perfect whose theatre despised Shakespeare and concentrated on "happenings" is as

---

where there is *clear evidence* that—as it sometimes has done, and in many countries still could do—it improves the quality of men's lives, diminishes mutual suspicion, enables men to devote themselves more freely to their loves, offers them opportunities for creative enterprise, or, in short, does what the Enlightenment hoped it would do.

[23] It can also be an expression of discontent, a wilful—as distinct from a playful—destruction of established forms and practices, directed against their authoritarian character, or what is presumed to be such. In this respect the "happening" in Heinrich Böll's novel *The End of a Mission* (tr. Vennewitz, 1968) may be more typical than it at first sight appears to be. Anarchism is an attempt to turn political action into a "happening," and in anarchism there is a peculiar mixture of rational criticism and mystical aspiration. It is only to be expected that the boundary lines I have been drawing will be ill-defined and often crossed.

clearly absurd as to suppose that a society would be more perfect whose art consisted only of propaganda for approved ideals.

In discussing *Hair* we have already noted some of the ways in which the experimental theatre of the 1960s is allied to mysticism. And whether or not *Hair* "lasts" is irrelevant to its interest as a cultural phenomenon, as giving expression in the twentieth century to old, but for long submerged, mystical ideals. Much recent theatre seeks to break down the distinction between audience and performer, to make of them a "single community," and to arouse in the audience physical sensations rather than to offer them occasion for thought. Like advertising, it seeks to kill thought, not to arouse it, by making a direct onslaught on its audience. It refuses to count a thinking audience as a participating audience; to "participate" is, the presumption runs, to be physically involved, to be touched, showered with confetti, moved amongst, fondled, or sat upon. Admittedly, a good many traditional theatre audiences neither think nor participate in any other way; but whereas Shaw tried to break down the lack of participation by making his audience think—and could only do so by thinking himself—thinking by no means suits the contemporary style.

Taking up the suggestions of Antonin Artaud, theatrical productions and experimental films have sought to "explore our nervous impressionability with rhythms, sounds, words, resonances and vocalisations." Theatre has abandoned the traditional stage for open halls reminiscent, in Artaud's words, "of certain temples of Upper Tibet."[24]

It is worth noting, once more, just how reactionary the new mysticism is. Such dramatic forms as comedy and tragedy gradually emerged out of ceremony and ritual; they became drama precisely by doing so. But the suggestion now is that the theatre ought to revert to the religious ceremony it once was—just as Heidegger would have human thinking revert to its pre-philosophical and pre-scientific stages. The current revival of interest in astrology, magic, the occult, witchcraft, is no less intellectually reactionary in character; it involves abandoning those habits of thinking scientifically and critically which men have slowly and painfully built up. Its recrudescence demonstrates just how little scientific thinking has penetrated our society, particularly, perhaps, the feminine segment of our society. (The women's journals are the great propagators of occultism.)

The fact is, or so I am suggesting, that there is nothing better than "loves." Some measure of "play" is certainly desirable. "Games" can be enjoyable and can contribute a great deal to the vigour and vitality of a community. Toil is in some measure unavoidable; self-sacrifice, action out of duty, unenjoyable work are bound up with—and can be justified by

---

[24] For Artaud see *Le théâtre et la cruauté* (*c.* 1935) and *Le théâtre de la cruauté—Premier Manifeste* (1932) included in *Le théâtre et son double* (Paris, 1964), pp. 133, 146.

reference to—our loves. But the quality of a society depends on the quality of the loves it exhibits and fosters.

"Man only plays," Friedrich Schiller once wrote, "when he is in the fullest sense of the word a human being, and he is only fully a human being when he plays." For "plays," in this passage, one should rather read "loves." Schiller is conscious of this in so far as he adds that "with beauty man shall only play, and it is with beauty only that he shall play." The "play" Schiller has in mind is a play in and through cherished forms. I should rather say, adopting for the nonce Schiller's style: "Man only loves when he is in the fullest sense a human being, and he is only a full human being when he loves; his loves man shall enjoy; these are not the only things he should enjoy, but they are the enjoyments in which he shows himself at his best."[25]

Quite certainly, if the loves society fosters are the love of power, of money, and of status, it is a low-grade society. Yet even these loves are relatively harmless compared with the "cosmic loves"—the activities which describe themselves as the love of God and the love of Humanity. These are the "loves"—on my view, the pseudo-loves—in the name of which human beings persecute, torture, censor, kill. Sometimes, of course, people describe as "the love of God" or "the love of Humanity" what is in fact love for persons: There are doctors, nurses, clergymen, men and women in every walk of life, whom one might in this sense describe as "loving humanity" and who might think of themselves as loving God. Again, we know what Wittgenstein is driving at when he tells us in the foreword to his *Philosophische Bemerkungen* that, except that he knows he would be misunderstood, he would like to say of his work that it is written for the "greater glory of God;" he goes on to add that in so far as it has been written not out of this motive but out of vanity, it ought to be condemned. To act out of love for God, or for the glory of God, can mean nothing more than to seek to make a contribution to human life, as distinct from satisfying one's vanity—love as distinct from self-love is sometimes thus described as "the love of God."

But often enough men have sought to demonstrate their love for God by loving nothing at all and their love for humanity by loving nobody whatsoever. These are the men to be feared above all others—the Robespierres who "love humanity," the Inquisitors who "love God." The loves which determine the quality of a society are not such pseudo-loves as these but what, relatively speaking, might be called the "little loves"— the love of one's work, of one's friends, of works of art, of scientific and technological achievements, of justice, of political freedom, of one's community, one's wife, one's children.

Another "cosmic love" is the "love of Nature." Man's relationship to

[25] See Friedrich Schiller, *On the Aesthetic Education of Man,* Fifteenth Letter (ed. Wilkinson & Willoughby, 1967), p. 107.

Nature exemplifies the contrasts I have been emphasising. It may be a relationship of toil: Nature is then an object to be exploited in the interests of profit. Or Nature may serve, as it does to the yachtsman and the mountaineer, as the opponent in a game. Or, finally, men may be said to "love" Nature. But two quite different attitudes are covered by this phrase. Nature may be loved as a farmer, a conservationist, a forester, loves it—as something to be cherished. Or it may be "loved," in Wordsworth's manner, as a purely sensual object; in my terminology, that is, man's relationship with Nature may be simply "play." In this latter form, significantly enough, it is often associated with mysticism. The "lover of Nature" feels himself "at one" with it, indistinguishable from it, in a kind of swooning enjoyment, not necessarily interpreted in religious terms. Even in this form, the "love of Nature" is perhaps the least harmful form of pseudo-love although one often finds it serving as a substitute for the love of care-creating human beings. Hermits often built their hermitages in settings of great natural beauty, and it would be difficult to excel, in this respect, the surroundings of Hitler's Berchtesgaden. But it is certainly the active form of love which is now called for, if this is to be a world worth living in.

THE PROCESS OF DEHUMANISATION

What of "love for one's neighbours?" It is quite misleading to use the word "love" in this context. The appropriate attitude to a neighbor—to another human being merely as such—is not love but that quite different relationship which one might call "consideration." It consists in treating a neighbour as another human being, taking his interests into account, coming to his aid if he is in difficulties, admitting his right to live his own life in his own way. Love, when it is a love for persons, includes consideration but goes much beyond it: it is a special relationship to other persons, which implies taking a peculiar interest in their growth and development.

A principal objection to the view that we ought to love our neighbours, love them as brothers, is that it is presumptuous to do so. They may properly resent any attempt on our part to take a peculiar interest in them, merely in virtue of their being our neighbours. We certainly do not wish to be loved by everybody: why should we imagine that everybody wishes to be loved by us? Affection—personal love—always carries with it some degree of intimacy, loss of privacy. Nowhere is there more talk about "the brotherhood of man" than in the Soviet Union: there it is used to justify the total rejection of the right to privacy, the denunciation of neighbours one by another, constant interference in one another's lives. That is why Orwell called his supreme ruler "Big Brother." And precisely the same phenomenon has occurred in rigidly Christian communities like, for example, Puritan New England or 16th-century Spain.

If, with these reservations, we think of "love" as the highest form of human activity we have still to grant to the perfectibilist that "loves," even the best of them, are not perfect in any of the classical senses. "Care" is essentially involved in them, discontent, anxiety, dependence on others, disunity, opposition, unhappiness. Herder sums up in his characteristically metaphorical fashion: "Nowhere upon Earth does the rose of happiness blossom without thorns: but what proceeds from these thorns is everywhere and under all its forms, the lovely though perishable rose of vital joy."[26] Lovely, perishable, joyous—such are the best human loves: but full of thorns.

To write, for example, can be a "vital joy," but a joy which is inevitably united with the thorns of anxious care. It is not a contribution to perfection, as perfection is classically understood. To write anything worth writing is to arouse opposition and controversy. Writing does not promote the classical perfectibilist ideals of unity and harmony or contentment. To write is to abandon all hope of self-sufficiency, to make oneself dependent on a multitude of other human beings, to surrender one's peace of mind, to stir up one's passions, to struggle with time. Love for persons is no less "imperfect" in the classical sense of the word.

On the other side, or so I have suggested, the classical ideals of perfection banish care only by dehumanising. No doubt they can be so interpreted as not to be destructive of humanity. Art and science have their own orders, the artist and the scientist seek particular forms of harmony: to that extent the love of order need not be dehumanising. If "simplicity" is interpreted to mean no more than "Do not unnecessarily complicate your life with possessions!"—it is an ideal any humanist would do well to adopt. Science, though itself a passion, must certainly be "dispassionate"; if freedom from passion means nothing more than objectivity, disinterestedness, it is certainly not a dehumanising ideal. Man needs to think of himself as "at one with the world," as the perfectibilist urges him to do, if this is to be contrasted with setting himself above, or apart from, the natural world. "Self-sufficiency" is vitally important to humanity, when it means no more than a capacity to do without such solaces as reputation and status.

But classical perfectibilists go a great deal further than this. They set out in search of a total order, a total harmony, and neither science nor art, as Plato saw and the dystopians have seen after him, could be freely operating loves within such a total order; science and art are by their very nature revolutionary, destructive of established orders. Perfectibilists tell us not only to abandon our possessions but to abandon our lives; to be not merely dispassionate but, what is very different, without passion; to seek a kind of unity which is destructive of that diversity which is the glory of the world and the secret of all man's achievements; to be self-sufficient in a sense which does not permit of love. That is precisely why perfectibilism is dehumanising. To achieve perfection in any of its classical senses, as so many perfectibilists have admitted, it would first be necessary to

---

[26] Herder, *Ideas,* Bk. VIII, ch. V, p. 222.

cease to be human, to become godlke, to rise above the human condition. But a god knows nothing of love, or science, or art, or craft, of family and friends, of discovery, of pride in work. And can we really count as perfection a condition which excludes all of these, for the sake of eternity, of order, or of unalloyed enjoyment?

MAN'S USEFUL PASSION

In spite of these reflections, which might lead us to reject perfectibilism in any of its forms, it is very hard to shake off the feeling that man is capable of becoming something much superior to what he now is. This feeling, if it is interpreted in the manner of the more common-sensical Enlighteners, is not in itself irrational. There is certainly no *guarantee* that men will ever be any better than they now are; their future is not, as it were, underwritten by Nature. Nor is there any device, whether skillful government, or education, which is certain to ensure the improvement of man's condition. To that extent the hopes of the Developmentalists or the Governmentalists or the Educators must certainly be abandoned. Nor is there the slightest ground for believing, with the anarchist, that if only the State could be destroyed and men could start afresh, all would be well. But we know from our own experience, as teachers or parents, that individual human beings can come to be better than they once were, given care, and that wholly to despair of a child or pupil is to abdicate what is one's proper responsibility. We know, too, that in the past men have made advances, in science, in art, in affection.

Men, almost certainly, are capable of more than they have ever so far achieved. But what they achieve, or so I have suggested, will be a consequence of their remaining anxious, passionate, discontented human beings. To attempt, in the quest for perfection, to raise men above that level is to court disaster; there is no level above it, there is only a level below it. "To be man," Sartre has written, "means to reach towards being God."[27] That is why he also describes man as a "useless passion." For certainly man is a "useless passion" if his passion is to be God. But his passions are not useless, if they help him to become a little more humane, a little more civilised.

[27] Jean-Paul Sartre, *Being and Nothingness* (tr. Barnes, 1957), p. 566.

Biographical Notes

CATHERINE DRINKER BOWEN is the distinguished author of numerous biographies. They include *Beloved Friend* (1937) about Tchaikowsky, *Yankee from Olympus* (1944) about Justice Oliver Wendell Holmes, *John Adams and the American Revolution* (1950), *The Lion and the Throne* (1957) about Sir Edward Coke of Elizabethan England, and *Francis Bacon: Temper of a Man* (1963).

SHEILA BURNFORD is a Canadian author whose special interests are mycology, hunting, and astronomy. Her book *The Incredible Journey* (1961) was published in seven countries and has been made into a series of Walt Disney nature films. *The Fields of Noon* (1964) and her latest book *Without Reserve* (1969) are collections of essays.

ROBERT CAMPBELL lives in Rockaway Township, New Jersey, because "a lot of auto mechanics also live there." A graduate of St. John's College in Annapolis, he now writes scripts for prize-winning corporate and documentary films. His special interests are philosophy and mathematics; as he puts it, "both subjects are relevant to Bugattis, the former when the car isn't running, the latter when it is."

LORD RITCHIE-CALDER of Balashanner, Scotland, is a British writer and professor who has served as a delegate or advisor to such varied agencies as UNESCO, the FAO Famine Conference, and United Nations commissions for Deserts, Southeast Asia, the Arctic, the Congo, and the United Nations Atoms for Peace Conference. He received the UNESCO Kalinga Prize in 1960 and has written twenty-six books about mankind and modern political and environmental problems.

HAROLD CLURMAN, author of *The Fervant Years* (1957), *Lies Like Truth* (1958), and *The Naked Image* (1966), is a stage director and professor of theater at Hunter College in New York. He is also theater critic for *The Nation*.

JOHN CORRY began his career as a writer on the national news desk of the New York *Times*. His studies of history, government, and politics as a

Nieman Fellow at Harvard led to his publishing *The Manchester Affair* (1967) and his collaborating on three other books about the Presidential elections of 1964, John Kennedy, and Adlai Stevenson. He has written articles as a contributing editor of *Harper's Magazine* where his topics ranged from politics and religion to portraits of unpublicized Americans. Now he is again with the staff of the *Times*.

EMILY AND OLA D'AULAIRE are a young American husband-and-wife writing team. After graduating from Mount Holyoke and Princeton respectively, they worked for several years on the *Reader's Digest* and then spent two and a half years traveling through Europe, Africa, Asia, and Australia as free-lance magazine writers. Among their special interests are wildlife and conservation.

NICK AARON FORD has been professor and head of the English Department at Morgan State College, Baltimore, Maryland, since 1945. He has also been a consultant on higher education for the United States Office of Education. His books, *The Contemporary Negro Novel: A Study in Race Relations* (1968) and *Black Insights: Significant Literature by Afro-Americans* (1971), an anthology, are examples of his scholarly interests in the Negro in American literature and in making Black literature an integral part of the literature curriculum.

IVAN ILLICH is the founder of the Center of Intercultural Documentation (CIDOC) in Cuernavaca, Mexico, an institution devoted to studying the cultural and social environment of Latin America. Mr. Illich has written many articles on Latin-American affairs, and his views on education are influenced by his intimate knowledge of the problems of developing countries. One of his principal concerns is "the commodity-nature of contemporary 'services' and the degradation of the social milieu which results from their production." His most recent book is *Deschooling Society* (1971).

NEIL H. JACOBY is professor of business economics and policy at the University of California in Los Angeles and was Dean of the Graduate School of Business Administration for twenty years. He has been a consultant to the Rand Corporation since 1951 and United States Representative in the Economic and Social Council of the United Nations since 1957.

ALFRED KAZIN, writer and educator, is at present Distinguished Professor of English at the State University of New York at Stony Brook. He is the author of such well-known books as *Starting Out in the Thirties* (1965) and *A Walker in the City* (1968). More recently he has written a great deal of literary criticism and literary biography.

ROBERT JAY LIFTON is the author of *Death in Life: Survivors of Hiroshima* (1968). He has also published books on the cultural revolution in China. Mr. Lifton served as captain in the Air Force in Korea from 1951 to 1953 and then spent five years as a research associate in both psychiatry and East Asian studies at Harvard. He has been professor of psychiatry at Yale Medical School since 1961. His "Beyond Atrocity" is adapted from his introduction to *Crimes of War* (1970), an anthology he edited with Richard Falk and Gabriel Kolko.

JOHN MC PHEE was born, raised, and educated at Princeton. He is the author of numerous profiles—ranging from Bill Bradley to the New Jersey Pine Barrens. These profiles have been collected in six separate volumes, which include *Pine Barrens* (1968) and *Roomful of Hovings and Other Profiles* (1969).

JACK NEWFIELD, Brooklyn born and a graduate of Hunter College in New York, is a politically active writer in his native city. His articles on national and city politics and, more recently, his series on prison reform have appeared in New York's weekly newspaper the *Village Voice* where he is assistant editor. Other articles have been published in nationally-known magazines as *Playboy, Life, The Nation,* and *New York Magazine.* He is the author of *Prophetic Minority* (1966), *Robert Kennedy: A Memoir* (1969), and a collection of essays, *Bread and Roses, Too* (1971). *The Populist Manifesto* (1972), his most recent book, presents Mr. Newfield's political philosophy and is an elaboration of his essay of the same title.

MICHAEL NOVAK, born in the mining country of Johnstown, Pennsylvania, in 1933, is a prolific and controversial liberal Catholic writer. A frequent contributor to numerous magazines, he is at present professor of philosophy at the State University of New York in Westbury. He is the author of *Belief and Unbelief* (1965) and *The Experience of Nothingness* (1970), and a novel, *Naked I Leave* (1970). His most recent book is *The Rise of the Unmeltable Ethnics* (1972).

PHILIP D. ORTEGO teaches English at the University of Texas at El Paso. He has had a varied career both in the Air Force and as a teacher of Spanish, French, and English. His literary works include several prize-winning short stories.

JOHN PASSMORE is an Australian philosopher and educator. He has been professor of philosophy at the Institute of Advanced Studies in Canberra, Australia, since 1956. Among his numerous publications are books about Hume, Joseph Priestley, T. S. Eliot, and Australian culture. His specialties are studies of the nature of philosophy, the philosophies of history and education, and British empiricism.

CHARLES REICH, author of the recent controversial book *The Greening of America* (1970), has been professor of law at Yale Law School for a number of years. He was born in 1928 and received his A.B. from Oberlin College in 1949.

IRVIN STOCK, professor of English at the University of Massachusetts in Boston, is the author of *William Hale White (Mark Rutherford): A Critical Study* (1956), the American Writers Series pamphlet *Mary McCarthy* (1968), and a number of critical essays on European and American fiction. He has also published short stories, and two of his plays have been produced.

ARTHUR H. WESTING is chairman of the Biology Department at Windham College in Putney, Vermont. He headed a study commission to Vietnam in August, 1970, to report on the ecological effects of the war. Westing is now doing research on the physical effects of herbicidal agents on animals.

JOSEPH WHITEHILL has written two novels, *The Angers of Spring* (1959) and *Precious Little* (1968), and two books of short stories. "The Convict and the Burgher" was first presented as a speech at the Annenberg School of Communications of the University of Pennsylvania.

MITCHELL WILSON is the author of numerous books, many of the more recent ones on scientific subjects. Among them are *Stalk the Hunter* (1943); *None So Blind* (1945); *My Brother, My Enemy* (1952); *American Science and Invention* (1954); and *Meeting at a Far Meridan* (1962).

YEVGENY YEVTUSHENKO is a world-famous Russian poet and an editor of the Russian journal *Yunost*. He travels extensively giving poetry readings from his eight published books of poetry to enthusiastic audiences. His most recent book of poetry is *Stolen Apples* (1971).

2
B 3
C 4
D 5
E 6
F 7
G 8
H 9
I 0
J 1